MEDICINE AND SHARIAH

MEDICINE AND SHARIAH

A DIALOGUE IN ISLAMIC BIOETHICS

EDITED BY
AASIM I. PADELA

FOREWORD BY
EBRAHIM MOOSA

University of Notre Dame Press
Notre Dame, Indiana

University of Notre Dame Press
Notre Dame, Indiana 46556
undpress.nd.edu

Published in the United States of America

Paperback edition published in 2022

Library of Congress Control Number: 2021931594

ISBN: 978-0-268-10837-3 (Hardback)
ISBN: 978-0-268-10838-0 (Paperback)
ISBN: 978-0-268-10840-3 (WebPDF)
ISBN: 978-0-268-10839-7 (Epub)

CONTENTS

Foreword vii
Ebrahim Moosa

Preface xiii

An Introduction to Islamic Bioethics: Its Producers and Consumers 1
Aasim I. Padela

ONE The Relationship between Religion and Medicine: Insights from the *Fatwā* Literature 39
Vardit Rispler-Chaim

TWO The Islamic Juridical Principle of Dire Necessity (*al-ḍarūra*) and Its Application to the Field of Biomedical Interventions 57
Abul Fadl Mohsin Ebrahim and Aasim I. Padela

THREE A Jurisprudential (*Uṣūlī*) Framework for Cooperation between Muslim Jurists and Physicians and Its Application to the Determination of Death 71
Muhammed Volkan Yildiran Stodolsky and Mohammed Amin Kholwadia

FOUR Considering Being and Knowing in an Age of Techno-Science 87
Ebrahim Moosa

FIVE Exploring the Role of Mental Status and Expert Testimony in the Islamic Judicial Process 121
Hooman Keshavarzi and Bilal Ali

SIX Muslim Perspectives on the American Healthcare System: The Discursive Framing of Islamic Bioethical Discourse 149
Aasim I. Padela

SEVEN Muslim Doctors and Islamic Bioethics: Insights from a National Survey of Muslim Physicians in the United States 193
Aasim I. Padela

EIGHT Jurists, Physicians, and Other Experts in Dialogue: A Multidisciplinary Vision for Islamic Bioethical Deliberation 227
Aasim I. Padela

List of Contributors 235

Index 241

FOREWORD

EBRAHIM MOOSA

The nineteenth-century Irish physicist John Tyndall, deliberating on the process of fermentation, observed what the art and practice of the brewer had in common with that of the physician: both were founded on empirical observation.[1] Today observation together with professional collaboration between scientists and inventors has resulted in far-reaching breakthroughs in science and medicine.

One area in which collaboration and observation had been lagging is medical ethics and bioethics, especially Muslim/Islamic bioethics. Professor Aasim Padela, a physician and bioethicist, in editing this volume took an important step toward facilitating this conversation, and I trust that others will follow his lead to further this dialogue. I am honored to have been asked to share a few thoughts by way of this foreword.

Bioethics in general, and Muslim bioethics in particular, faces a range of challenges in an age of acceleration and speed. Not only is medical science rapidly changing, but also the growing role of techno-science in medicine raises new questions for the practitioners of medicine and ethicists, as well as for patients, caregivers, families, policymakers, and the healthcare industry at large. The truth is that techno-science and healthcare policies together are shaping our bodies and minds, wittingly and unwittingly. We certainly do have altered natures compared to our forebears centuries ago, and if this bold claim is unacceptable, then at least our subjectivities—how we think of ourselves as persons—have clearly shifted from the subjectivities cultivated by those before us.

Emerging forms and new patterns of existence are pressed onto our bodies and souls with the help of invasive mechanical and chemical treatments of the body. Even though I use the word "invasive," I use the term advisedly and in a purely descriptive sense, not in an evaluative sense, since I am not prejudging mechanically and chemically intrusive therapeutic treatments. Chemical treatments might not be new. However, mechanical treatments, regenerative therapies, and genetically based interventions are increasingly becoming more sophisticated and refined and will most likely become more commonplace once medical therapies in conjunction with economic factors facilitate their optimal use.

At every stage of human development, scientists and medical practitioners, theologians and philosophers, ethicists and jurists are inclined to ask these fundamental questions: What does it mean to be human, to seek remedy and relief through treatment? Or what does it mean in certain instances to refuse treatment or decline specific forms of treatment? What is the meaning of life, and how do medical remedies, surgical interventions, and other forms of intervention add to or subtract from the meaning of life? Surely there is no single answer to any of these pressing questions, but the plurality of inquiries as well as the outcomes ensure that an ethical vitality will prevail. At the heart of any form of ethical vitality are the questions: How does one measure one's quality of life? Who makes that decision ultimately? Individuals alone or together with their families? Do policymakers and governments have a say in our healthcare and treatment options? These are critical questions that this foreword cannot pursue but ought to remain foremost in the minds of the readers of this volume. Critical thinking in pursuit of ethical vitality in Muslim bioethics, to my mind, will surely advance the discipline in numerous ways and guide scholars, ethicists, and practitioners to more complex and insightful modes of deliberation and hopefully more adequate solutions.

Muslim bioethics is advancing in the direction of complexity and excellence. Juristic theology, a domain nurtured by the traditional *'ulamā*,' still plays a critical role in guiding our attention in ethical matters. However, this monopoly of traditionalist jurist theologians is not an entirely totalizing one, since a more critical and diverse array of voices are rising to the challenge of presenting a plurality of robust perspectives. Yet the truth is that the field of Muslim bioethics is still largely dominated by soothing scriptural approaches that readily offer revealed texts and scripts of religious authority as definitive solutions to complex problems in bioethics. In search of authenticity, some end users view any traditional opinion and interpretation as a solution based on the face value of a claim or advocacy. Often practitioners have to deal with anachronisms and the absence of empirical evidence, which could potentially have harmful ethical outcomes for patients. Commitment to tradition does not mean that the past has a solid veto on the present. The surest way to suffocate tradition is to fawn over it with unthinking admiration.

Another way of putting this is to say that Muslim bioethics requires an intake of a serious dose of philosophical thinking. For this reason, I have advocated an approach called critical traditionalism, in which tradition is always part of the conversation but never a conversation stopper. Often Muslim ethicists and jurists shy away from philosophical thinking for multiple reasons. One is that philosophical inquiry requires deliberative, systematic, and analytical thinking, often in itself an onerous process. It requires the acquisition of a variety of skills and the mastery of multiple literacies in the service of bioethics. Another reason is that, in the minds of some gatekeepers of the moral discourse of Islam, especially some in the quarters of traditional *'ulamā*,' as well as in the minds of those who identify with "traditionalist" perspectives, philosophical thinking has been stigmatized by polemics spawned by past Muslim theologians. This is also true of those who espouse tradition and engage ancient philosophical discourses; for many among this group, any discussion of contemporary philosophy that relates to our human predicament today is dismissed with the justification that the realms of the "modern" and the "secular" are equal to a fallen human condition. This tendency is not exclusive to Muslim ethics, for it has its equivalent in other faith traditions too.

Perhaps the more promising way forward is to revitalize the conversation with tradition by ensuring that there are solid and inclusive perspectives drawing on experiences of the present in the mix. This will allow for the dialectic and dialogic processes to deliver the multiple outcomes and possibilities such opportunities promise. Hence, the dialogue between practitioners of medicine and the proponents of juristic theology, which this volume attempts to facilitate, should be lauded. Ancient and contemporary philosophical traditions and contemporary knowledge traditions more broadly ought to be integral to the ethical endeavors of the medical practitioner and the practitioner of Muslim ethics. The lacunae in the field of Muslim bioethics can be addressed by a deliberative process of critical thinking, one that takes seriously knowledge of the tradition as a discursive component while not ignoring the fact that tradition requires updating and renewal.

Past Muslim philosophers, theologians, and ethicists engaged the world as it best appeared to them, and they took the picture of reality seriously as a point of departure. Their worldview was a complex one. Muslim theologians of the past were adept at dealing with the most complex conceptions of the body, in which metaphysics, medicine, and philosophy overlapped in distinctive and complex ways.

Contemporary Muslim jurist theologians are fond of the Arabic term *fiqh*, which means deep discernment and understanding. Often discernment/*fiqh* is narrowly defined as limited to "insider" knowledge traditions. However, readers are asked to consider that *fiqh* is also synonymous with *ḥikma*, a term used to denote sagely wisdom. Muḥibbullāh Ibn 'Abd al-Shakūr al-Bihārī (d. 1119/1707), a jurist theologian, judge, and leading administrator in Awrangzeb's Mughal empire in precolonial India, unabashedly wrote that the discipline of juristic ethics, known as *fiqh*, is a "derivative form of revealed wisdom" (*al-fiqh ḥikma far'īya shar'īya*).[2] Bihārī indicates that *fiqh* is more in line with a deep and critical thinking process with strong affinities to philosophy.

Past Muslim theologians were fond of posing critical questions as to how one grapples with health, healing, disease, and disability. The theologians Aḍud al-Dīn al-Ījī (757/1356) and his commentator Sayyid Sharif al-Jurjānī (d. 816/1413) thought of questions of health, disease, and illness in relation to our relationship as humans with God's character and nature. How do believers make sense of God as the source of health and goodness, and what is the purpose of illness, deterioration, restoration, or ultimately the destruction of the body that is made ready for the reaper? In terms of that which brings us closer to mortality, how does one explain disease and convalescence?

Ījī and Jurjānī unhesitatingly do their theology by drawing on the intellectual legacy that the noted philosopher-physician Ibn Sīnā, also known as Avicenna (d. 1037), had bequeathed to posterity. They construe their theology on health and illness around Avicenna's idea that a state of health means the performance of the unimpaired and embodied actions of a person. Either health is a temporal condition or one continuously develops that condition until it becomes a normal habit; hence, one strives to keep oneself in optimal health. This acquired state of health is what Avicenna calls a faculty or an acquired habit (*malaka*).[3] For this reason health and illness impact the physical body and impair our perceptive senses in the way a fever or a headache impacts the sensory system.

What is most interesting is that these Muslim theologians did not deem illness and health to affect the quality of the soul or the quality of sentient human life (*kayfiyāt nafṣānīya*). Physicians, they conceded, sometimes took poetic license and loosely used the term "quality of the soul" to describe the condition of a patient, and by so doing confused things. Illness and disease, in their view, are caused when the physical, structural, and corpuscular functions of the body are impaired.

A reduced bodily condition is what we learn to grapple with in the process of aging, in enduring an illness, in a battle with terminal illness, and in conditions of palliative care. We are reassured by the theologians just mentioned that when experiencing the poorest of health our personhood remains intact, with all the moral and ethical implications such a position requires us to meet.

Friedrich Nietzsche, the most critical figure among German philosophers, also had something to say about health since he personally experienced illness at different phases of his life. Nietzsche spoke and wrote extensively about the "will to power." In simple terms, this means that humans ought to develop a sensibility as to how they can experience force and make things matter and be valued. Nietzsche also analyzed things in terms of active force as an enabling power and reactive force that disables us and separates us from such positive force. French philosopher Gilles Deleuze provides an interesting reading of Nietzsche on health and illness. "Illness for example," writes Deleuze, "separates me from what I can do, as reactive force it makes me reactive, it narrows my possibilities and condemns me to a diminished milieu to which I can do no more than adapt myself. But in another way, it reveals to me a new capacity, it endows me with a new will that I can make my own, going to the limit of a strange power."[4]

Where Avicenna, Ījī, Jurjānī, Nietzsche, and Deleuze meet is their concern with the sensory-bodily sphere of human existence, albeit in the context of health and illness, where affect and experience are primary emotions. Conditions of power, as in health, and states of powerlessness and impaired conditions, as in illness, "bring us new feelings and teach us new ways of being affected," writes Deleuze.[5] Crucially, emotions and affect are the product of our corporeal and sensory bodies. Here there is very little mystification about the meaning of health and illness. Muslim theologians are clearly predisposed to empirical verification in medical science as well as being critical realists in their engagement with ethics and the world. What the practice of medicine and bioethics teaches us is that not only is care for the body indispensable, but we experience our ethical registers in our bodies in the most complex manner conceivable. The conversation between physicians and jurist theologians is a worthy one because it tells us more about ourselves and existence in the world. Dialogue lends both the art of conversation and ethics a unique nobility as a mode of being in the world.

NOTES

1. James Bryant Conant, *Modern Science and Modern Man* (Garden City, NY: Doubleday, 1953), 41.

2. Muḥibbullāh Ibn ʻAbd al-Shakūr, *Kitāb Musallam Al-Thubūt*, 2 vols. (Kafr al-Ṭammāʻīn: Al-Maṭbaʻa al-Ḥusaynīya al-Miṣrīya), 1:5.

3. ʻAḍud al-Dīn ʻAbd al-Raḥmān ibn Aḥmad al-Ījī, ʻAlī ibn Muḥammad al-Jurjānī, and ʻAbd al-Raḥmān ʻUmayra, eds., *Kitāb Al-Mawāqif Bi Sharḥ Al-Sayyid Al-Sharīf ʻalī B. Muḥammad Al-Jurjānī*, 3 vols. (Beirut: Dār al-Jīl, 1417/1997), 2:172.

4. Gilles Deleuze, *Nietzsche and Philosophy*, trans. Hugh Tomlinson (New York: Columbia University Press, 1983), 66.

5. Ibid.

REFERENCES

al-Ījī, ʻAḍud al-Dīn ʻAbd al-Raḥmān ibn Aḥmad, ʻAlī ibn Muḥammad al-Jurjānī, and ʻAbd al-Raḥmān ʻUmayra, eds. *Kitāb al-Mawāqif Bi Sharḥ al-Sayyid Al-Sharīf ʻalī B. Muḥammad Al-Jurjānī*. 3 vols. Beirut: Dār al-Jīl, 1417/1997.

al-Shakūr, Muḥibbullāh Ibn ʻAbd. *Kitāb Musallam Al-Thubūt*. 2 vols. Kafr al-Ṭammāʻīn: al-Maṭbaʻa al-Ḥusaynīya al-Miṣrīya.

Conant, James Bryant. *Modern Science and Modern Man*. Garden City, NY: Doubleday, 1953.

Deleuze, Gilles. *Nietzsche and Philosophy*. Translated by Hugh Tomlinson. New York: Columbia University Press, 1983.

PREFACE

Recent years have witnessed burgeoning interest in "Islamic" bioethics. Much ink has been spilled by scholars and thinkers in generating "Islamic" responses to bioethical questions and critiquing this literature; in this process, there have been multiple symposia, workshops, and conferences dedicated to the topic. Nonetheless, Islamic bioethics as a cohesive field of inquiry and an academic discipline remains very much in its infancy. Indeed, the parameters of the field remain ill defined, as its essential issues remain unaddressed and many core questions remain unresolved. For example: What features mark the "Islamic" within the various writings that advance Islamic bioethical perspectives? And do such writings of an explicitly religious nature belong in academic bioethics discourse?

In addressing the current state of Islamic bioethics, this book brings together diverse scholars to address theoretical questions and practical aspects of this developing field. Specifically, this book focuses on two groups of Islamic bioethics stakeholders, Muslim physicians and Islamic jurists, and examines their discursive interaction and outputs. Aligned with a multidisciplinary approach, the chapter authors include Islamic studies experts and Muslim theologians, as well as clinicians, and the volume contains analytic, empirical, and normative essays. While each individual chapter offers its author's own unique insights into the interactions between Muslim clinicians and jurists and their ethico-legal reasoning exercises, as a whole the book argues for moving beyond jurists and clinicians to incorporate other disciplinary experts (and thereby other fields of knowledge) in Islamic bioethical deliberation. As the discussion circles widen and different perspectives are brought into the conversation, methodological questions about how to bring different disciplinary perspectives into alignment and derive holistic Islamic ethico-legal positions will arise.

Developing such models and attending to such questions will mark the next phase of development for the field of Islamic bioethics. In tandem, the field's disciplinary parameters and research methods will be mapped out and better delineated. The authors of this book foresee such a future and provide here definitions, typologies, and frameworks that may serve as foundations for a multidisciplinary Islamic bioethics.

The intellectual seeds of this project were sown many years ago when I began avidly reading the writings of Muslim physicians and the *fatāwā* of Islamic jurists providing guidance on bioethical issues. My quest was a personal one, as I wanted to carry out my clinical practice, as far as possible, in accord with such religious guidelines. My personal and professional search shortly transformed into an academic one as I came to realize that physicians and jurists applied different methods of reasoning to derive "Islamic" bioethics, used different vocabularies to explain it, and arrived at different conclusions about it. Furthermore, when physicians and jurists worked together—for example, in *fiqh* academies—it appeared to me that they often talked past each other and misunderstood concepts and constructs from each other's disciplines. Unfortunately, I discovered that there was no cohesive and comprehensive literature of Islamic bioethics that could be readily applied to clinical practice or used to advise Muslim patients; critical gaps in knowledge and incomplete understandings led to a very flawed discourse and literature. My concern thus became to demystify Islamic ethics and law for Muslim clinicians, to decode biomedical science and clinical practice for Islamic jurists, and ultimately to bring them together with social scientists and bioethicists in educational workshops, research working groups, and academic conferences. In this book I have collected the outputs of discussions and ideas presented during several such ventures across multiple institutions.

Most immediately, however, the volume includes several chapters that started as papers presented at a conference titled "Interfaces and Discourses: A Multidisciplinary Conference on Islamic Theology, Law, and Biomedicine," which was held at the University of Chicago in April 2016, and captures ideas that were germinated at that meeting. The conference was hosted by my program, the Initiative on Islam and Medicine, and was co-organized by the University Muslim Medical Association (UMMA) Community Clinic, supported by the American Islamic College, and partially funded by the John Templeton Foundation. I would like to convey my gratitude to Dr. Shaheen Nageeb, Veronica McCoy, and Akila Ally, all of whom spent countless hours making the conference a success, and to Adel Syed (UMMA Clinic) and Dr. Ali Yurtsever (formerly of American Islamic College), who brought their organizations on board to underwrite the conference.

With respect to this volume, another group of individuals needs to be acknowledged and thanked. It could not have been put together without, in addition to all of the chapter authors, the expert copyediting and writing assistance of Dr. Don Fette (of Barrett, the Honors College at Arizona State University) and the formatting work of Dr. Shaheen Nageeb and Khadija Snowber. I also want to thank my hosts, Professors Nizami and al-Akiti at the Oxford Centre for Islamic Studies, who provided me with the space to undertake the final revisions of the manuscript in late 2017. Moreover, I want to acknowledge the friendship and support of Dr. Michael Murray, formerly of the John Templeton Foundation and now with the Arthur Vining Davis Foundation, who helped me secure the grant funding needed to take time away from my clinical obligations so that I can devote myself to this and other ventures at the intersection of Islam and biomedicine.

Finally, this book represents one phase in an ongoing personal, professional, and academic journey into Islamic bioethics. I have had many teachers, confidants, collaborators, interlocutors, and students along the way. I know that when these individuals read this book, they will no doubt find traces of ideas we discussed, analyses we conducted, and understandings we came to. I want to thank you all for your continued role in my journey and hope the book brings each of you satisfaction as we all share in our contributions to the field. Among this large group, I want to acknowledge my deep gratitude to several who have profoundly influenced and informed the development of this volume and are listed in alphabetical order: Ustadh Taha Abdul Basser; Professor Mohammed Ghaly; Shaykh Mohammed Amin Kholwadia; Professors Ingrid Mattson, Ebrahim Moosa, Omar Qureshi, and Abdulaziz Sachedina; Dr. Hasan Shanawani; and Dr. Dan Sulmasy.

I owe the most profound gratitude to my wife, Maryam, along with my children, Aaleeyah, Maaria, Ahmed Fateh, and Faathima, who make sacrifices on a daily basis to allow me to engage in such intellectual pursuits. I owe all praise and gratitude to God, who enables, facilitates, and creates all of this. And may the finest of blessings be upon His Messenger, Prophet Muhammad, who showed us the path to felicity and instructed us on it.

An Introduction to Islamic Bioethics

Its Producers and Consumers

AASIM I. PADELA

This volume covers a topic of increasing interest in public, professional, and academic circles—Islamic bioethics. One needs only to look at the newspapers to observe the relevance of "Islamic bioethics" to current controversies. For example, the proliferation of American press reports, expert commentaries, and editorials related to the trial of Dr. Jumana Nagarwala—a Shia Muslim physician who performed a religious genital cutting procedure on children—illustrates how religious views on the body and Muslim customs can impact physicians' practices. The case brought into focus how Islamic views and ethical notions play a role in contemporary political, legal, and ethical debates.[1] More recently, the COVID-19 crisis has also revealed the need to harmonize public health guidance and religious obligations, such as communal Friday prayers. These policy- and community-level debates have also highlighted the need for a class of experts who can bridge the religious and the biomedical sciences in order to furnish accurate Islamic bioethical guidelines.

Interest in such perspectives is burgeoning in the health professional and academic sectors. Over the past decade in the United States, Islamic bioethics conferences have been held at Penn State, the University of Michigan, Yale, the University of Florida, and the University of Chicago. Similarly, on the global scene, the past ten years have witnessed Islamic bioethics conferences at institutions such as Haifa University in Israel, Ankara University in Turkey, Georgetown University in Qatar, the University of Hamburg in Germany, and the International Islamic University in Malaysia. Drawing upon the scholarship and interest generated by these initiatives, leading academic journals such as the *Journal of Bioethics*, the *Eubios Journal of Asian and International Bioethics*, *Theoretical Medicine and Biomedicine*, *Die Welt des Islams*, the *Journal of Religion and Health*, and *Zygon* have all published articles on thematic issues related to Islamic bioethics.[2] Further, the growing body of Islamic bioethics literature has spurred grant agencies to action. For example, the Qatar Foundation funded the Kennedy Institute of Ethics' initiative to develop a resource library on Islamic medical and scientific ethics, and it is also supporting plans to publish an encyclopedia of Islamic bioethics.[3] These disparate ventures aim at generating a body of work that can enable further academic research and field development.

By glancing at the preceding activities a casual observer may suppose that Islamic bioethics is an established field and that a home for Islamic bioethics within the academy has been secured. One may assume that because "bioethics began in religion"[4] and that theological perspectives, particularly Christian ones, have long been part and parcel of the academic bioethics discourse, Islamic bioethics sits alongside other faith traditions well ensconced in institutions and well represented in academic journals and books.[5]

Yet if one were to move beneath the surface to examine the literature more closely, one would find that the foundations of an academic Islamic bioethics have yet to be laid and concepts that demarcate the field remain undefined; for instance, what are the "Islamic" aspects of Islamic bioethics? Furthermore, the blueprint for the building remains incomplete, as important actors such as seminary-trained theologians and congregational *imāms* are often left out of academic forums. Consequently, their insights into how the ethical teachings and values of Islam are to be transmitted to, and translated for, biomedical actors such as patients and clinicians are largely unknown and unexamined. A more overarching issue is that even the land on which to build an academic institution of Islamic bioethics is argued about; debates rage over whether religious perspectives on bioethical questions should be considered a part of bioethics or whether they should be relegated to the province of religious studies.[6]

Consequently, Islamic bioethics remains very much a field in and under construction. What is Islamic bioethics? What are the source materials and outputs of Islamic bioethics? Who are Islamic bioethics experts? All of these questions remain open to discussion and debate. Thus, individuals seeking out Islamic bioethical perspectives, whether they are academicians, patients, or physicians, find it difficult to locate and make sense of the diversity of Islamic bioethical writings. Similarly, those seeking to set up Islamic bioethics-related courses, certificate programs, and centers for research also struggle in their attempts to formulate pedagogical parameters and research methods.

In addressing the complexity of this developing and, as suggested earlier, potentially perplexing nexus of discourses, this introductory chapter adopts a sociological perspective. The goal is to set forth as clearly as possible the major components of the discourse. I will begin by providing a foundational definition for Islamic bioethics and a brief history of the nascent field. I will next outline major conceptual and analytic questions that impact Islamic bioethics as it develops into an academic field of inquiry. Subsequently, I will provide a typology of the principal consumers and producers of Islamic bioethics discourse, discuss their respective roles, and identify illustrative outputs. Finally, I will close by introducing the chapters and themes of the book in light of the preceding typology.

DEVELOPING AN ISLAMIC BIOETHICS

Definitions

As noted earlier, much ink is being spilled in writing on Islamic bioethics. To quantify the matter, Hasan Shanawani and Mohammad Hassan Khalil undertook a review of the Medline-indexed health literature on the topic over a decade ago. Using the search terms "Islam" or "Muslim" or "Arab" and "Bioethics," they uncovered 497 articles published between 1950 and 2005 on these topics, 112 of which they found to be genuinely related to Islamic bioethics.[7] The same search string yields over three times as many articles today, suggesting a rapidly growing body of discourse. But what is Islamic bioethics, and what sort of relationship between Islam and bioethics does the conjunction refer to?

While I along with others have offered somewhat overlapping answers to these questions over the years, defining Islamic bioethics in the following way allows us to bring together these varied approaches and disparate writings. *Islamic bioethics* is a discourse that uses the Islamic tradition to address moral questions and ethical issues arising out of the biomedical sciences and allied health practice. At the center of this discourse is a discursive pairing: an individual (or institution) from the biomedical arena that seeks "Islamic" guidance and resources and an expert respondent (or group) representing the Islamic tradition. Most often this pair is a Muslim physician and an Islamic jurist. Surrounding this dyad are other scholars (biomedical scientists, health practitioners, policy experts) who provide information that clarifies the issues at hand and thereby complements the interaction. Moving further outward from this locus of question and answer are myriad scholars who use different methodologies to study and opine on the interaction(s) between Islam/Muslims and biomedicine/bioethics.

This figuration of Islamic bioethics, which is a multidisciplinary discursive enterprise, allows us not only to identify voices in the field but also to identify their outputs. For example, if the central pairing in Islamic bioethics is a seeker of a moral opinion and an Islamic scholar respondent, then *fatāwā* literature becomes the principal source material for the study of Islamic bioethics.[8] Similarly, other texts that document dialogue between solicitors and advisors are important sources; court proceedings or reports from ethics bodies that involve expert testimony/commentary from an Islamic perspective are often neglected but nonetheless important materials of the field. At the same time, *fatāwā* and *fatāwā*-like materials are not the only sources for studying Islamic bioethics. The writings of clinicians, social scientists, researchers, and others are also valuable. These experts may also offer Islamic bioethical perspectives, synthesize and critique the genre, or otherwise provide pertinent insights on, and for, the developing field. It also bears mention that texts are not the only source materials for Islamic bioethics discourse. Video and audio recordings of lectures, sermons, and *fatwā* sessions may detail Islamic views on various bioethics issues. Furthermore, in many cases *fatāwā* are not written down; rather, the response is given verbally to the seeker.[9] Similarly, ethics case consultations and committee deliberations in hospitals are not routinely recorded, although a consultation note in the patient chart might record the consensus view. Accordingly, it is important for the researcher to recognize that the discourse is broader than texts and that some sources might otherwise be inaccessible. These limitations must be accounted for when conducting research into Islamic bioethics. To guide researchers along their paths, a working typology of the consumers and producers of the discourse and illustrative outputs will be provided later in this chapter.

Before moving on to provide a brief history of Islamic bioethics discourse, I would like to distinguish Islamic bioethics from Muslim bioethics. I consider Islamic bioethics to be anchored to the ethico-legal sciences of Islam, which in turn ground the moral guidance and ethical opinions rendered. Accordingly, Islamic bioethics considers scripture and tradition, along with the associated class of scholars of both, to be sources of normativity.[10] Muslim bioethics, in my view, represents the sociological and anthropological study of how Muslims act when encountering moral challenges and ethical questions related to medicine and biotechnological advances. Within Muslim bioethics the "normative" is a descriptive rather than an evaluative term. Thus the normative is what people routinely do, not what "Islam" calls upon them to do. Said another way, Islamic bioethics concerns itself with the study of Islamic scriptural texts and moral traditions along with those who produce ethico-legal guidance based on these sources. Muslim bioethics studies human actors who may or may not engage these texts, traditions, and rulings while facing bioethical dilemmas. This distinction, albeit not absolute and not without zones of overlap, can be helpful for researchers delving into the vast literature related to the encounter of Islam and Muslims with biomedicine.

History

When defined as a discourse seeking scripture-based guidance for moral issues related to biomedicine, the history of Islamic bioethics is as old as the history of Islam.[11] Indeed one could credibly argue that the earliest discourse of Islamic bioethics is captured by *ḥadīth* that record statements from the Prophet Muhammad about the ontology of healing as well as his responses to individuals' querying about the permissibility of various therapies. Such reports are vast in scope and many in number and are contained within the *kitāb al-ṭibb* (chapter on medicine) sections of the canonical *ḥadīth* collections. For example, an oft-cited narration from the Prophet reads "Allah has sent down both the disease and the cure, and He has appointed a cure for every disease, so treat yourselves medically, but use nothing unlawful."[12] Moving beyond the Prophet's time, Islamic scholars in every succeeding epoch made moral assessments of biomedicine. Indeed, nearly every *fatwā* collection, classical or modern, contains rulings about the permissibility of various therapeutic modalities. Hence one might say that Islamic medical jurisprudence has always been part of, and has developed alongside, the tradition.

In addition to legal, or *fiqh*-related, writings on Islamic bioethics,[13] another subgenre has deep roots within the tradition. This ethical subgenre is known as *adab* literature. This literature, in general, focuses on moral formation and goodly comportment toward God and humankind. While there are multiple definitions of *adab*, they all focus on the relationship between the inner being and the outward action. *Adab* writers seek to instill the practice of doing good works and the adoption of virtues as a means of molding an inner disposition inclined toward good action.[14] Not all of their works apply to humanity in general; some are manuals aiming at specific professional virtues. These manuals focus on emulating the best exemplars of the field and on the specific virtues needed to become a "goodly" practitioner. With respect to the medical field, the treatise *Adab al-Tabīb* (Practical Ethics of the Physician), by Ishaq ibn Ali al-Ruhawi (d. 931), a ninth-century physician residing under the Islamic caliphate in modern-day Iraq, represents the crowning achievement of this genre.[15] Other prominent Muslim physicians of the classical period, such as 'Ali ibn al-'Abbas al-Majusi (d. 982–94) and Abū Al-Faraj 'Alī ibn al-Husayn ibn Hindū (d. 1019–32), also included sections on the virtues and the ethical practice of medicine in their clinical tomes.[16] Such writings remain very much a part of contemporary Islamic bioethics discourse today and are reflected in the Islamic codes of medical ethics and writings on the duties of an "Islamic" physician.[17]

While I have shared the origins and early history of Islamic ethical discourse related to medicine and clinical practice, one could also argue that Islamic bioethics is a more recent development. Such a view considers Islamic bioethics to be part of a discourse that arose in response to predominately secular global bioethics discourses. To be sure, the story of bioethics originated in the 1970s with the term coined by Van Rensselaer Potter in his "Bioethics, the Science of Survival." In that article Potter argues for the development of a moral philosophy that integrates biology, ecology, medicine, and human values.[18] Following the publication of Potter's article, the moral philosopher Daniel Callahan argued for the establishment of bioethics as a discipline, and thereafter he institutionalized the field by co-founding the Hastings Center.[19] After the establishment of this seminal foothold, the next few decades saw bioethics become part of the fabric of American healthcare delivery and health policymaking, with clinical medical ethics centers and committees finding homes in academic medical centers and hospitals. While initially dominated by theologians and philosophers, the discourse has become a multidisciplinary one that includes lawyers, clinicians, social scientists, and others.[20] Furthermore, bioethics represents a global community of scholars and transnational enterprises, with bodies such as the United Nations' Educational, Scientific and Cultural Organization forming bioethics advisory groups, and training programs and bioethics being studied in universities around the globe.

Witnessing the rise of bioethics and the rapid pace of biotechnological advancements in the so-called West, Muslim stakeholders sought to address moral questions of biomedicine in a transnational way from an Islamic vantage point. Petrodollars had already been used to establish *fiqh* academies in the Muslim World League and the Organisation of Islamic Cooperation (known at the time as the Organisation of the Islamic Conference) in the late 1960s and early 1970s. In the 1980s, Islamic jurists of these academies were increasingly tasked with questions of a bioethical nature.[21] Prominent Muslim physicians with a religious bent and often with training in the West were thus brought in to assist with answering these questions, and an Islamic bioethics discourse, albeit a transnational and legalistic one, was born.[22] These transnational *fiqh* academies were complemented by other institutions, such as the Islamic Organization for Medical Sciences, founded in 1984, which drew largely from the same jurist and physician pool but also brought in transnational healthcare stakeholders for dialogue over an Islamic bioethics.[23] Such bodies engage bioethical questions through the process of collective *ijtihād*, which involves joint discovery of the ethical issues and collaborative moral assessment between jurists, physicians, and other biomedical scientists or healthcare stakeholders.[24] The outcomes of deliberation are judicial decisions, *qararāt*, which serve as a nonbinding *fatwā*. Since the 1980s this process of Islamic bioethical assessment has been undertaken, more or less, in *fiqh* academies in different organizations and countries, such as the Department of Islamic Development Malaysia (JAKIM).[25] One could arguably trace the scholarly origins of a multidisciplinary Islamic bioethics to these institutions and hold that the judicial decisions of such academies represent the most impactful Islamic bioethics writings. Viewed in this way, Islamic bioethics is roughly forty years old and is beginning to experience the insecurity of what might be deemed a kind of midlife crisis.

Critical Questions and Contestations

Before moving on to describe a typology of consumers and producers of Islamic bioethics discourse, I would like to outline several broad conceptual questions that affect the field's development. As with the earlier issues, scholars make different arguments not only about the history of Islamic bioethics, but also about what it comprises, its authority structures, and its boundaries. Although a scholarly consensus on these issues is untenable and may constrain healthy debate, clarity about the points of contention is useful. Indeed, as Islamic bioethics develops into a cohesive field of inquiry and academic discipline, defining the content, scope, and research methods of the field necessitates attending to the issues outlined below.

What is the "Islamic" in Islamic bioethics?

This question can be rephrased in many different ways: What is the source of the Islamic content of Islamic bioethics? What features of the discourse make it distinctly Islamic? How does one distinguish Islamic bioethics from other types of bioethics? What connection does Islamic bioethics have with the Islamic tradition? Ambiguities regarding the contours of an Islamic bioethics do not stem from the lack of a moral theology outlined by scripture or from a dearth of ethico-legal judgments pertaining to medicine and healthcare formulated by Islamic jurists.

Rather, the principal challenge has been to articulate the Islamic character of the field given that notions about moral norms, the good, and the ethical are scattered across many Islamic sciences, including moral theology (*uṣūl al-fiqh*), scholastic theology (*'ilm al-kalām*), jurisprudence, and law (*fiqh*). Furthermore, these notions are conceived of differently in the genres related to spiritual and moral formation (for example, *taṣawwuf* and *adab*).

As noted earlier, when invoking "Islamic" to describe a field, one is attempting to move beyond the anthropological/sociological, that is, the individual Muslim actor, to the study of the lived tradition and its source proper. In other words, by attaching the label "Islamic" one seeks to move past invoking a "purely" human construct and on to examining practices and texts that draw on revelation. While this rhetorical move might allow for classifying studies of the organ transplantation practices of Muslims in Malaysia as *Muslim bioethics*, and therefore not central to *Islamic bioethics* discourse, the dividing line is not as clear as one would like. For example, a researcher might study the transplantation attitudes of Muslims in Malaysia and find that they are heavily influenced by understandings of Islamic scriptural texts and/or Islamic juridical verdicts on the matter. Thus the so-called Muslim bioethical attitudes are informed by hermeneutical understandings and traditional Islamic authorities. Would such work belong to Muslim studies or to Islamic bioethics?

Recognizing this challenge, I conceive of such studies as straddling Muslim and Islamic bioethics and classify them as belonging to a subgenre of Islamic bioethics: applied Islamic bioethics.[26] Applied Islamic bioethics, in my view, refers to (1) studies of how Muslims at the ground level, that is, the end users, interpret and apply Islamic bioethics rulings and (2) how Islamic scholars derive normative values and make moral assessments based on scriptural texts and religious traditions to address bioethics questions. This is somewhat separate from Islam and bioethics as subjects of study, either where rulings are the primary sources of study (as in Islamic bioethics) or where peoples and societies are primary sources of study (as in Muslim bioethics). Some scholars, particularly those from religious studies, might argue that the bounding conditions are ambiguous and that, since religious traditions are embodied, one cannot divorce the study of the religious texts from the study of the people who interpret and live out the teachings in those texts. Indeed, the ongoing and lively debates pertaining to the methods and sources for the study of religion in Western academies suggest that Muslim versus Islamic versus applied Islamic bioethics terminology might be similarly debated as the discourse matures.

I admit that these classifications do not fully resolve ambiguities but assert that they are useful for the developing field, and may at the least differentiate Muslim studies where "Muslim" is simply a demographic descriptor from studies where the religious tradition is under study. To return to our question at hand: What makes Islamic bioethics "Islamic"? If the Islamic in Islamic bioethics refers to something more or other than Muslim identity, what does it refer to? The forgoing discussion suggests that the Islamic refers to drawing from the scriptural sources of Islam and that the focus on revelation is a defining feature of Islamic bioethics discourse. Revelation, or *waḥy*, in Islam, refers to two sources: the Qur'an and the *Sunnah*. The former refers to the revelation that is recited in prayer and the latter to the revelation that is not recited. All of the moral sciences of Islam—indeed, all of Islam—spring forth from these scriptures as they separate the Islamic message and tradition from other systems of knowledge and *weltanschauungen* (worldviews). Islamic bioethics, therefore, is tied to the revelatory texts of Islam and to the tradition that is formed on the bases of these scriptural sources. Yet, as noted earlier, there are many different moral and ethical sciences within the Islamic tradition. Some are heavily rooted in scriptural texts, for example, *fiqh*, and others less so, for instance, *adab*; and it remains to be seen how holism will emerge and how normativity will be negotiated as the discipline of Islamic bioethics is established.

Organizing the various Islamic moral sciences at play in Islamic bioethics is important because it has methodological implications for the derivation of an Islamic bioethical vision. For example, if Islamic bioethics is merely about the moral assessment of human actions based on revelatory guidance, then Islamic law is the principal science involved and the methods and devices of Islamic law are those that must be used to author Islamic bioethics perspectives. Should Islamic bioethics instead focus more on the moral formation of the agent, *adab* discourse must be generated. Alternatively, if Islamic bioethics pertains to generating theologically defined outcomes in society (that is, the generation of healing or reduction of illness among humankind), frameworks from other sciences of moral theology, such as the *maqāṣid* (the overarching objectives of Islamic law), might need to be applied to biomedicine, and/or ideas from scholastic/dialectic theology about God, theodicy, illness, and healing might furnish theological parameters for healthcare delivery. Identifying and delineating the Islamic sciences at play is important not only for deriving Islamic bioethical guidance but also for studying the field, since different texts and authors are implicated as source material. In other words, as Islamic bioethics expands beyond law, it moves from the study of *fatāwā* and ethico-legal manuals to studying the outputs of theologians and other scholars.

What is the ethical scope of "Islamic bioethics"?

This question aims at delineating the scope and levels of analyses for the emerging field. Academic bioethics incorporates many different subfields, and contemporary bioethics discourse likewise is comprised of several different subgenres.[27] Medical ethics, environmental ethics, and animal ethics were all traditionally subsumed under bioethics, and more recent additions include public health ethics, genethics, and biomedical research ethics. Furthermore, courses on law and policymaking related to biomedicine are often included in bioethics training. Each of these specific areas brings into focus a particular topic and level of analysis. For example, medical ethics is primarily concerned with the clinical domain and focused on resolving ethical issues at the patient-doctor level. Public health ethics, on the other hand, focuses on the health of populations and the ethical underpinnings of public policy. Genethics and animal ethics have special topics of interest but analyze ethical questions at many different levels—individual, institutional, societal, and transnational.

Islamic bioethics literature is not yet vast enough, nor does Islamic bioethics have multiple academic programs dedicated to its study. Because of this, little concern has been generated about the organizational structure of the field and its potential subdisciplines/genres. Nonetheless, these are important questions. If Islamic bioethics were to mirror the structure of bioethics, certain types of literature would become mainstays for some subfields and not others. For example, health policies and laws promulgated by Muslim governments that consider Islamic law as a legal source—that is, Pakistan, Iran, and Saudi Arabia—would become sources of study for an Islamic public health ethics should such a subfield exist. Alternatively, if Islamic bioethics were constructed such that state policy was not within its purview, such material would become unimportant. Perhaps it is more important to consider the practice of Islamic bioethics and its scope along similar boundary lines. Much of the *fatwā* literature used to discuss Islamic bioethics focuses on individual-level ethico-legal analyses. Beyond considering whether Islamic law could deem an act morally licit, jurists do not routinely comment on or consider how that act implicates the medical profession, social policy, or law. Are such rulings somehow incomplete in their exposition of an Islamic bioethical norm? In other words, should rendering an Islamic bioethical opinion necessarily involve adjudicating societal or national-level ramifications? Certainly any critical discourse involves hierarchies in which certain voices and concerns reside at the margins. As Islamic bioethics develops, delineating the orders in its discourse will become important for researchers and practitioners.

Who is an "Islamic bioethics" expert?

This question is connected with two preceding questions and transitions us to the subsequent typology of producers of Islamic bioethics material. There are several questions that relate to the question of expertise and affect the development of the field and its literature. For example, prior to developing educational training programs to certify and produce "Islamic bioethicists," program developers must decide what the core competencies of the field are. Moving from education to resource development, when organizations convene Islamic experts to address questions of bioethics they must consider whom to invite to the deliberations based on their assessment of the various types of Islamic ethical and biomedical knowledge needed. Similarly, individuals and institutions, such as patients, doctors, and policymakers, who seek out Islamic bioethical guidance have to sort out what content expertise is needed and locate trustworthy experts.

At present, Islamic bioethics literature is primarily based on the output of Islamic jurists (*fatāwā*), with other disciplinary experts playing, at best, complementary roles. Seeing jurists as Islamic bioethics experts accords with the view that the main ethical science of Islam is law.[28] Following this path would lead to the view that Islamic bioethics training should consist primarily of the Islamic legal sciences. Yet Islamic law is not the only science of ethics in Islam. An Islamic bioethical vision should focus on more than the moral status of acts at the individual level, and an Islamic response to the secular, multidisciplinary field of bioethics requires a multidisciplinary approach. Consequently, a purely legal vision does not suffice for the field. Indeed individual *fiqh* experts have recognized the limitations of their own knowledge in addressing bioethical issues; they have addressed these by convening *fiqh* academies where multiple jurists issue collective opinions and fill in each other's knowledge gaps. Some of these academies have included biomedical scientists and health policy stakeholders in order to obtain a better handle on the various biomedical and bioethical dimensions of the issue. Beyond expert testimony, some *fiqh* academies have given biomedical content experts greater roles in collective *ijtihād*, so much so that they co-author judicial decisions and offer their own Islamic ethical analyses.[29] Thus the practice of issuing Islamic bioethical positions is evolving to address individual limits in knowledge of the relevant biomedical and legal contexts.

This move from individual to collective and from a purely legal adjudication of ethics toward a multidisciplinary ethico-legal vision was anticipated by Tariq Ramadan. He has called for a "radical reform" in *ijtihād* where "scholars of the [scriptural] texts" and "scholars of the context" come together to provide a holistic Islamic ethico-legal vision for contemporary society.[30] In addition to multidisciplinarity, he also calls for reform in the process of ethical assessment so that the scriptural sciences will be placed on an equal footing with the natural and social sciences and so that natural theology informs moral theology.[31] In his view, all of the sciences belong at the expert table, and all have (partial) Islamic bioethical expertise. Ramadan further suggests that the traditional methods of generating *fiqh* be discarded in favor of a *maqāṣid*-based approach to develop ethico-legal rulings. In his view, the *maqāṣid* (overarching objectives of Islamic law) are to be revised and better specified in light of the contemporary sciences. While this approach has both merit and shortcomings, it attends to the need to broaden conceptions of the ethical and of the expert in Islamic bioethics. As the process of Islamic bioethical assessment evolves, so too will the Islamic bioethics literature, along with the definition of Islamic bioethical expertise.

As the disciplinary parameters and methods of Islamic bioethics take shape, answering the preceding questions will help stakeholders mark the evolution of the field. The distinguishing features that make Islamic bioethics "Islamic," the scope and levels of analyses related to the "bioethical," and a delineation of Islamic bioethics experts and expertise will come into clearer view. It is to be expected that leaders in the field will answer these questions differently and that paradigm shifts will occur. Observing how these questions are addressed by different scholars over time will allow for marking the field's growth.

While the preceding three questions are not the only ones that bear upon the construction of the field, they foreshadow critical epistemic concerns and impending authority crises. For example, one area of heated debate will focus on normative theorization, engaging the question of how the "what is" should inform the "what should be." In other words, what is the extent to which, and how might, realities on the ground (what is) inform the development of an Islamic bioethical philosophy for the right-ordering of society (what should be). This question is central to Islamic ethico-legal theory and has generated intense, continued debate among Islamic scholars. Islamic bioethical theoreticians will need to weigh in on this debate. And by doing so they will help organize the disciplines that inform Islamic bioethical rulings, delineate potential hierarchies among content experts, and identify research methods and source materials for the field.

Consumers of the Discourse

Islamic bioethical judgments and resources are sought out by many groups for somewhat different reasons (see table I.1). In what follows, I classify the principal consumers by type and describe their respective underlying motivations for seeking Islamic bioethics resources. While the list is neither exhaustive nor the classes described mutually exclusive, the typology allows us to appreciate different stakeholders and the broader significance of the discourse.

Muslim patients and their surrogate decisionmakers

Numerous studies have documented that Islam strongly influences the health behaviors and healthcare decisions of diverse groups of Muslims.[32] Muslims may look to Islamic authorities to advise them on the moral dimensions of healthcare, which include Islamic views on the act of seeking healthcare, those pertaining to clinical therapeutics, and the manner of seeking treatment. Said another way, Muslim patients and their surrogate decisionmakers might want to know whether they are obligated to seek a certain type of treatment, which of the available

TABLE 1.1 A Typology of Islamic Bioethics Consumers

Consumers	*Motivations for Seeking Islamic Bioethics Resources*
Muslim patients and their surrogate decisionmakers	• To establish concordance between medical care and Islamic values
Muslim clinicians and their professional organizations	• To determine what types of treatment they are morally obligated to provide and which they can conscientiously refuse to provide • To inform an "Islamic" ethos for their clinical practice
Religious leaders, *imāms*, and Muslim chaplains	• To ensure that their advice is theologically sound before imparting it to patients and/or providers
Hospitals and healthcare systems	• To understand the needs of the Muslim patient population and ensure that culturally sensitive healthcare is being provided
Health policy- and lawmakers	• To advocate for a more culturally accommodating healthcare system
Academicians and researchers	• To establish the pedagogical parameters for the field of Islamic bioethics • To study, synthesize, develop, and critique literature in the field
Islamic/Muslim bioethicists	• To inform their practice as ethics advisors on research and clinical ethics committees and on advisory councils • To inform their scholarship in the field

Source: Author's construction.

clinical therapies are licit, and whether certain ways of seeking healthcare are morally sanctioned. While not all Muslims incorporate Islamic bioethical guidance into their medical decisionmaking process, some do, and when confronted with life-threatening illnesses and end-of-life care choices, many seek spiritual support.

Muslim clinicians and their professional organizations

Just as Muslim patients might desire Islamic bioethical perspectives on seeking healthcare, Muslim clinicians often seek moral guidance about delivering healthcare. As biotechnological advancements portend increased capabilities for intervening in illness and shaping the human body, clinicians desire to know if they ought to do so. At the patient-provider level, what types of treatment are Muslim clinicians morally obligated to provide, and which can they conscientiously (on the basis of religion) refuse? In addition to answering questions about matters of practice, Islamic bioethical guidance is also sought to inform ethos. What are the moral duties of a Muslim physician toward his or her patients, how should a Muslim carry him- or herself in the clinical realm, and what character virtues must be adopted and inculcated to live out an Islamic bioethics? Importantly, Muslim clinicians are often sought out by Muslim patients for guidance on patient-level religious obligations. For example, Muslim clinicians might be sought out for advice on when illnesses are severe enough that Muslim patients are exempted from fasting the month of Ramadan or when certain allowances can be made in performing ritual prayers and the like. Indeed, Islamic jurists often cede ethical authority to Muslim clinicians when it comes to matters of the severity of illnesses necessitating exemptions and allowances in matters of worship. Hence Muslim clinicians themselves seek Islamic bioethics guidance from jurists in order to be better informed about the religious rationale behind, and considerations involved in, rendering exemptions and allowances on account of illness. As noted earlier, the professional associations of Muslim clinicians have been at the forefront of jurist-physician collaboration to furnish Islamic bioethics guidance. In addition to generating resources that can be used by Muslim clinicians in practice, the Islamic bioethical understandings generated by such partnerships help these organizations set policy and issue position statements in accordance with Islam.

Religious leaders, imāms, *and Muslim chaplains*

When confronting ethical challenges in medicine, patients and providers alike often turn to local religious leaders, *imāms*, and chaplains for advice. Often these religious advisors are tasked not only with providing spiritual support but also with informing clinicians, patients, families, and others about Islamic bioethical rulings that pertain to a clinical situation at hand. Indeed, as Islamic bioethics "experts," local religious leaders are sometimes invited by clinical care teams and hospital ethics committees to participate in family meetings (upon the advice and permission of Muslims patients and families). Given these roles, local religious leaders, *imāms*, and Muslim chaplains, in turn, seek Islamic bioethics literature to secure their knowledge bases.

Hospitals and healthcare systems

Modern healthcare delivery is increasingly moving toward being more responsive to and respectful of patient needs and values. To illustrate, movements toward patient-centered and culturally sensitive healthcare are championed by stakeholders across the board and motivate hospital and healthcare system leaders to learn about the beliefs, values, norms, and healthcare needs of the patient populations they serve. After obtaining such knowledge, healthcare administrators and policymakers must decide what patient needs ought to be accommodated and how to do so. Against this backdrop, hospital and healthcare system leaders seek out Islamic bioethical guidance in order to understand the norms, values, and needs of Muslim patients. Moreover, many hospitals and healthcare systems desire to operate out of an Islamic vision for healthcare and therefore take Islamic bioethical guidelines into consideration as they design and structure their healthcare services. These institutions are therefore also consumers of Islamic bioethics.

Health policy- and lawmakers

Policies and laws help to ensure the functioning of society and ideally reflect the values of its citizens. As politicians and lawmakers structure healthcare delivery and set the health laws of the areas they already represent or hope to, the religion-related attitudes, norms, and values of Muslim communities in society become important to them. Policies and laws regulate the boundaries of the biomedical enterprise, and Islamic bioethical assessments of permitted forms of health services delivery and biomedical research provide data that can help legislators set boundaries that meet the needs of society and minimize conflict. Islamic bioethical determinations obviously become more important as the numbers of Muslims in a given society grow, and these are, of course, of the utmost importance to policy- and lawmakers in Muslim-majority nations where Islam is a legislative source.

Academicians and researchers

Every academic field is built on research activities and a growing body of literature. As Islamic bioethics comes into its own, the field will be followed by academicians who set out its pedagogical parameters as well as researchers who study, synthesize, develop, and critique its literature. There are many motivations underlying current research on Islamic bioethics, from intellectual curiosity about how Islamic moral traditions engage with modern biomedical science and practice, to interest in collating material for the consumers noted earlier. Some are drawn to Islamic bioethics because they want to reform Islamic ethical thinking and the production of sacred law; others desire to map out the growth of religious bioethics in different faith traditions; and still others desire to furnish common morality-based universalist frameworks for global bioethics that also align with Islamic morality.[33] All of the groups require material to work with and thus seek out Islamic bioethics-related materials with which to conduct their academic work.

Islamic/Muslim bioethicists

For the sake of completeness it is worth mentioning the emergence of a class of experts who represent both consumers and producers of the discourse. Just as secular bioethicists are a diverse group, individuals within this group include individuals with clinical, Islamic studies, legal, and other backgrounds. These are Muslim physicians, lawyers, philosophers, and social scientists who are working as practicing ethicists and doing research and writing on Islamic bioethics. Since there are relatively few institutions that offer coursework in Islamic bioethics, and perhaps a handful of certificate or graduate programs on Islamic bioethics,[34] the expertise and core competencies of members of this group are far from uniform. For example, individuals who obtain graduate degrees in bioethics can be included in this group, as can individuals who obtain formal training in Islamic law. Their consumer role is tied to their professional activities. Individuals from this group who serve on clinical and research ethics committees or in bioethics advisory groups seek literature on Islamic bioethics in order to offer expert guidance to the larger group from an Islamic lens. Those who work primarily as researchers and educators study the literature to inform their scholarship.

Producers of the Discourse

Although there remains definitional ambiguity regarding Islamic bioethics and critical questions for the field remain unaddressed, there are a great number of "producers" of material on Islamic bioethics (see table I.2). In what follows I outline the principal producers of Islamic bioethics literature, discuss their primary role(s) in the field, and provide examples of their respective outputs or of writings about their outputs.

TABLE I.2 A Typology of Islamic Bioethics Producers

Producers	*Primary Roles*	*Textual Outputs*
Islamic jurists	• To serve Muslims by enabling their continued adherence to the faith	• *Fatāwā* • Judicial opinions (*qararāt*)
Muslim clinicians	• To serve as biomedical experts helping jurists understand the biomedical science and context that surround bioethical questions • To serve as conduits of Islamic bioethical knowledge to patients who might ask for religiously informed opinions on medical treatments and decisions	• Peer-reviewed journal articles
Academic Islamic/religious studies experts	• To study and address dialectics between Islam and biomedicine by analyzing the literature and drawing on aspects of the Islamic tradition	• Normative essays • Books and book chapters • Peer-reviewed journal articles
Social scientists	• To describe how Muslims engage with bioethical questions • To focus on the negotiation of Islamic values and identities in healthcare systems and within individual societies	• Books • Peer-reviewed journal articles • Policy reports and briefs

(*continues*)

TABLE 1.2 *Continued*

Producers	*Primary Roles*	*Textual Outputs*
Islamic/Muslim bioethicists	• To serve on clinical and research ethics committees, as well as bioethics advisory groups, offering Islamic and Muslim ethical insights • To author scholarly articles and papers to advance the field of Islamic bioethics	• Books • Peer-reviewed journal articles • Normative essays
Muslim health professional organizations	• To convene scholars to deliberate about bioethical questions • To generate bioethics primers and policies	• Books • Articles • Judicial opinions (*qararāt*)
Juridical academies	• To bring jurists together to render Islamic ethico-legal opinions	• Books • *Fatāwā* • Judicial opinions (*qararāt*)
State authorities	• To use Islamic ethics and law as sources in crafting policies and laws	• Policies • Laws

Source: Author's construction.

Islamic jurists

Islamic jurists are individuals with advanced training in Islamic law whose primary concern is to serve Muslims by enabling their continued adherence to the faith. They are formally authorized *muftīs* or those with comparable credentials who draw on Islamic jurisprudential frameworks to render *fatāwā*. This is a heterogeneous group of scholars in that they are variably trained through Islamic seminaries and colleges and render judgments based on different schools of law and ethico-legal approaches. Their service to the community is likewise diverse, as some serve in mosques or community-based colleges, others have leadership roles on regional or national juridical councils, and others have formal governmental positions. They are united by their engagement in the dialogical *muftī* : *mustaftī* (religious advisor : seeker of religious law opinion) relationship to render Islamic opinions. The ethico-legal opinions of these scholars are issued verbally in person or via public media, online in virtual forums, or in public media or books. The output of jurists is thus a key to and rich resource for the study of Islamic bioethics. For example, Vardit Rispler-Chaim was arguably the first scholar to carry out systematic *fatāwā* research for the purpose of understanding Islamic bioethics. Based on the *fatāwā* of Egyptian scholars, she authored *Islamic Medical Ethics in the Twentieth Century*.[35] With respect to online *fatāwā*, Stef Van den Branden and Bert Broeckaert have conducted multiple studies on the bioethical rulings of jurists issuing verdicts on internet forums (e-fatwās) to better understand Islamic positions on organ donation, euthanasia, and other critical questions.[36] *Fatāwā* research remains very much a cornerstone of Islamic bioethics research today, even though it has significant methodological limitations.[37]

Muslim clinicians

As noted earlier, Muslim clinicians play multiple roles in the field. They serve as biomedical experts who help jurists understand the biomedical science and clinical context of a bioethical question, and they often serve as conduits of Islamic bioethical knowledge to patients who ask for a religiously informed opinions on medical treatments and decisions. In addition, they might render their own Islamic bioethical opinions. The Islamic bioethics–related outputs of Muslim clinicians are consequently diverse. As source material for the field, certain types of writings stand out. Muslim clinicians often speak to their profession through peer-reviewed journal articles and in this medium deliver Islamic bioethical guidance. Such works transmit and collate extant *fatāwā* on a particular issue (or critique them), or they might make Islamic bioethical arguments *de novo*. Medline is a particularly rich database for researching the Islamic bioethics outputs of Muslim clinicians because it is the largest bibliographic database for the life sciences and is globally accessible to both clinicians and researchers. In addition, the journals indexed by Medline are the main venue of publication for academic clinicians and health researchers.[38] Illustrating the importance of Muslim clinician outputs for the field of Islamic bioethics, Hasan Shanawani and Mohamed Hasan Khalil, as referenced at the opening of this chapter, reviewed all Islamic bioethics–related papers in Medline from 1950 to 2005 in order to characterize the authors of this genre and examine their expertise.[39]

Academic Islamic/religious studies experts

This diverse group is marked by their normative research into Islamic bioethics. Using a variety of methods from religious studies and comparative ethics, they analyze writings at the intersection of Islam and biomedicine, such as *fatāwā*, or draw on other aspects of Islamic tradition, such as theology, to study and address dialectics between Islam and biomedicine. Their focus can be historical or contemporary, their research descriptive or analytic, and their interests broad or topical. Vardit Rispler-Chaim can be classified as part of this group, as can Abdulaziz Sachedina. In his book *Islamic Biomedical Ethics: Principles and Application*, Sachedina takes a theological ethics approach to outlining a form of moral reasoning that is related to, but different from, the traditional legal approach to generating Islamic bioethical rulings.[40]

Social scientists

Given the preceding distinction between Islamic and Muslim bioethics, I separate out social scientists as producers of Islamic bioethics from religious studies experts, as the former focus primarily on describing how Muslims engage with bioethical questions. They focus on the negotiation of Islamic values and identities in healthcare systems and in individual societies. These are generally anthropologists, sociologists, scholars of policy (economics, political science), and others who rely on empirical data obtained from and/or about Muslims. This group is increasingly invited to Islamic bioethical deliberations to inform jurists about the societal ramifications and the particular contexts that generate bioethical dilemmas. In this way "thick" descriptive analyses can, variably, facilitate normative theorization (moving from what is to what ought to be). The distinguishing feature of scholars who work on Islamic bioethics and those who are content with describing Muslim bioethical decisionmaking is the analytic interest of the former in the relationship between scriptural understandings and lived reality. Examples from this group of producers include Sherine Hamdy and Farhat Moazam. Both scholars take an ethnographic approach to studying the lives of individuals confronting ethical challenges related to organ donation and transplantation in Muslim countries.[41] Notably, both scholars interrogate the self-understandings of their study participants as to what Islam calls them to do and investigate how jurists reason about the ethico-legal permissibility of organ donation and transplantation.

Islamic/Muslim bioethicists

As mentioned earlier, this somewhat ambiguous and relatively new class of experts are both consumers and producers of the discourse. They can come from almost any disciplinary background yet are distinguished by their formal training in bioethics or in Islamic ethics and law. In other words, this group includes individuals who have pursued advanced training (master's and/or doctoral degrees or postgraduate fellowships) in bioethics or, alternatively, have pursued certificates and degrees in Islamic ethics and law with a focus on bioethical issues. They are either professional bioethicists conducting research and teaching in the field or practicing ethicists on clinical, research, governmental, and hospital committees. Thus their writings can appear in the peer-reviewed press, in public media, or in policy and position papers. To my knowledge, there has been no formal research into the formation of such experts, nor has there been in-depth study of how this group's writings compare to those of other producers. Such work will be invaluable to establishing the field of Islamic bioethics and its experts.

Muslim health professional organizations

Muslim health professional organizations are important contributors to Islamic bioethics because they convene scholars to deliberate over bioethical questions and thereby generate primers and policies. They may also provide Islamic bioethics education to their membership and interface with other organizations (healthcare institutions, policymakers, pharma representatives, and others) to advocate on behalf of Islam and Muslims. Examples include the Islamic Organization for Medical Sciences (IOMS) in Kuwait, which has convened deliberative Islamic bioethics meetings with jurists, health policy stakeholders, and biomedical scientists for decades. Their conference proceedings and consensus-based juridical verdicts are found in book form. Another prominent organization is the Federation of Islamic Medical Associations (FIMA), which comprises more than thirty-five different organizations located throughout the world. Part of FIMA's vision is to serve the Islamic ethics needs of Muslim clinicians and providers. To this end, they publish books dedicated to Islamic bioethics.[42] Similarly, one of the constituent members of FIMA, the Islamic Medical Association of North America, has laid out its own Islamic views on bioethical issues.[43] The output of such organizations provides insight into their conceptions of Islamic ethics and how they can go about motivating policymakers and the broader public to support various health policies.[44]

Juridical academies

This group is represented by transnational Islamic *fiqh* councils such as the *fiqh* academies belonging to the Organisation of Islamic Cooperation (OIC), the Muslim World League (MWL), and the European Council for Fatwā and Research (ECFR); national bodies such as the Islamic *Fiqh* Academy of India, the Majlis Ulama of South Africa, or the Department of Islamic Development Malaysia (JAKIM); and similar local bodies. These organizations aggregate jurists to produce Islamic ethico-legal opinions on a variety of matters, and they use different deliberative methodologies. Some operate on the basis of specific schools of law, some align themselves with state authorities, and others allow nonjurists to participate in deliberation. Their outputs, like those of jurists themselves, can be found online or in book form. In the extant Islamic bioethics literature, the *fiqh* academies of the OIC and MWL and, more recently, the JAKIM are prominently featured. These councils are expansive in scope and use innovative multidisciplinary methods to generate their positions. For example, Mohammed Ghaly studied the proceedings of the *fiqh* academies of the OIC and MWL and concluded that instead of using traditional methods for collective *ijtihād* where clinicians provide expert testimony, these academies gave Muslim clinicians greater latitude to the extent that they could be considered "co-*muftīs*," authoring and generating Islamic bioethical positions alongside traditional jurists.[45]

State authorities

A final group of Islamic bioethics producers are Muslim state authorities who consider Islam a legislative source. For example, ministries of health in Pakistan, Iran, and Saudi Arabia routinely craft health policies with reference to Islam. These materials also provide insight into Islamic bioethical determinations and how Islamic ethical values can generate public policy. Given the complicated relationship between Islamic ethics, state policy, and law, it can sometimes be a challenge to tease out what Islamic norms are being advanced and why. Yet research such as that conducted by Mehrunisha Suleman illustrates the promise of such materials for the study of Islamic bioethics. She analyzed biomedical research policies in several Muslim countries to assess whether and how Islam influences research ethics.[46]

Like any descriptive typology, the preceding lists of consumers and producers of Islamic bioethics are not exhaustive, and there may be overlap between the various roles delineated. Nonetheless, after identifying the principal voices in the discourse, along with their respective textual outputs, I hope scholars will be better equipped to engage the field and fill in gaps in the literature.

THE BOOK CHAPTERS

In subsequent chapters of this book the authors analyze the interplay between biomedical and Islamic concepts, discuss the forms of interactions between jurists and physicians in the production of Islamic bioethics, and comment on frameworks that can be used to develop a multidisciplinary Islamic bioethics.

The first chapter, "The Relationship between Medicine and Religion: Insights from the *Fatwā* Literature," is authored by an Islamic studies expert and leading figure in *fatwā*-based Islamic bioethical analyses, Professor Vardit Rispler-Chaim. She conducts a *fatāwā* review in order to delineate how jurists analyze the theological implications of biomedical science. She records how the jurists' techno-scientific imaginations inform their assessments of the morality of biomedical practices. Surely the ways in which jurists resolve the perceived conflicts between scriptural knowledge and theological doctrines, on one side, and biomedical science and medical practice, on the other, have implications for their advice to practitioners and patients. Professor Rispler-Chaim's work sheds light on Islamic jurists' biomedical imaginations.

The second chapter, "The Islamic Juridical Principle of Dire Necessity (*al-ḍarūra*) and Its Application to the Field of Biomedical Interventions," details the scriptural basis of the ethico-legal construct of dire necessity. *Ḍarūra* is an oft-cited device in Islamic bioethics writings, as it is widely used by jurists and clinicians to justify the permissibility of controversial therapeutics and practices.[47] *Ḍarūra* is an incredibly important construct in the Islamic ethico-legal sciences; it has many legal maxims (*qawāid*) associated with it, an entire category of *maqāṣid* (the overarching objectives of Islamic law) are categorized as necessities (*ḍarūrī*), and within *uṣūl al-fiqh* the construct translates the lived reality of dire need into an ethico-legal tool. In this chapter Professor Abul Fadl Mohsin Ebrahim, an Islamic studies expert with both academic and seminary training, and I offer further operative insight into how the construct can assist with Islamic bioethical decisionmaking about the use of vaccines and abortion.

The third chapter, "A Jurisprudential (*Uṣūlī*) Framework for Cooperation between Muslim Jurists and Physicians and Its Application to the Determination of Death," is authored by two Islamic scholars, Muhammed Volkan Yildiran Stodolsky and Mohammed Amin Kholwadia. Dr. Stodolsky is an Islamic studies expert who has studied Islam in both the academy and the seminary, while Shaykh Kholwadia is a traditionally trained Islamic theologian and jurist. In their chapter they present a framework by which jurists and clinicians can collaborate to generate Islamic bioethical verdicts. Drawing on the model of *ijtihād* described by the thirteenth-century Maliki jurist Abu Ishaq al-Shāṭibī, they identify the respective roles of jurists and biomedical scientists and illustrate how such a process would work. They also critically (re)evaluate the permissibility of using brain death as the standard for legal death in Islamic law. In their view, the *fiqh* academies—for example, the Islamic Organization for Medical Sciences (IOMS) and the Organisation of the Islamic Conferences' Islamic *Fiqh* Academy (OIC-IFA)—erred in their ethico-legal assessment of brain death because clinicians overstepped by speaking on matters of Islamic law rather than simply on medical "fact."

The fourth chapter, "Considering Being and Knowing in an Age of Techno-Science," also uses an Islamic lens to evaluate the moral significance of the brain-dead state. In this chapter, Ebrahim Moosa, a professor of Islamic Studies at the University of Notre Dame, muses on relationships between epistemology and ontology and argues that juridical writings on the permissibility or impermissibility of declaring someone legally dead by neurological criteria miss the mark because of an inattention to such relationships in both the classical and the modern eras. He takes a historical-analytic approach by sifting through the writings of Muslim theologians who wrestled with questions of being and knowing and personhood. After revisiting various classical views on these relationships, he suggests that an Islamic literacy that is more complete and sophisticated than contemporary juridical analyses can inform physicians, patients, families, and religious counselors on the personhood of a medically irreparably damaged person and the ethical duties owed to the "brain-dead."

The fifth chapter, "Exploring the Role of Mental Status and Expert Testimony in the Islamic Judicial Process," is a qualitative study. Hooman Keshavarzi (a clinical psychologist) and Bilal Ali (an Islamic seminarian) report on findings from twelve semi-structured interviews with Islamic jurists. These interviews aimed at exploring participants' views on the relationship between clinical advice about mental status and the final ethico-legal verdict on moral culpability, as well as their views on how jurists should engage with other disciplinary experts in making determinations about mental status. Using a grounded theory approach to qualitative content analysis, they describe the categories of mental status in Islamic law and the scope of expert testimony their participants discuss and also offer a best-practice judicial process model for the assessment of mental capacity.

In the sixth chapter, "Muslim Perspectives on the American Healthcare System: The Discursive Framing of 'Islamic' Bioethical Discourse,"[48] I hone in on the differing ways in which Islamic bioethics producers conceive of, construct, and speak about Islamic morality. In the context of public policy debates about US healthcare reform that took place in the late 2000s, I compare the discursive outputs of American Muslim health organizations—reports, sermon guides, and press releases—in support of reform with the *fatāwā* of US-based jurists on the permissibility of health insurance. My analysis focuses on the moral arguments used by these producers and also the types of external discourses present in, as well as absent from, their textual outputs. Press releases and reports in support of healthcare reform and *fatāwā* providing religious guidance about health insurance may appear to be sufficiently dissimilar as discursive genres to render a comparative examination of their "Islamic" nature and bioethical framing methodologically contestable. However, the materials are conceptually linked in multiple ways. Both types of producers make "Islamic" moral assessments of the prevailing American healthcare system and seek to motivate Muslim behavior by means of their arguments. Aside from Muslims, both sets of Islamic bioethics producers have disseminated their material in such a way as to engage multiple publics and represent the "Islamic" to broader society. Consequently, examining these respective outputs provides both data on the connections and disconnections between different Islamic bioethics producers and also insight into the social forces that shape the outputs of the field.

In the seventh chapter, "Muslim Doctors and Islamic Bioethics: Insights from a National Survey of Muslim Physicians in the United States," I describe the ways in which Muslim physicians engage with Islamic bioethics resources. I further discuss and analyze their understandings of brain death and the concept of *ḍarūra*. The chapter situates arguments presented by other chapter contributors in light of data from Muslim clinicians.

In the concluding chapter, "Jurists, Physicians, and Other Experts in Dialogue: A Multidisciplinary Vision for Islamic Bioethical Deliberation," I present a schematic model for Islamic bioethics deliberation and describe the various disciplines that need to come together for a more holistic ethical evaluation of biomedicine. This multidisciplinary approach attends to the knowledge gaps and shortcomings of jurists and clinicians working in isolation, and indeed even when combining forces, to furnish Islamic bioethics guidance.

NOTES

1. Tresa Baldas, "Report: Girl's Genital Mutilation Injury Worse than Doctor Claims," *USA Today*, April 27, 2017; Alyza Zavala-Offman, "Penalties Worsen as More Female Genital Mutilation Victims Are Suspected," *Detroit Metro Times*, June 9, 2017; Janice Williams, "Nearly 100 Girls May Have Had Genitals Cut by Doctors in Michigan, Prosecutor Says," *Newsweek*, June 6, 2017; Samantha Schmidt, "Detroit-Area Doctors Indicted in 'Brutal' Genital Mutilation Case," *Washington Post*, April 28, 2017; A. I. Padela and R. Duivenbode, "Medicine, Morals, and Female Genital Cutting," Hastings Center, https://www.thehastingscenter.org/medicine-morals-female-genital-cutting/.

2. Mustafa Ahmed, "Muslims and Medical Ethics: Time to Move Forward by Going Back," *Journal of Religion and Health* 55, no. 2 (2016); Morgan Clarke, Thomas Eich, and Jenny Schreiber, "The Social Politics of Islamic Bioethics," *Die Welt des Islams* 55, no. 3–4 (2015); Mohammed Ghaly, "Islamic Bioethics in the Twenty-First Century," *Zygon* 48, no. 3 (2013); "Islamic Bioethics: The Inevitable Interplay of 'Texts' and 'Contexts,'" *Bioethics* 28, no. 2 (2014); A. I. Padela, "Islamic Bioethics: Between Sacred Law, Lived Experiences, and State Authority," *Theoretical Medicine and Bioethics*, April 16, 2013.

3. Islamic Bioethics Project, "Encyclopedia of Islamic Bioethics (EIB)," http://ibp.georgetown.domains/en/encyclopedia/; Kennedy Institute of Ethics, *Islamic*

Medical and Scientific Ethics (Doha, Qatar: Georgetown University Press), https://bioethics.georgetown.edu/library-materials/bioethics-research-library-databases/islamic-medical-and-scientific-ethics/.

4. A. R. Jonsen, "A History of Religion and Bioethics," in *Handbook of Bioethics and Religion*, ed. David E. Guinn (Oxford: Oxford University Press, 2006), 23.

5. Although this volume does not contain chapters that compare Islamic bioethical perspectives with Christian, Jewish, or other religious views, such work enriches our understandings of the moral values at stake. There are several institutes dedicated to inter-religious bioethics dialogue and many noteworthy articles and books that take this approach. Some important works in the area include E. D. Pellegrino and A. I. Faden, *Jewish and Catholic Bioethics: An Ecumenical Dialogue* (Doha, Qatar: Georgetown University Press, 1999); M. Cherry, *Religious Perspectives on Bioethics* (London: Taylor and Francis, 2013); J. Tham, K. M. Kwan, and A. Garcia, *Religious Perspectives on Bioethics and Human Rights* (Cham, India: Springer International, 2017). Additionally, if the reader is interested in Christian and Jewish bioethics primers, the following texts may be useful: F. Rosner, J. D. Bleich, and M. M. Brayer, *Jewish Bioethics* (Brooklyn, NY: KTAV Publishing House, 2000); D. F. Kelly, G. Magill, and H. Have, *Contemporary Catholic Health Care Ethics*, 2nd ed. (Doha, Qatar: Georgetown University Press, 2013); H. T. Engelhardt, *The Foundations of Christian Bioethics* (Engelhardt-Lisse, Netherlands: Swets and Zeitlinger, 2000); C. B. Mitchell and D. J. Riley, *Christian Bioethics: A Guide for Pastors, Health Care Professionals, and Families* (Nashville, TN: B&H Publishing Group, 2014).

6. Udo Schuklenk, "On the Role of Religion in Articles This Journal Seeks to Publish," *Developing World Bioethics* 18, no. 3 (2018); Judah Goldberg and Alan Jotkowitz, "In Defense of Religious Bioethics," *American Journal of Bioethics* 12, no. 12 (2012): 32–34; Timothy F. Murphy, "In Defense of Irreligious Bioethics," *American Journal of Bioethics* 12, no. 12 (2012): 3–10; William E. Stempsey, "Bioethics Needs Religion," *American Journal of Bioethics* 12, no. 12 (2012): 17–18; Audrey Chapman, "In Defense of the Role of a Religiously Informed Bioethics," *American Journal of Bioethics* 12, no. 12 (2012): 26–28; J. Cayenne Claassen-Lüttner, "How Religious Ethics Can Be Intelligible and Compatible with Bioethics," *American Journal of Bioethics* 12, no. 12 (2012): 30–31; R. De Vries, "Good without God: Bioethics and the Sacred," *Society* 52, no. 5 (2015).

7. Hasan Shanawani and Mohammad Hassan Khalil, "Reporting on 'Islamic Bioethics' in the Medical Literature," in *Muslim Medical Ethics: From Theory to Practice*, ed. Jonathan Brockopp and Thomas Eich (Columbia: University of South Carolina Press, 2008).

8. Typically *fatāwā* (singular *fatwā*) are nonbinding ethico-legal opinions about the moral status of actions that are issued by a trained Islamic scholar (jurist or *mufti*). These opinions are derived from values found in the Qur'an and *Sunnah* using conventional methodologies of *uṣūl al-fiqh*. For more details on the various

types of *fatāwā*, see Jakob Skovgaard-Petersen's "A Typology of Fatwas," *Die Welt des Islams* 55, nos. 3–4 (2015): 278–85.

9. For a discussion of how "unwritten" *fatāwā* contribute to methodological limitations in Islamic bioethics research, see A. I. Padela et al., "Using Fatawa within Islamic and Muslim Bioethical Discourse: The Role of Doctrinal and Theological Considerations—a Case Study of Surrogate Motherhood," in *Islam and Bioethics*, ed. B. Arda and V. Rispler-Chaim (Ankara: Ankara University Press, 2011).

10. A. I. Padela, H. Shanawani, and A. Arozullah, "Medical Experts and Islamic Scholars Deliberating over Brain Death: Gaps in the Applied Islamic Bioethics Discourse," *Muslim World* 101, no. 1 (2011); A. I. Padela et al., "Dire Necessity and Transformation: Entry-Points for Modern Science in Islamic Bioethical Assessment of Porcine Products in Vaccines," *Bioethics* 28, no. 2 (2014).

11. For the purposes of this academic chapter, the historical event marking the "birth" of Islam is the conferral of Prophethood upon Muhammad when the first portion of the Qur'an was revealed to him. Devotional audiences may argue that Islam as a tradition originated with the first human and Prophet, Adam. For the purposes of this chapter, this latter historical lineage is not critically important.

12. Abu Dawud Sulayman ibn al-Ash'ath as-Sijistani, "Sunan Abi Dawud 3874," Book 29, Hadith 20 (English translation: Book 28, Hadith 3865), https://sunnah.com/abudawud/29/20.

13. *Fiqh*, literally "understanding or discerning," refers to Islamic jurisprudence or law in general. *Fiqh* spans both moral theology and jurisprudence, as the objects of *fiqh* (as understanding) are either religious values or sources of law. *Fiqh* as law represents the formulated legal ruling on a subject matter and/or the moral value assigned to a particular action.

14. E. Sartell and A. I. Padela, "Adab and Its Significance for an Islamic Medical Ethics," *Journal of Medical Ethics* 41, no. 9 (2015).

15. M. Levey, "Medical Ethics of Medieval Islam with Special Reference to Al-Ruhawi's 'Practical Ethics of the Physician,'" *Transactions of the American Philosophical Society* 57, no. 3 (1967).

16. "Advice to a Physician, Advice of Haly Abbas (Ahwazi) [Tenth Century A.D.]," in *Encyclopedia of Bioethics*, revised edition, vol. 5, ed. W. T. Reich (New York: Simon and Schuster Macmillan, 1995); Abu al-Faraj 'Ali ibn al-Husayn ibn Hindu, *Key to Medicine and a Guide for Students* (*The Great Books of Islamic Civilization*), trans. Aida Tibi (Reading, UK: Garnet Publishing, 2011).

17. Thalia A. Arawi, "The Muslim Physician and the Ethics of Medicine," *Journal of the Islamic Medical Association of North America* 42, no. 3 (2010); International Organization of Islamic Medicine, *Islamic Code of Medical Ethics: Kuwait Document* (Kuwait City: Islamic Organization for Medical Sciences, 1981).

18. Van Rensselaer Potter, "Bioethics, the Science of Survival," *Perspectives in Biology and Medicine* 14, no. 1 (1970).

19. D. Callahan, "Bioethics as a Discipline," *Hastings Center Studies* 1, no. 1 (1973).

20. Albert R. Jonsen, *A Short History of Medical Ethics* (New York: Oxford University Press, 2000); H. Brody and A. Macdonald, "Religion and Bioethics: Toward an Expanded Understanding," *Theoretical Medicine and Bioethics* 34, no. 2 (2013).

21. J. Grundmann, "Shari'ah, Brain Death and Organ Transplantation: The Context and Effect of Two Islamic Legal Decisions in the Near and Middle East," *American Journal of Islamic Social Sciences* 22, no. 4 (2005).

22. Mohammed Ghaly, "Biomedical Scientists as Co-Muftis: Their Contribution to Contemporary Islamic Bioethics," *Die Welt des Islams* 55, nos. 3–4 (2015).

23. Ibid.; Grundmann, "Shari'ah, Brain Death and Organ Transplantation"; Ole Martin Bøe Stokke, "The Construction of Modern Islamic Authority: Analyzing the Medical Ethics of the Islamic Organization for Medical Sciences," PhD dissertation, University of Oslo, Oslo, 2014. https://www.duo.uio.no/handle/10852/41451.

24. Collective *ijtihād*, *ijtihād jamāʿī*, brings together groups of scholars to issue *fiqh* rulings via joint deliberation. Such joint forums are increasingly being used in the Muslim world because of growing scientific and social complexities that are critical to the rendering of juridical verdicts. The methodology for such deliberation remains unsettled. For an overview of the history and methodology of collective *ijtihād*, see Aznan Hasan's "An Introduction to Collective Ijtihad (Ijtihad Jamai): Concept and Applications." *American Journal of Islamic Social Sciences* 20, no. 2 (2003): 26–49.

25. Shaikh Mohd Saifuddeen Bin Shaikh Mohd and Kuala Lumpur Salleh, "The Role of Diverse Stakeholders in Malaysian Bioethical Discourse," paper presented at an international conference in 2013: Health Related Issues and Islamic Normativity, hosted by the University of Hamburg and organized by the Department of Islamic Studies and South East Asian Studies at the Asia Africa Institute of the University of Hamburg and funded by the German Federal Ministry of Health and the Koerber Foundation.

26. Padela, Shanawani, and Arozullah, "Medical Experts and Islamic Scholars Deliberating over Brain Death"; A. I. Padela, A. Arozullah, and E. Moosa, "Brain Death in Islamic Ethico-Legal Deliberation: Challenges for Applied Islamic Bioethics," *Bioethics* 27, no. 3 (March 2013).

27. John-Stewart Gordon, "Bioethics," in *Internet Encyclopedia of Philosophy*, ed. James Fieser and Bradley Dowden. https://iep.utm.edu/bioethic/.

28. A. K. Reinhart, "Islamic Law as Islamic Ethics," *Journal of Religious Ethics* 11, no. 2 (1983).

29. Ghaly, "Biomedical Scientists as Co-Muftis."

30. Tariq Ramadan, *Radical Reform: Islamic Ethics and Liberation* (Oxford and New York: Oxford University Press, 2009).

31. Ibid.

32. A. Padela and F. Curlin, "Religion and Disparities: Considering the Influences of Islam on the Health of American Muslims," *Journal of Religion Health*, June 1, 2012; Aasim I. Padela and Afrah Raza, "American Muslim Health Disparities: The State of the Medline Literature," *Journal of Health Disparities Research and Practice* 8, no. 1 (2015).

33. A. Sachedina, *Islamic Biomedical Ethics: Principles and Application* (Oxford and New York: Oxford University Press, 2009); Ramadan, *Radical Reform*; T. Ramadan, "The Challenges and Future of Applied Islamic Ethics Discourse: A Radical Reform?," *Theoretical Medicine and Bioethics* 34, no. 2 (April 2013); Jonsen, "A History of Religion and Bioethics."

34. The Markfield Institute of Higher Education in the United Kingdom previously offered a certificate program in Islamic bioethics. I have heard that a similar graduate program is being launched in Saudi Arabia under the guidance of Dr. Abdullah Al-Joudi.

35. Vardit Rispler-Chaim, *Islamic Medical Ethics in the Twentieth Century* (Leiden, Netherlands: E. J. Brill, 1993).

36. Stef Van den Branden and Bert Broeckaert, "The Ongoing Charity of Organ Donation: Contemporary English Sunni Fatwas on Organ Donation and Blood Transfusion," *Bioethics* 25, no. 3 (2011); Stef Van den Branden and Bert Broeckaert, "Living in the Hands of God: English Sunni E-Fatwas on (Non-)Voluntary Euthanasia and Assisted Suicide," *Medicine, Health Care and Philosophy* 14, no. 1 (2011).

37. Padela et al., "Using Fatawa within Islamic and Muslim Bioethical Discourse."

38. M. E. Falagas et al., "Comparison of Pubmed, Scopus, Web of Science, and Google Scholar: Strengths and Weaknesses," *Federation of American Societies for Experimental Biology Journal* 22 (2008).

39. Shanawani and Khalil, "Reporting on 'Islamic Bioethics' in the Medical Literature."

40. Sachedina, *Islamic Biomedical Ethics*.

41. S. F. Hamdy, *Our Bodies Belong to God: Organ Transplants, Islam, and the Struggle for Human Dignity in Egypt* (Berkeley: University of California Press, 2012); F. Moazam, "Sharia Law and Organ Transplantation: Through the Lens of Muslim Jurists," *Asian Bioethics Review* 3, no. 4 (2011).

42. Federation of Islamic Medical Associations, *Encyclopedia of Islamic Medical Ethics*, part I, ed. H. E. Fadel et al. (Amman, Jordan: Jordan Society for Islamic Medical Sciences, 2013).

43. Islamic Medical Association of North America (IMANA) Ethics Committee, ed., "Medical Ethics: The IMANA Perspective" (Lombard, IL, 2005).

44. Asim I. Padela, "Muslim Perspectives on the American Healthcare System: The Discursive Framing of 'Islamic' Bioethical Discourse," *Die Welt des Islams* 55, nos. 3–4 (2015).

45. Ghaly, "Biomedical Scientists as Co-Muftis."

46. Mehrunisha Suleman, "Contributions and Ambiguities in Islamic Research Ethics and Research Conducted in Muslim Contexts: A Thematic Review of the Literature," *Journal of Health and Culture* 1, no. 1 (2016); Mehrunisha Suleman, "Biomedical Research Ethics in the Islamic Context: Reflections on and Challenges for Islamic Bioethics," *Islamic Bioethics: Current Issues and Challenges* 2 (2017).

47. Padela et al., "Dire Necessity and Transformation"; N. M. Isa, "Darurah (Necessity) and Its Application in Islamic Ethical Assessment of Medical Applications: A Review on Malaysian Fatwa," *Science and Engineering Ethics* 22, no. 5 (2015).

48. Padela, "Muslim Perspectives on the American Healthcare System"; Isa, "Darurah (Necessity) and Its Application in Islamic Ethical Assessment of Medical Applications."

REFERENCES

"Advice to a Physician, Advice of Haly Abbas (Ahwazi) [Tenth Century A.D.]." In *Encyclopedia of Bioethics*, rev. ed., vol. 5, ed. W. T. Reich. New York: Simon and Schuster Macmillan, 1995.

Ahmed, Mustafa. "Muslims and Medical Ethics: Time to Move Forward by Going Back." *Journal of Religion and Health* 55, no. 2 (2016): 367–68.

Arawi, Thalia A. "The Muslim Physician and the Ethics of Medicine." *Journal of the Islamic Medical Association of North America* 42, no. 3 (2010): 111–16.

Baldas, Tresa. "Report: Girl's Genital Mutilation Injury Worse Than Doctor Claims." *USA Today*, April 27, 2017.

Brody, H., and A. Macdonald. "Religion and Bioethics: Toward an Expanded Understanding." *Theoretical Medicine and Bioethics* 34, no. 2 (April 2013): 133–45.

Callahan, D. "Bioethics as a Discipline." *Studies of the Hastings Center* 1, no. 1 (1973): 66–73.

Chapman, Audrey. "In Defense of the Role of a Religiously Informed Bioethics." *American Journal of Bioethics* 12, no. 12 (2012): 3.

Cherry, M. *Religious Perspectives on Bioethics.* London: Taylor and Francis, 2013.

Claassen-Lüttner, J. Cayenne. "How Religious Ethics Can Be Intelligible and Compatible with Bioethics." *American Journal of Bioethics* 12, no. 12 (2012).

Clarke, Morgan, Thomas Eich, and Jenny Schreiber. "The Social Politics of Islamic Bioethics." *Die Welt des Islams* 55, nos. 3–4 (2015): 265–77.

De Vries, R. "Good without God: Bioethics and the Sacred." *Society* 52, no. 5 (2015): 438–47.

Engelhardt, H. T. *The Foundations of Christian Bioethics.* Amsterdam: Swets and Zeitlinger Publishers, 2000.

Falagas, M. E., E. I. Pitsouni, G. A. Malietzis, and G. Pappas. "Comparison of Pubmed, Scopus, Web of Science, and Google Scholar: Strengths and Weaknesses." *Federation of American Societies for Experimental Biology Journal* 22 (2008): 338–42.

Federation of Islamic Medical Associations. *Encyclopedia of Islamic Medical Ethics*, part I, ed. H. E. Fadel, A. A. Misha'l, A. F. M. Ebrahim, and M. M. Nordin, 129. Amman, Jordan: Jordan Society for Islamic Medical Sciences, 2013.

Ghaly, Mohammed. "Biomedical Scientists as Co-Muftis: Their Contribution to Contemporary Islamic Bioethics." *Die Welt des Islams* 55, nos. 3–4 (2015): 286–311.

———. "Islamic Bioethics: The Inevitable Interplay of 'Texts' and 'Contexts.'" *Bioethics* 28, no. 2 (2014): ii–v.

———. "Islamic Bioethics in the Twenty-First Century." *Zygon* 48, no. 3 (2013): 592–99.

Goldberg, Judah, and Alan Jotkowitz. "In Defense of Religious Bioethics." *American Journal of Bioethics* 12, no. 12 (2012).

Gordon, John-Stewart. "Bioethics." In *Internet Encyclopedia of Philosophy*, ed. James Fieser and Bradley Dowden. https://iep.utm.edu/bioethic/.

Grundmann, J. "Shari'ah, Brain Death and Organ Transplantation: The Context and Effect of Two Islamic Legal Decisions in the Near and Middle East." *American Journal of Islamic Social Sciences* 22, no. 4 (2005): 1–25.

Hamdy, S. F. *Our Bodies Belong to God: Organ Transplants, Islam, and the Struggle for Human Dignity in Egypt*. Berkeley: University of California Press, 2012.

Hasan, Aznan. "An Introduction to Collective Ijtihad (Ijtihad Jamai): Concept and Applications." *American Journal of Islamic Social Sciences* 20, no. 2 (2003): 26–49.

Hindu, Abu al-Faraj 'Ali ibn al-Husayn ibn. *Key to Medicine and a Guide for Students* (*The Great Books of Islamic Civilization*). Trans. Aida Tibi. Reading, UK: Garnet Publishing, 2011.

ibn al-Ash'ath as-Sijistani, Abu Dawud Sulayman. "Sunan Abi Dawud 3874." Book 29, Hadith 20 (English translation: Book 28, Hadith 3865). https://sunnah.com/abudawud/29/20.

International Organization of Islamic Medicine. *Islamic Code of Medical Ethics: Kuwait Document*. Kuwait City: Islamic Organization for Medical Sciences, 1981.

Isa, N. M. "Darurah (Necessity) and Its Application in Islamic Ethical Assessment of Medical Applications: A Review on Malaysian Fatwa." *Science and Engineering Ethics* 22, no. 5 (2015): 1319–32.

Islamic Bioethics Project. "Encyclopedia of Islamic Bioethics (EIB)." http://ibp.georgetown.domains/en/encyclopedia/.

Islamic Medical Association of North America (IMANA) Ethics Committee, ed. "Medical Ethics: The IMANA Perspective." Lombard, IL: IMANA, 2005.

Jonsen, A. R. "A History of Religion and Bioethics." In *Handbook of Bioethics and Religion*, ed. David E. Guinn, 23–36. Oxford: Oxford University Press, 2006.

Jonsen, Albert R. *A Short History of Medical Ethics.* New York: Oxford University Press, 2000.

Kelly, D. F., G. Magill, and H. Have. *Contemporary Catholic Health Care Ethics.* 2nd ed. Doha, Qatar: Georgetown University Press, 2013.

Kennedy Institute of Ethics. "Islamic Medical and Scientific Ethics." Doha, Qatar: Georgetown University Press. https://bioethics.georgetown.edu/library-materials/bioethics-research-library-databases/islamic-medical-and-scientific-ethics/.

Levey, M. "Medical Ethics of Medieval Islam with Special Reference to Al-Ruhawi's 'Practical Ethics of the Physician.'" *Transactions of the American Philosophical Society* 57, no. 3 (1967): 1–100.

Mitchell, C. B., and D. J. Riley. *Christian Bioethics: A Guide for Pastors, Health Care Professionals, and Families.* Nashville, TN: B&H Publishing Group, 2014.

Moazam, F. "Sharia Law and Organ Transplantation: Through the Lens of Muslim Jurists." *Asian Bioethics Review* 3, no. 4 (2011): 316–32.

Mohd, Shaikh Mohd Saifuddeen Bin Shaikh, and Kuala Lumpur Salleh. "The Role of Diverse Stakeholders in Malaysian Bioethical Discourse." Paper presented at an international conference in 2013: Health Related Issues and Islamic Normativity, hosted by the University of Hamburg and organized by the Department of Islamic Studies and South East Asian Studies at the Asia Africa Institute of the University of Hamburg and funded by the German Federal Ministry of Health and the Koerber Foundation.

Murphy, Timothy F. "In Defense of Irreligious Bioethics." *American Journal of Bioethics* 12, no. 12 (2012): 3–10.

Padela, A., and F. Curlin. "Religion and Disparities: Considering the Influences of Islam on the Health of American Muslims." *Journal of Religion Health*, June 1, 2012.

Padela, A. I. "Islamic Bioethics: Between Sacred Law, Lived Experiences, and State Authority." *Theoretical Medicine and Bioethics*, April 16, 2013.

Padela, A. I., A. Arozullah, and E. Moosa. "Brain Death in Islamic Ethico-Legal Deliberation: Challenges for Applied Islamic Bioethics." *Bioethics* 27, no. 3 (March 2013): 132–39.

Padela, A. I., and R. Duivenbode. "Medicine, Morals, and Female Genital Cutting." Hastings Center. https://www.thehastingscenter.org/medicine-morals-female-genital-cutting/.

Padela, A. I., S. W. Furber, M. A. Kholwadia, and E. Moosa. "Dire Necessity and Transformation: Entry-Points for Modern Science in Islamic Bioethical Assessment of Porcine Products in Vaccines." *Bioethics* 28, no. 2 (February 2014): 59–66.

Padela, A. I., H. Shanawani, and A. Arozullah. "Medical Experts and Islamic Scholars Deliberating over Brain Death: Gaps in the Applied Islamic Bioethics Discourse." *Muslim World* 101, no. 1 (2011): 53–72.

Padela, A. I., H. Shanawani, M. A. Kholwadia, and A. Arozullah. "Using Fatawa within Islamic and Muslim Bioethical Discourse: The Role of Doctrinal and

Theological Considerations—a Case Study of Surrogate Motherhood." In *Islam and Bioethics*, ed. Berna Arda and Vardit Rispler-Chaim. Ankara: Ankara University Press, 2011.

Padela, Aasim I. "Muslim Perspectives on the American Healthcare System: The Discursive Framing of 'Islamic' Bioethical Discourse." *Die Welt des Islams* 55, nos. 3–4 (2015): 413–47.

Padela, Aasim I., and Afrah Raza. "American Muslim Health Disparities: The State of the Medline Literature." *Journal of Health Disparities Research and Practice* 8, no. 1 (2015): 1–9.

Pellegrino, E. D., and A. I. Faden. *Jewish and Catholic Bioethics: An Ecumenical Dialogue*. Doha, Qatar: Georgetown University Press, 1999.

Potter, Van Rensselaer. "Bioethics, the Science of Survival." *Perspectives in Biology and Medicine* 14, no. 1 (1970): 127–53.

Ramadan, T. "The Challenges and Future of Applied Islamic Ethics Discourse: A Radical Reform?" *Theoretical Medicine and Bioethics* 34, no. 2 (April 2013): 105–15.

Ramadan, Tariq. *Radical Reform: Islamic Ethics and Liberation*. Oxford and New York: Oxford University Press, 2009.

Reinhart, A. K. "Islamic Law as Islamic Ethics." *Journal of Religious Ethics* 11, no. 2 (1983): 186–203.

Rispler-Chaim, Vardit. *Islamic Medical Ethics in the Twentieth Century*. Leiden, Netherlands: E. J. Brill, 1993.

Rosner, F., J. D. Bleich, and M. M. Brayer. *Jewish Bioethics*. Brooklyn, NY: KTAV Publishing House, 2000.

Sachedina, A. *Islamic Biomedical Ethics: Principles and Application*. Oxford and New York: Oxford University Press, 2009.

Sartell, E., and A. I. Padela. "Adab and Its Significance for an Islamic Medical Ethics." *Journal of Medical Ethics* 41, no. 9 (September 2015): 756–61.

Schmidt, Samantha. "Detroit-Area Doctors Indicted in 'Brutal' Genital Mutilation Case." *Washington Post*, April 27, 2017.

Schuklenk, Udo. "On the Role of Religion in Articles This Journal Seeks to Publish." *Developing World Bioethics* 18, no. 3 (2018): 207.

Shanawani, Hasan, and Mohammad Hassan Khalil. "Reporting on 'Islamic Bioethics' in the Medical Literature." In *Muslim Medical Ethics: From Theory to Practice*, ed. Jonathan Brockopp and Thomas Eich, 213–28. Columbia: University of South Carolina Press, 2008.

Skovgaard-Petersen, Jakob. "A Typology of Fatwas." *Die Welt des Islams* 55, nos. 3–4 (2015).

Stempsey, William E. "Bioethics Needs Religion." *American Journal of Bioethics* 12, no. 12 (2012).

Stokke, Ole Martin Bøe. "The Construction of Modern Islamic Authority: Analyzing the Medical Ethics of the Islamic Organization for Medical Sciences."

PhD dissertation, University of Oslo, Oslo, 2014. https://www.duo.uio.no/handle/10852/41451.

Suleman, Mehrunisha. "Biomedical Research Ethics in the Islamic Context: Reflections on and Challenges for Islamic Bioethics." *Islamic Bioethics: Current Issues and Challenges* 2 (2017): 197.

———. "Contributions and Ambiguities in Islamic Research Ethics and Research Conducted in Muslim Contexts: A Thematic Review of the Literature." *Journal of Health and Culture* 1, no. 1 (2016): 46–57.

Tham, J., K. M. Kwan, and A. Garcia. *Religious Perspectives on Bioethics and Human Rights*. Cham, Switzerland: Springer International, 2017.

Van den Branden, Stef, and Bert Broeckaert. "Living in the Hands of God: English Sunni E-Fatwas on (Non-)Voluntary Euthanasia and Assisted Suicide." *Medicine, Health Care and Philosophy* 14, no. 1 (2011): 29–41.

———. "The Ongoing Charity of Organ Donation: Contemporary English Sunni Fatwas on Organ Donation and Blood Transfusion." *Bioethics* 25, no. 3 (2011).

Williams, Janice. "Nearly 100 Girls May Have Had Genitals Cut by Doctors in Michigan, Prosecutor Says." *Newsweek*, June 6, 2017.

Zavala-Offman, Alyza. "Penalties Worsen as More Female Genital Mutilation Victims Are Suspected." *Detroit Metro Times*, June 9, 2017.

ONE

The Relationship between Religion and Medicine

Insights from the *Fatwā* Literature

VARDIT RISPLER-CHAIM

Islamic medical ethics is the scholarly field in which the permissibility of certain medical treatments and procedures is evaluated by Islamic ethico-legal criteria. The purpose of this evaluation is to clarify for devout Muslims, patients, and doctors whether the resort to a certain treatment or medication conforms to Islamic legal principles, rulings, and theology. If the ethical assessment is positive, devout Muslims can be assured that they may apply the given medical treatment or medication without fear of violating the lawful rulings of their religion. The questions covered by Islamic medical ethics today are similar in content and scope to those covered by medical ethics in "the West." The answers, however, are not identical, since Islamic bioethics must abide by guidelines laid down in the Qur'an, the *Sunnah* of the Prophet Muhammad, Islamic law, and the independent decisions (*ijtihād*) of Muslim jurists made over the course of fourteen centuries and down to the present.

INTRODUCTION

Islamic medical ethics is thus formulated mainly by religious scholars and jurisconsults,[1] and is often issued in the format of a *fatwā*. A *fatwā* is essentially an answer to a real or fictitious question posted by lay Muslims, Islamic authorities and institutions, or even by the scholars themselves. The accumulation of the thousands of *fatāwā* collected through all these centuries of Islamic legal activity is what constitutes the "*fatwā* literature." This can be classified according to the period when a *fatwā* was issued: fifteenth century, nineteenth century, or twenty-first century; according to the individual jurist who issued the *fatāwā*; or according to the legal institution/council with which a group of *muftīs* is affiliated.

The *fatwā* literature can also be classified according to the topic under discussion. For the present chapter I analyze what I call "medical *fatāwā*"—that is, *fatāwā* on medicine, surgery, pharmacology, general health, and mental health. My aim is to depict the characteristics of the relationship between religion and medicine or, more accurately, between the agents of medicine—the physicians and scientists, on the one hand, and the Muslim religious ethicists–Islamic jurists, on the other. Through this lens it might be possible to resolve the dilemma of whether the Islamic religion is an obstacle to scientific progress—a query raised against Islam in recent decades. This study also provides insight on the extent to which Muslims are likely to be "consumers" of modern advanced medicine and its technology. So what, at present, can we learn about the Muslim jurists' attitudes concerning medicine from the medical *fatāwā*?

The abundance of *fatāwā* on medical issues, at least during the past four decades, in itself attests to the interest today in the achievements of medicine and the intense wish of Muslims—patients, scholars, and physicians alike—to welcome the achievements of medicine into their daily lives.

A traditional historian and thinker, ʻAbd al-Raḥmān ʻAlī al-Ḥajjī, stated that any scientific idea or "valid truth" cannot be contradictory to Islam. Since God created the world as well as everything in it, it is impossible for the world and "truth" (science and medicine, for example, both created by God and stemming from the same source of power and wisdom) to be in dissonance.[2] Therefore, Muslim jurists attempt to reconcile newly introduced medical innovations with the spirit of Islamic law so that these innovations may be embraced in practice by Muslim physicians and patients. This relationship is also the interest of non-Muslim physicians who care for Muslim patients if they wish to continue offering modern medicine to Muslim patients as well as to non-Muslims.

The general difficulty for Muslims with modern medicine is that they view it as a "Western European and American" product that, as such, may introduce into Islamic communities undesirable Western byproducts such as materialism, secularism, and promiscuity. The role of Muslim ethicists is sometimes to obliterate such fears.

Islamic bioethics today is formulated by three groups of people:

1. Muslim physicians, who are graduates of medical schools all over the world.
2. *Muftīs*, who are jurisconsults from the circles of *'ulamā'* (religious scholars) in various Islamic societies whose duty is to evaluate medical procedures and decide whether they can be approved or must be prohibited according to Shariah criteria. Unlike in the past, in recent years *muftīs* have worked in larger consultative bodies, such as those at the IFA (Islamic *Fiqh* Academy, New Delhi), the IIFA (International Islamic *Fiqh* Academy, Jeddah), the CSS (Council of Senior Scholars/*'ulamā'* of Saudi Arabia), the ECFR (European Council for *Fatwā* and Research, Dublin), and so on.
3. Muslim jurists and lawyers, who frequently react to aspects of human rights and international law that arise from medical and ethical issues.

We now turn to the relationship between the first two groups, 1 and 2, since most *fatāwā* on medical issues are the outcome of their deliberations. As already mentioned, in these *fatāwā* the *muftī* represents Islamic law and the physician the science of medicine.

For his Muslim "clients" the *muftī* is the bridge between the proposed medical treatment and Shariah norms. Usually the *muftī* consults a physician or a scientist who, before the *muftī* issues the *fatwā*, explains to the *muftī* the proposed medical treatment as regards the steps involved, the prognosis for recovery, and more. Then the *muftī* alone, or joined by an assembly of *muftīs*, will weigh the pros and cons and present his decision in the form of a *fatwā* that is announced to the public. The medical *fatwā* often contains a section that provides the relevant medical information in simplified scientific language.

This "dialogue" between the doctor and the *muftī* that precedes the announcement of a *fatwā* constitutes collaboration between two ways of thinking to set out "Islamic" behavioral norms in medicine. Although the *muftī* is often the one who initiates the discussion with the doctor, sometimes the reverse is the case. At times, the doctor's personality, gender, religious affiliation, and moral conduct are themselves the subjects of the *fatāwā* (e.g., regarding doctor-patient relations and the doctor's liability). For example, often a Muslim woman asks the *muftī* whether she can be treated by a male physician when a female physician is unavailable or too far away to reach; the answer is not always affirmative. However, when the male physician is a specialist, the situation is of medical urgency, precautions are taken to avoid *khālwa* (forbidden seclusion between a stranger male and a female), and the physician is trustworthy (*thiqa*)—treatment by the male physician is legitimized.[3] The physician's good manners and moral character are crucial for such legitimization.

ATTITUDES ABOUT MEDICINE AND PHYSICIANS THAT *MUFTĪS* HAVE REFLECTED IN THEIR *FATĀWĀ*

The Information and Knowledge of the Medical Staff Is Limited When Compared to the Knowledge of God

The knowledge available to doctors will always remain inferior to the knowledge available to God; therefore, doctors should demonstrate humility with regard to the knowledge they have accumulated.

Representing traditional Islamic seminary scholarship, the popular Egyptian Muftī Muhammad Mutawalli al-Sha'rāwī (1911–98) commented on artificial insemination, test-tube babies, and the ability to foretell the sex of a fetus still in the womb.[4] He stated that medical achievements in the above fields did not attest that medicine "knows what is in the womb"—a phrase attributed to God in Qur'an 31:34. Medicine, he continues, knows the little it knows only when a fetus is already in the womb and with the help of instruments and tests. God knows the fate of each fetus even before fertilization, without tests and technology. Furthermore, God knows the characteristics of the fetus once born, whether it will grow up to be tall or short, wise or stupid, happy or miserable, and so on. A similar opinion was given by Shaykh 'Aṭiyya Ṣaqr (1914–2006), head of the al-Azhar *Fatwā* Committee in Egypt.[5] With regard to the genetic cloning that led to the birth of the sheep Dolly, an anonymous *muftī* claimed that the experiment had a success rate of only 0.36 percent.[6] The mention of this low rate was meant to emphasize the limitations of scientific knowledge, and possibly to attribute the birth of Dolly to luck rather than to actual scientific mastery.

As to whether fetuses diagnosed as suffering from genetic disorders may be aborted, Dr. Yūsuf al-Qaraḍāwī claims that since doctors sometimes err, their conclusions must not be taken as final, and therefore such fetuses should not be aborted.[7] In other words, since diagnostics during pregnancy are not unequivocal, the results of such tests are not fully reliable. On the other hand, in Saudi Arabia the Council of Senior Scholars (CSS) judged that—if (a) a fetus is severely malformed, (b) three expert physicians concur (c) that it cannot be cured of this deformity, (d) no more than 120 days have passed since gestation, and (e) the parents so wish—the fetus may be aborted.[8] The Iranian parliament similarly passed a law in 2003 allowing abortion of a malformed fetus if certain circumstances (similar to those required in Saudi Arabia) materialized. Given the relation between religious jurists and lawmakers in Iran, this law must have received approval from senior *Shi'i* scholars.[9]

Most of the examples shown so far seem to belong to the general domains of beginning and end of life, birth and death. Physicians are often attacked on these issues for attempting to "play God" when they suggest abortion of a fetus or disconnection of life-saving machines from the terminally ill. The medical *fatāwā* stress the inferiority of physicians' knowledge compared to that of God and attack the physicians' "pretensions" that they know what the actual fate of a fetus or a patient may be and consequently act on that (mistaken) premise.

In all the cases in which the success of a medical treatment or procedure is below 100 percent, the *muftīs* attribute the "missing" percentages to God's intervention and powers. For example, it is permissible to resort to sex preselection of a fetus under certain conditions, since the sex-preselection procedure is 98 percent successful. The remaining 2 percent represents God's will, thus indicating that *only* God decides if the goal desired by the parents and the doctors is realizable in practice. The 98 percent success rate is therefore the result of God's will.[10] This last justification for sex selection refutes a major counterclaim that, given the choice, most parents in traditional societies will choose to produce sons and thereby cause an imbalance between males and females in society as well as further social problems. Such an imbalance is, of course, undesirable in any society, the Islamic society included. However, when the success rate is below 100 percent, we must deduce that God reserves to Himself the place to intervene in the "man-planned" technique and change its results to others more desirable for society at large.

The same motif—that God can interfere in humanity's plans—applies to fertility and contraception: not all people who use contraceptives manage to control their pregnancies with 100 percent success, while not everyone who wishes to bear children succeeds. The gap between the human desire and the final results testifies that God is in charge of every birth, even when it appears "natural."[11]

Medical Knowledge Is Wisdom That God Has Previously Graciously Placed in the World for Humankind to Discover and Use

The *fatwā* literature also seems to underscore that scientific discoveries are only the belated recoveries of the knowledge and understanding of natural phenomena that God placed in the world at its creation. Human discoveries are not proof of excellence and creativity on the part of humankind and scientists but are indications of the limitations of the human brain. Only recently, with God's assistance, has the human brain matured to a level that enables scientists to understand some of the natural phenomena better than before. "Innovations" in medicine are new only with respect to the time they are disclosed to present-day scientists compared with scientists of previous generations. God placed these "innovations" in the universe, perhaps at the creation, in readiness for the right moment, when He decides to render them accessible to scientists to understand and apply. The human brain develops according to God's plan and pace, and what scientists understand today is only what God allows their brains to comprehend. No "innovation" is "man-made."

On cloning, for example, as much as theologians fear that scientists will eventually be able to interfere in determining the characteristics of a "desired person," it is stated that nothing is new about the creation of people by means other than intercourse between a man and a woman. The Qur'an is invoked to prove that Adam was created from earth, without having a father or a mother, and Isa (Jesus) was created from a mother without a father. This implies that "unnatural" births have been known to exist as early as the creation of the world. Also, God created all the elements used in the cloning process beforehand. Thus, cloning—any cloning—rather than being a "creation" of a new living creature is an assembly process using existing elements that God has created.[12] The preselection of a fetus's sex is also attributed to knowledge God has enabled humans to obtain. In other words, if God did not want man to have certain pieces of knowledge, that scientific "discovery" regarding preselection would never have been made by man.[13]

The encouragement to avoid consanguinity, and hence to reduce the chances of producing children with genetic disorders, was addressed by Muftī 'AbdAllāh al-Mushidd (1903–90) when he was head of the *Fatwā* Committee at al-Azhar in Cairo. He asserted that the Qur'anic verse 4:23, which lists all the possible degrees of women related to a man whom a man may not marry, had already taken into consideration the genetic perils of consanguinity. In the Qur'an, revealed in the seventh century, God had already taught what science came to know only many centuries later.[14]

With regard to in vitro fertilization (IVF) treatments and whether the doctors who practice them interfere with acts of God, the answer is that the sperm and the ovum are created by God. All that the doctors can do today is to ease the way for sperm and ovum to meet. Again, it is actually God who provided the knowledge necessary to circumvent problems in the reproductive system. God's knowledge preceded that of the physicians.[15] The fact that for most medical inventions religious scholars can show similar precedents in the Qur'an and the *ḥadīth*, the two divinely ordained sources in Islam, indicates that God attended to human needs and healing processes more than thirteen centuries ago at least—long before the modern human mind became capable even of conceiving them.

Medicine Is a Useful Tool That Allah Created for the Benefit of the Human (*maṣlaḥa*)

As a sign of God's compassion and mercy toward His human creatures, He revealed the art of medicine as professional knowledge to certain people who should, in turn, transfer this knowledge to laypeople in order to heal them and ease their pain. Medicine is classified in Islamic law and ethics as *farḍ kifāya*, meaning that the service extended by physicians to the community is a religious duty (communal obligation). Consequently, a nation (*umma*) that does not care to train a number of its members as physicians is committing a sin. Medicine is so important and useful for a Muslim community that physicians, even when they make mistakes, are not held liable (unless proven negligent) lest, afraid of erring, they avoid extending medical help altogether.[16]

Muftīs often use the ethico-legal construct of *maṣlaḥa* to legitimize modern medications and means of treatment when they cannot find legitimacy for them in classical legal or medical literature. Such is the case, for example, with organ transplantation. Shaykh Muḥammad Sayyid Ṭanṭāwī, Shaykh al-Azhar and *muftī* of the Republic of Egypt until his death in 2010, declared that he wished to donate all of his organs after his death. Yet he did not rule on a critical issue, namely, the dilemma of what exactly is the moment of death, but left it to the doctors to decide. The subject of brain death is still debated in Egypt today, as Sherine Hamdy explained in an interview on the publication of her book *Our Bodies Belong to God: Organ Transplants, Islam, and the Struggle for Human Dignity in Egypt.*[17]

By pledging to donate his organs and avoiding precarious pitfalls such as the brain death debate, Shaykh Ṭanṭāwī recognized the pragmatic value of organ transplantation in saving life. The debate in the Islamic world between the two methods of determining death (brain death or cessation of heartbeat and breathing) continues; but Ṭanṭāwī hurried to embrace the transplant technique itself, recognizing its overall benefit.[18]

Strong encouragement to donate organs, from both the living and the dead, was reiterated again in 2006 by the Grand Muftī of the Republic of Tunisia, Kameleddine Djaït, who declared organ transplantation both a huge scientific achievement and a great benefit to humankind.[19]

Autopsies, too, although they involve undesirable issues from an Islamic legal perspective, such as delaying burial, moving the body from the place of death, and possibly violating its integrity, are mostly legitimized based on *maṣlaḥa*. The benefits that might accrue from autopsies are both educational and ethical. On the one hand, they can help us learn about the causes of diseases and death, which can help us prevent plagues and diseases in the future. On the other hand, autopsies can also bring about justice: for example, if a death is suspected of having been caused by a criminal act, the autopsy can reveal this, and the criminals responsible will be brought to justice.

Similarly, the use that medical students make of human skeletons, and even the sale and purchase of skeletons, are legitimized on grounds of the pragmatic understanding that what medical students learn from a human cadaver, as well as the scientific benefit that accrues to the public, take precedence over the damage that may be caused to the body during dissection.[20] Similarly, medical students are permitted to observe in medical textbooks explicit "provocative" pictures of female organs because they need to know what these organs look like and where exactly in the body they are located.[21] The pragmatism here overcomes the prohibition against *ʿawra*—exposure of female or male body parts to members of the other sex unless they are of certain blood or marital relations.

Muftīs largely permit the use of contraceptive pills by women who wish to postpone their monthly periods in order to successfully complete with the rest of their families a hajj that they have embarked on or the fast of Ramadan. This is an interesting adaptation of a scientific advance—the hormonal contraceptive pill. Muslim jurists do not object to "the pill" as a means of family planning, but in relation to the hajj and the fast they permit taking it for a purpose entirely different from that for which it was originally intended. This means that the pill, a contraceptive first and foremost, has been transformed, due to its side effect, into a useful tool to control menstruation. In religious terms, the pill can aid women in maintaining their purity (menses are considered ritual impurity), without which women cannot perform the hajj, the fast, or ritual prayer.[22]

Through the ethico-legal construct of *maṣlaḥa* many more medical advances have entered into the realm of Islamic legal permissibility.

Medicine and Religion Serve the Same Purposes

The establishment of a medical school in 1961 at al-Azhar University, an institution that had represented the fortress of *ʿulamāʾ* and a leading center of seminary studies, in itself represents a bridge that connects religion and science.

Several *muftīs* praise the performance of religious duties as instruments to preserve or improve both physical and mental health. Shaykh 'Aṭiyya Ṣaqr states that observing the religious duties prevents mental illness and psychological complications. He relies on Qur'anic verse 13:38 to support his claim.[23] It is clear from the *fatwā* that Ṣaqr is aware of the existence of medical treatments for mental diseases, but he is probably referring to the preventive stage when he says he believes that religious devotion may have a healing impact. Medical doctors would undoubtedly agree that it is easier and more useful to prevent a disease than to try to cure it once it has occurred. There is a popular saying in Arabic: "*al-wiqāya khayr min al-'ilāj*"—prevention is better than treatment. And, although the adage is not attributed directly to the Prophet Muhammad, it is supposedly based on the Prophet's instructions on how to prevent diseases by maintaining cleanliness, avoiding the places of disease and impurity, and seeking health in supplications to God.[24]

Some doctors eagerly seek to prove that religious duties and Shariah laws contribute to good health. Dr. al-Sayyid Nijm, head of a faculty at al-Azhar, explains that the fast is the best instrument for letting the body eliminate waste accumulated in it during the previous year, for reorganizing eating times, for giving the stomach a rest, and so on. In any case, he adds, doctors recommend eating less for better health.[25]

A booklet published in London in 1982 explains "how scrupulous standards of personal hygiene are attained by a Muslim following the injunctions of the Qur'an and the example of God's Prophet, Muhammad upon whom be peace." Thus, by performing the religious duties that are preceded by specific purification rituals, the Muslim believer enhances his or her health and avoids diseases—without even being aware of it.[26]

The personality of the Muslim doctor, especially if he or she is a devout Muslim, renders him or her sufficiently reliable, trustworthy, and morally upright to mediate between medical and Islamic practices.

In one case, a physician advised a woman who had already undergone four C-sections to undergo tubal ligation to protect her health. This advice seems to contravene the prohibition of permanent sterilization. However, Muftī al-Mushidd, then head of the *Fatwā* Committee at al-Azhar, stated that if a trustworthy physician (*tabīb 'adl*) ruled it necessary, that ruling should be followed.[27] Thus medical testimony and *ḍarūra* (dire necessity) appear to mediate religious injunctions.

Whenever a contradiction arises between conventional medical judgment and Shariah norms, a "trustworthy Muslim physician" (*tabīb thiqa* or *tabīb ʿadl*) is called upon to decide. In one such case, a person was admitted to hospital during Ramadan and needed blood transfusions to save his life. The doctor in charge asked donors to break their fasts so that the donated blood would be of good quality. The question at stake was "Can a physician order another human being to break the fast and violate a duty imposed by God?" Dr. Sayyid Rizq al-Ṭawīl, then chair of the Faculty of Islamic Studies at al-Azhar, concluded that if the doctor was Muslim and had weighed the benefit of giving the donation against the loss of a day of fasting, the doctor's recommendation should be accepted, and the donors would have to make up for the missed fast after Ramadan.[28]

Conflict between one's religious conscience and medical practices is also noted in *fatāwā*. Here it seems that religious duties prevail over medical ones. One doctor reported to Lajnat al-Fatwā at al-Azhar that he was employed at a public hospital where he was sometimes required to perform sterilization surgery (with the patient's consent). He inquired whether such a surgery was permitted by the Shariah and if he could receive a monthly salary from that hospital for performing these operations. The answer was that such a surgery was condemned, and earning from an illicit act was forbidden, too. In sum, the hospital director could not oblige that doctor to perform such a surgery.[29] In this case it was the doctor who tried to stop the contravention of religious mores by obstructing a medical treatment that the Shariah does not tolerate.

Similarly, in a *fatwā* posted on April 22, 2010, by Darul Iftaa of the United Kingdom, a physician who was asked to perform abortions against his conscience was advised that if the abortion was justified by Shariah criteria, the doctor could perform it, and if not, or if he objected to abortions altogether, he could refer the patient desiring the abortion to another doctor who did not object to the procedure. The *fatwā* did not mention whether the patient herself was Muslim or not, nor does it seem to matter from an ethical point of view.[30]

In Sweden, for example, it is non-Muslim physicians who are approached by Muslim (and other) girls to perform hymen restorations, or so-called re-virgination procedures. Swedish physicians are divided over whether to accede, thereby saving the girls' lives, or to refuse and not let "traditional norms" and "patriarchal norms" take over modern lives, imposing controversial ancient customs in a "free modern society."[31] Muslim *muftīs* are often more negatively inclined toward hymen restoration than the Swedish doctors are, albeit not for the same reasons. While the Swedish doctors oppose these surgeries because they do not want to give in to "anti-feminist customs," *muftīs* object to them lest young women enjoy promiscuity in their sexual behavior, then resort to hymen restoration time and again, deceiving prospective husbands who believe their young wives are virgins, while their virginity has been falsified.[32]

Apparently Iranian physicians, too, aware of the moral and legal detriments of hymenoplasty, confessed that they had reluctantly performed the surgery on girls who turned to them for this purpose, just to save those women's lives, despite the fear of possible punitive measures awaiting them if caught.[33]

Nowadays we are becoming accustomed to seeing medical documents presented and considered in court in matters of marriage, divorce, custody of children, and so on. The Swedish doctors' debates on hymenoplasty, the Iranian doctors' confessions, and many more similar events show that Shariah has entered the hospital corridors as well. This is a fact, and it is hard to conclude whether anyone benefits from these encounters, and if someone does, who it is. In the majority of cases, when doctors and lay Muslims meet, whether in the hospitals or the clinics, one may assume that the meetings end in ways satisfactory to both. (Negative encounters usually end up in court.)

As for the relationships between *muftīs* and doctors, for the most part their collaboration seems to work satisfactorily for both, as the plethora of medical *fatāwā* may attest. However, recently an article was published about *muftīs* complaining that Muslim physicians and biomedical scientists have transgressed their limits and, instead of merely informing the *muftīs* about the scientific aspects of a phenomenon, they have started issuing "*fatāwā*" of their own, using *ijtihād* (even offering their own commentaries to the Qur'an and the *Sunnah*) without being trained in them. The "accused" scientists did not retreat in the face of the religious scholars' complaints. Defending themselves, they claimed that, as "Muslim scientists," not just scientists, they were eligible to participate in the process of *ijtihād* leading to bioethical solutions.[34]

CONCLUSION

From the analysis of medical *fatāwā* several themes emerge: (a) A physician's knowledge is limited compared with that of God; doctors can err, but God never errs. (b) Whatever physicians know is a grace from God, who down the generations has let them understand some of His miracles in His creation, which doctors mistakenly consider "their own discoveries." (c) All in all, the science of medicine carries benefits for humankind; therefore, learning medicine is encouraged, and it is legally graded *farḍ kifāya*.

Medicine is not a science alien to Muslims, nor is it new to them. Muftī Ṭanṭāwī of Egypt nicely phrased the situation as follows: "Medicine entered Europe with an *'imāma* [Islamic turban] and returned to us with a *qubā'a* [European rimmed hat]." By so saying he concisely expressed the frustration with and even bitterness toward Muslims, who, having led the medical sciences until the twelfth and thirteenth centuries, lost their hegemony to Europe and the West. A paradigmatic example of this loss and appropriation by the West is the *siwāk*—a natural toothbrush that the Prophet, already in the seventh century, encouraged Muslims to use for hygienic purposes as part of their purification rituals. The *siwāk* is a toothbrush that, unlike the contemporary toothbrush, does not need toothpaste. But, out of ignorance, Muslims let it go. Then, in recent centuries, European companies started producing toothpastes from the same ingredients embedded in the *siwāk*, and nowadays Muslims have to purchase this toothpaste—something that originally belonged to them.[35]

The originally Islamic medicine returning to Islamic societies from Europe and the West today is indeed garbed in European attire. Many of the medical *fatāwā* contain full citations from medical textbooks, which have largely originated in the West. Thus Muslim medical students and doctors rely on Western medical literature for their educations. But this does not mean that they never encounter ethical difficulties in prescribing "Western" medicine for Muslim clients. Nor does it mean that Muslims are against science. It does mean that the medicine suggested for Muslims must be presented and explained in terms that assure them that, although they use "Western" technology and knowledge, they still remain within the domain of Islamic theological and legal legitimacy. Muslims need this assurance, just as they need assurances that the banks they use and the jobs they hold respect certain basic Islamic tenets. This is where the role of the *muftī* becomes critically important, as he brings the science of medicine into alignment with Islamic values by using ethico-legal devices of law and by being informed of the biomedical science by clinicians. Accordingly, Muslims for the great part enjoy the general benefits of medicine along with the rest of the world, but make minor adjustments to medical practice on the basis of Islamic bioethics.

NOTES

1. By this term I mean a trained Islamic jurist, or *muftī*.

2. 'Alī al-Ḥajjī, in Yvonne Yazbeck Haddad, *Contemporary Islam and the Challenge of History* (Albany: State University of New York Press, 1982), 172.

3. Markaz al-Fatwa, "Tadāwī Al-Mar'a 'Ind Al-Rajul in Lam Tūjad Ṭabība (Fatwa 148487)," Fatawa Islam Web, http://fatwa.islamweb.net/fatwa/printfatwa.php?Id=148487&lang=A; "Ḍawābiṭ Takashshuf Al-Mar'a Amām Al-Ṭabīb (Fatwa 165873)," Fatawa Islam Web, http://www.islamweb.net/fatwa/printfatwa.php?Id=165873&lang=A; "Qarār Al-Majma' Al-Fiqhī Bi-Sha'n Aṭfāl Al-Anābīb (Fatwa 153375)," Fatawa Islam Web, http://www.islamweb.net/fatwa/printfatwa.php?Id=153375&lang=A.

4. Muḥammad Mutawallī Al-Sha'rāwī, *Kull Mā Yahimm Al-Muslim Fi Ḥayātihi Wayawmihi Wa-Ghaddihi* (*All That Interests the Muslim in His Life, Daily Life, and Future*), vol. 1 (Cairo: Maktabat al-Qur'an, 1981), 24–25.

5. *Māyū* (in Egypt, an organ of the National Democratic Party), November 28, 1994, p. 4.

6. *Al-Nūr* (in Egypt, an organ of the Liberal party Al-Aḥrār), February 18, 1998, p. 6.

7. al-Qaraḍāwī (b. 1926) is an Egyptian scholar who has resided for many years in Qatar and is known to be a fervent supporter of the Muslim Brotherhood in Egypt, for which he was sentenced to death in absentia in Egypt after the fall of Mohamed Morsi's regime. He was accused by his opponents from the Salafi movement of being too independent in his decisions, and not sufficiently reliant on the holy scriptures. The *fatwā* appears in *Sayyidatī* no. 778, February 3–9, 1996, p. 84 (the journal was published in London with Saudi financing).

8. Saleh al-Alaiyan and Khalid M. Alfaleh, "Aborting a Malformed Fetus: A Debatable Issue in Saudi Arabia," *Journal of Clinical Neonatology* 3, no. 4 (2014): 242.

9. K. M. Hedayat, P. Shooshtarizadeh, and M. Raza, "Therapeutic Abortion in Islam: Contemporary Views of Muslim Shiite Scholars and Effect of Recent Iranian Legislation," *Journal of Medical Ethics* 32, no. 11 (2006): 652–57.

10. Vardit Rispler-Chaim, "Contemporary Muftis between Bioethics and Social Reality: Selection of the Sex of a Fetus as Paradigm," *Journal of Religious Ethics* 36 (2008): 53–76.

11. This is emphasized in many *fatāwā* that permit using contraceptives in Islam. The answers often rely on the "quiet" permission that Prophet Muhammad gave for using *coitus interruptus* (*'azl*), explaining that "a soul would not be created if God has not created it." In other words, pregnancy can occur *despite the use of 'azl*, or may not occur even when *'azl* is not used and pregnancy is desired. See http://hadith.al-islam.com/Page.aspx...ID=34&PID=4289, July 2010, accessed October 24, 2017. Reference is made to *Ṣaḥīḥ Muslim* in particular.

12. "Mashrū' bayān al-istinsākh al-basharī li-majma' al-buḥūth al-Islāmiyya." *Majallat al-Azhar* 7 (November 1997): 1066–74. A fatwā issued in *al-Mujtama'* (published in Kuwait on January 25, 2003, pp. 40–41) states that "al-istinsākh laysa khalqan jadīdan" (cloning is not equal to a new creation), meaning that cloning is a scientific experiment with material that God has created. Objections to human cloning stem from fear of eugenics and of "changing what God created," but this does not include cloning of certain organs to replace a defective organ, which is permissible. Dr. 'Alī Jum'a, "Istinsākh juz' aw 'uḍw lil-'ilāj jā'iz," *al-Liwā' al-Islāmī,* September 30, 2004, p. 7.

13. Umar Sulaymān al-Ashqar, Muḥammad Uthmān Shubayr, 'Abd al-Nāṣir Abū al-Basal, 'Ārif 'Alī 'Ārif, and 'Abbās Aḥmad Muḥammd al-Bāz, *Dirāsāt Fiqhiyya fī Qaḍāyā Ṭibbiyya Mu'āṣira* (Amman: Dār al-Nafā'is, 2001), 2:870.

14. *Al-Ahrām* (a daily newspaper that, at the time, represented a wide range of opinions), April 4, 1986, 15; *Māyū*, March 25, 1996, 9.

15. *Al-Liwā' al-Islāmī,* April 2, 1987, "Ṭifl al-anābīb wal-talqīḥ al-ṣinā'ī."

16. On the importance of medical treatment, see also Majma' al-Ṭibb al-Islāmī, "al-'ilāj al-ṭibbī," http://islamtoday.net/bohooth/artshow-32-4705.htm, March 5, 2012, accessed June 7, 2014.

17. Steven Viney, "Q&A with Sherine Hamdy: Organ Transplants, Islam and the Struggle for Human Dignity in Egypt," *Egypt Independent*, January 15, 2012.

18. *Al-Naba' al-Waṭanī*, May 11, 1997, p. 1. "Fī qaḍiyyat zar' al-a'ḍā'" As M. Albar wrote: "The subject of brain death was discussed for the first time in the Second International Conference of Islamic Jurists held in Jeddah in 1985. No decree was passed at that time, until further studies and consultations were obtained. In the Third International Conference of Islamic Jurists (Amman 1986), the historic resolution (No. 5) was passed with a majority of votes, which equated brain death to cardiac and respiratory death." M. Albar, "Organ Transplantation: A Sunni Islamic Perspective," *Saudi Journal of Kidney Diseases and Transplantation* 23, no. 4 (2012).

19. Cheikh Kameleddine Djaït, "La fatwa Tunisienne" (translated into French in January 2009), *Don et Vie*, Bulletin 4, January 2009.

20. *Majallat al-Azhar*, July 1997, 3:408. Lajnat al-Fatwa bil-Azhar. See also Ḥasanayn Muḥammad Makhlūf in *al-Ahrām*, January 26, 1990, 13.

21. http://www.iislamqa.com/paging_fatawa.php?bid=3353&tid=7325, accessed March 28, 2008. The *fatwā* is dated October 28, 1424H.

22. *Al-Liwā' al-Islāmī*, April 18, 1996, p. 7; *al-Aḥrār*, February 8, 1996, p. 6; *Majallat al-Tawḥīd* (a monthly published by Jamā'at Anṣār al-Sunna al-Muḥammadiyya), no. 3, Rabı' al-Awwal 1411, 23–24; "Al-'aqāqīr liman' al-dawra," *Majallat al-Azhar*, August 2011, p. 1531.

23. *Minbar al-Islām* (an Egyptian monthly published by the Ministry of Endowments), May–June 1994, p. 84. The verse reads: "Who have believed and whose hearts have rest in the remembrance of Allah. Verily in the remembrance of Allah do hearts find rest" (M. M. Pickthall, N.D. *The Meaning of the Glorious Koran*, USA).

24. http://hassan22.7olm.org/t321-topic. Published in October 2015, accessed October 15, 2017.

25. *Al-Jumhūriyya* (a daily Egyptian newspaper since 1953; since 1970 it has held a leftist ideology), February 9, 1996, p. 8; *Māyū*, February 14, 1994, p. 4.

26. Ghulam Mustafa Khan, *Personal Hygiene in Islam* (London: Ta Ha Publishers and Islamic Medical Association, 1982).

27. *Al-Nūr*, September 27, 1989, p. 8; *al-Liwā' al-Islāmī*, September 5, 1991, p. 17.

28. *Al-Jumhūriyya*, April 2, 1991, p. 7.

29. *Majallat al-Azhar*, November 1981, p. 174.

30. Muhammad ibn Adam al-Kawthari, "How Should Muslim Physicians Deal with the Issue of Abortion with Their Patients? (Fatwa)," http://www.islamopediaonline.org/fatwa/how-should-muslim-physicians-deal-issue-abortion-their-patients, accessed September 25, 2017. Al-Kawtharī is a traditional *muftī*, residing presently in Leicester, UK. He is a teacher of various traditional Islamic sciences in Leicester, London, and other locations and is a director and researcher at the Institute of Islamic Jurisprudence.

31. Niklas Juth and Niels Lynoe, "Zero Tolerance against Patriarchal Norms? A Cross-Sectional Study of Swedish Physicians' Attitudes towards Young Females Requesting Virginity Certificates or Hymen Restoration," *Journal of Medical Ethics* 41, no. 3 (2015): 215–19.

32. Vardit Rispler-Chaim, "The Muslim Surgeon and Contemporary Ethical Dilemmas Surrounding the Restoration of Virginity," *Hawwa: Journal of Women of the Middle East and the Islamic World* 5, nos. 2–3 (2007): 324–49. Hymen restoration was generally permitted by the *muftīs* only for girls raped as children or those who had been injured in accidents. In an article published in 2017, Mohammad H. Bawany and Aasim I. Padela noticed that there was more leniency in the *muftīs'* permitting hymenoplasty. They also allowed it for Muslim women who regretted their sexual misbehavior, repented, and never repeated it. Mohammad H. Bawany and Aasim I. Padela, "Hymenoplasty and Muslim Patients: Islamic Ethico-Legal Perspectives," *Journal of Sexual Medicine* 14, no. 8 (2017): 1003–10.

33. Azal Ahmadi, "Ethical Issues in Hymenoplasty: Views from Tehran's Physicians," *Journal of Medical Ethics* 40, no. 6 (2014): 429–30.

34. Mohammed Ghaly, "Biomedical Scientists as Co-Muftis: Their Contribution to Contemporary Islamic Bioethics," *Die Welt des Islams* 55, nos. 3–4 (2015): 286–311.

35. 'Aṭiyya Ṣaqr, "Al-siwāk wa-ma'jūn al-asnān," *Minbar al-Islām*, June 2006, no. 5 ;Vardit Rispler-Chaim, "The Siwak: A Medieval Islamic Contribution to Dental Care," *Journal of the Royal Asiatic Society* 2, no. 1 (1992): 13–20.

REFERENCES

Ahmadi, Azal. "Ethical Issues in Hymenoplasty: Views from Tehran's Physicians." *Journal of Medical Ethics* 40, no. 6 (2014): 429–30.

Al-Ahrām, April 4, 1986, p. 15.

al-Alaiyan, Saleh, and Khalid M. Alfaleh. "Aborting a Malformed Fetus: A Debatable Issue in Saudi Arabia." *Journal of Clinical Neonatology* 3, no. 4 (2014): 242.

al-Ashqar, Umar Sulaymān, Muhammad Uthmān Shubayr, A. al-Basal, A. 'Ārif, and A. al-Bāz. *Dirāsāt Fiqhiyya fī Qaḍāyā Ṭibbiyya Mu'āṣira*. Amman: Dār al-Nafā'is, 2001.

Albar, M. "Organ Transplantation: A Sunni Islamic Perspective." *Saudi Journal of Kidney Diseases and Transplantation* 23, no. 4 (2012): 817–22.

al-Fatwa, Markaz. "Ḍawābiṭ Takashshuf Al-Mar'a Amām Al-Ṭabīb (Fatwa 165873)." Fatawa Islam Web, http://www.islamweb.net/fatwa/printfatwa.php?Id=165873&lang=A.

———. "Qarār Al-Majma' Al-Fiqhī Bi-Sha'n Aṭfāl Al-Anābīb (Fatwa 153375)." Fatawa Islam Web, http://www.islamweb.net/fatwa/printfatwa.php?Id=153375&lang=A.

———. "Tadāwī Al-Mar'a 'Ind Al-Rajul in Lam Tūjad Ṭabība (Fatwa 148487)." Fatawa Islam Web, http://fatwa.islamweb.net/fatwa/printfatwa.php?Id=148487&lang=A.

al-Kawthari, Muhammad ibn Adam. "How Should Muslim Physicians Deal with the Issue of Abortion with Their Patients? (Fatwa)." Daruliftaa.com/node/6267, accessed July 28, 2020.

al-Sha'rāwī, Muḥammad Mutawallī. *Kull Mā Yahimm Al-Muslim Fi Ḥayātihi Wayawmihi Wa-Ghaddihi* (*All That Interests the Muslim in His Life, Daily Life, and Future*). Vol. 1. Cairo: Maktabat al-Qur'an, 1981.

Bawany, Mohammad H., and Aasim I. Padela. "Hymenoplasty and Muslim Patients: Islamic Ethico-Legal Perspectives." *Journal of Sexual Medicine* 14, no. 8 (2017): 1003–10.

Djaït, Cheikh Kameleddine. "La fatwa Tunisienne" (translated into French in January 2009). *Don et Vie*, Bulletin 4, January 2009.

Ghaly, Mohammed. "Biomedical Scientists as Co-Muftis: Their Contribution to Contemporary Islamic Bioethics." *Die Welt des Islams* 55, nos. 3–4 (2015): 286–311.

Haddad, Yvonne Yazbeck. *Contemporary Islam and the Challenge of History*. Albany: State University of New York Press, 1982.

Hedayat, K. M., P. Shooshtarizadeh, and M. Raza. "Therapeutic Abortion in Islam: Contemporary Views of Muslim Shiite Scholars and Effect of Recent Iranian Legislation." *Journal of Medical Ethics* 32, no. 11 (November 2006): 652–57.

Jum'a, 'Alī. "Istinsākh juz' aw 'uḍw lil-'ilāj jā'iz." *Al-Liwā' al-Islāmī*, September 30, 2004, p. 7.

Al-Jumhūriyya, April 2, 1991, p. 7.

Juth, Niklas, and Niels Lynoe. "Zero Tolerance against Patriarchal Norms? A Cross-Sectional Study of Swedish Physicians' Attitudes towards Young Females Requesting Virginity Certificates or Hymen Restoration." *Journal of Medical Ethics* 41, no. 3 (2015): 215–19.

Khadduri, M. "Maṣlaḥa." In *Encyclopaedia of Islam*. 2nd ed. Leiden, Netherlands: E. J. Brill: 1954–2005.

Khan, Ghulam Mustafa. *Personal Hygiene in Islam*. London: Ta Ha Publishers and Islamic Medical Association, 1982.

Majma' al-Ṭibb al-Islāmī, "al-'ilāj al-ṭibbī." http://islamtoday.net/bohooth/artshow-32-4705.htm. March 5, 2012. Accessed June 7, 2014.

"Mashrū' bayān al-istinsākh al-basharī li-majma' al-buḥūth al-Islāmiyya." *Majallat al-Azhar* 7 (November 1997): 1066–74.

Māyū, November 28, 1994, p. 4.

———, March 25, 1996, p. 9.

Al-Naba' al-Waṭanī, May 11, 1997, p. 1.

Al-Nūr, February 18, 1998, p. 6.

Rispler-Chaim, Vardit. "Contemporary Muftis between Bioethics and Social Reality: Selection of the Sex of a Fetus as Paradigm." *Journal of Religious Ethics* 36 (2008): 53–76.

———. "The Muslim Surgeon and Contemporary Ethical Dilemmas Surrounding the Restoration of Virginity." *Hawwa: Journal of Women of the Middle East and the Islamic World* 5, nos. 2–3 (2007): 324–49.

———. "The Siwak: A Medieval Islamic Contribution to Dental Care." *Journal of the Royal Asiatic Society* 2, no. 1 (1992): 13–20.

Ṣaqr, 'Aṭiyya. "Al-siwāk wa-ma'jūn al-asnān." *Minbar al-Islām*, June 2006, no. 5.

Viney, Steven. "Q&A with Sherine Hamdy: Organ Transplants, Islam and the Struggle for Human Dignity in Egypt. *Egypt Independent*, January 15, 2012.

TWO

The Islamic Juridical Principle of Dire Necessity (*al-ḍarūra*) and Its Application to the Field of Biomedical Interventions

ABUL FADL MOHSIN EBRAHIM
AND AASIM I. PADELA

In an era of rapidly advancing biomedical technology, a substantial number of Muslims, both patients and physicians, when confronted with bioethical challenges, consult religious scholars who apply juridical tools in order to address their ethico-legal concerns. What is important to note is that in the past three decades or so there has been a move in the Muslim world to transcend the issuance of a *fatwā* (a nonbinding legal verdict) by a single jurist to the issuance of *qarārāt* (collective resolutions) of multiple jurisconsults affiliated with national and international Islamic juridical academies, or *Majmaʿāt* (sing. *Majmāʿ*) *al-Fiqh al-Islāmī*.[1] At meetings called for this purpose, jurisconsults are briefed by the medical team on the issues in question before they begin their *ijtihād* in the hope of making them better informed of the biomedical science prior to using the instruments of

Islamic law to judge the situation. Such a briefing, theoretically, addresses the issue of a single medical view or an inaccurate interpretation of science impacting the *fatwā* of a single jurist. Yet misrepresentations and misunderstandings can still occur, and how exactly medical science interfaces with Islamic ethico-legal constructs remains obscure.

This chapter will focus on such juridical deliberations and the interplay between medical science and Islamic law through the lens of the construct of *ḍarūra* (dire necessity). Often when conflict arises between a medically indicated procedure and a religious dictate, Islamic jurists invoke the concept of *ḍarūra* to overturn a normative prohibition and allow for the procedure in question. Thus the construct of *ḍarūra* is critical for Islamic bioethics, as it brings medical perspectives into the edifice of Islamic law. But, as we will point out, *ḍarūra* is a complex notion. It is a term that reflects a state or condition present in social (medical) reality; it is an ethico-legal construct that grounds the overturning of prohibitions, as it is included in some Islamic ethico-legal maxims (*al-qawā'id al-fiqhiyyah*); and it is also tied to the higher objectives of Islamic law (*maqāsid al-Shariah*).

THE THEOLOGICAL CONSTRUCT OF ḌARŪRA

The Arabic word *ḍarūra* is derived from another Arabic word, *ḍarar*, which implies an injury that cannot be avoided.[2] Technically, *ḍarūra* legitimizes, on the basis of *qiyās* (analogical deduction), the suspension of what has been deemed prohibited in terms of the Shariah on the ground of necessity. The scriptural basis for *ḍarūra* is in both the Qur'an and the *Ḥadīth*. In fact, there are five verses of the Qur'an—namely, *al-Baqarah* 2:173; *al-Mā'idah* 5:3; *al-An'ām* 6:119; *al-An'ām* 6:145; and *al-Naḥl* 16:115—that discuss the concept. These stipulate that Muslims may consume that which is *ḥarām* (prohibited) out of *ḍarūra*. For example:

> Prohibited to you are dead animals, blood, the flesh of swine, and that which has been dedicated to other than Allah, and [those animals] killed by strangling or by a violent blow or by a headlong fall or by the goring of horns, and those from which a wild

> animal has eaten, except what you [are able to] slaughter [before its death], and those which are sacrificed on stone altars, and [prohibited is] that you seek decision through divining arrows. That is grave disobedience. This day those who disbelieve have despaired of [defeating] your religion; so fear them not, but fear Me. This day I have perfected for you your religion and completed My favor upon you and have approved for you Islam as religion. But whoever is forced by severe hunger with no inclination to sin then indeed, Allah is Forgiving and Merciful.[3]

This Qur'anic verse clarifies the types of meat that Muslims are censured from consuming. However, the concluding part of the verse states that if Muslims happen to find themselves in a dire situation when the nonconsumption of what they have been interdicted from eating would jeopardize their survival, it would be permissible for them to consume such meat to stave off death. On the basis of this verse, jurists developed the ethico-legal maxim *al-ḍarūrāt tubīḥu al-maḥẓurāt*—"circumstances of dire necessity make the unlawful lawful." Muhammad Abū Zahrah clarifies limits imposed by the verse, stating that the quantity of food that is made licit is that minimal amount needed to stave off death.[4] In other words, Muslims may not consume more than necessary or relish that which has been prohibited when invoking dire necessity. Relaxation of prohibitions via invoking *ḍarūra* when life is at stake further conforms with one of the five overarching objectives of the Shariah, namely, the preservation of life.

Imām Abū Ḥāmid al-Ghazālī classified the five overarching objectives (*maqāṣid*) of the Shariah into the following order: protection of faith (*al-dīn*), life (*al-nafs*), mind (*al-'aql*), offspring (*al-nasl*), and wealth (*al-māl*). He further notes that these interests can be categorized as *ḍarūriyāt* (necessities). In other words, Islamic law aims at the "preservation" (*al-ḥifẓ*) of these interests above all else. Hence the connection of *ḍarūra* to these *maqāṣid* is that when one of these interests is significantly threatened the ethico-legal construct of *ḍarūra* can, arguably, be invoked as the legal basis for relaxing a certain normative prohibition or rule.

Indeed, there are a number of traditions from the Prophet Muhammad that extend the rule of necessity beyond the preservation of life and incorporate the preservation of other objectives of the Shariah. For example, the Prophet is reported to have said: "He who is killed while protecting his property is a martyr, and he who is killed while defending his family, or his blood, or his religion is a martyr."[5] In other words, while Islamic law censures suicide, the status of a Muslim who is driven by necessity and puts his life in danger to protect his property or to defend his family, his own life, or his religion is raised to the grade of a martyr (*shahīd*).

Mansour Al-Mutairi points out that the point of contention between the contemporary Muslim scholars and the classical ones is precisely the restriction of *ḍarūra* to the preservation of life.[6] For example, Abū Bakr al-Jaṣṣās (d. 370/981), a proponent of the Ḥanafī school of Islamic law, defined "necessity" as "the fear of injury (to one's life or some of one's organs)." Likewise, al-Zarkashī (d. 794/1392), al-Suyūṭī (d. 911/1505), and al-Hamawī al-Ḥanafī (d. 1098/1687) defined "necessity" as "a situation in which one reaches a limit where if one does not take a prohibited thing, one will die." Al-Dardīr (d. 1201/1786), a proponent of the Mālikī school, understood "necessity" to be "the preservation of lives from being lost or from being greatly injured." Contemporary Muslim scholars, on the other hand, advocate that *ḍarūra* should encompass all the five objectives of Islamic law, namely, protection of faith (*al-dīn*), life (*al-nafs*), mind (*al-'aql*), offspring (*al-nasl*), and wealth (*al-māl*). However, attention must be drawn to the fact that *ḍarūra* (the ethico-legal principle of necessity) is not absolute. While the aim of *ḍarūra* is to ease a *mashaqqa* (difficulty), its relevance is contingent on the condition that allowed the infringement of the Shariah prohibition in the first place. Hence, once that condition no longer exists, the exceptional rule of dire necessity is no longer applicable.[7]

Certainly, one of us (A.I.P.) has demonstrated that for bioethical issues that cannot be resolved on the basis of the *uṣūl* (sources of Islamic jurisprudence), jurisconsults resort to arguments based on *al-qawā'id al-fiqhiyyah* (Islamic ethico-legal maxims) and the *maqāṣid al-Shariah*.[8] Since contemporary biotechnology and bioethical issues are often ones that are not addressed by the *uṣūl*, *ḍarūra* turns up in a substantial amount of the Islamic bioethics writing.

In what follows, two bioethical dilemmas are analyzed with the aim of elucidating how they could be resolved on the basis of the ethico-legal maxim of *ḍarūra* and in conjunction with the objectives of Islamic law.

VACCINES WITH PORCINE COMPONENTS AND THE CONSTRUCT OF DIRE NECESSITY

In the context of vaccination, *ḍarūra* arguably exists because vaccines have, over the years, proven to be successful in reducing mortality and morbidity from infectious diseases globally. They have saved the lives of millions, and, in light of this, taking them can be seen as a medical and moral necessity. The ethical dilemma associated with vaccination revolves around the fear, on the one hand, that vaccinations have the potential to harm individuals or their children versus the potential of subjecting to greater harms these individuals, their family members, and society should they contract the disease the vaccine is designed to prevent.

Within an Islamic context, Qur'anic injunctions—for example, *al-An'ām* 6:145 against consuming pork—add to the reservations some Muslims have over vaccinations. Indeed, many Muslims become uncomfortable when they learn that porcine components are present in, or used to manufacture, many standard vaccines, including those for rotavirus, polio, and measles, mumps, and rubella. Thus what may be a dilemma to non-Muslims amounts to a trilemma for Muslims because of the prohibition of consuming pork and Prophetic reports prohibiting the use of ritually impure materials for medicinal purposes.[9]

To be sure, there are Muslim scholars who hold that "transformation of pork products into gelatin alters them sufficiently to make them permissible for observant Muslims to receive vaccines containing pork gelatin and to take medicines packaged in gelatin capsules" (John Bloomberg School of Public Health, 2013). But in another work one of us (A.I.P.) referenced Islamic juridical authorities who contend that "transformation does not apply to the pig products artificially transformed in vaccine production."[10] Thus, in order to resolve this added issue for Muslims, Ahmked Khaleel Babakr reports that in 2009 the International Islamic *Fiqh* Academy, under the auspices of the Organisation of Islamic Cooperation, issued a detailed declaration encouraging Muslims to be vaccinated against polio.[11] That judicial opinion went as far as to declare that according to the Qur'an (*al-Baqarah*, 2:195), it is a duty for everyone to protect one's body and that of his or her dependents, to ensure their safety, and to keep them from any imminent harm. In other words, when there is an outbreak of a particular disease that imperils one's health or life but can be prevented by vaccination, it becomes imperative for a Muslim to respond positively toward vaccination even if the vaccine contains porcine products.

Moreover, al-Ghazālī regards the five objectives of Islamic law as falling within the ambit of *ḍarūriyāt* (fundamental necessities). In other words, these objectives assist one to fulfill one's religious and worldly needs that one cannot do without. Their nonfulfillment may jeopardize the upholding of one's religious obligations and hamper one's worldly affairs to the extent that one's life and the lives of one's progeny may come to an end. In light of the above, that vaccination in general fulfills all of the five objectives of Islamic law—namely, protection of faith (*al-dīn*), life (*al-nafs*), mind (*al-ʿaql*), offspring (*al-nasl*), and wealth (*al-māl*)—may be elucidated as follows. First, insofar as preservation of their religion is concerned, Muslims who are vaccinated against vaccine-preventable diseases will be in a better position to uphold and practice all the *farā'id* (obligatory acts of worship) of their religion. Secondly, vaccination initiatives have succeeded in the preservation of life by reducing global morbidity and mortality from a variety of diseases. Third, parents who opt to have their children vaccinated will have fulfilled the preservation of their progeny by safeguarding them from succumbing to vaccine-preventable diseases. Fourth, preservation of intellect is achieved through vaccination because people enjoy peace of mind knowing that their community and citizens have been protected from contracting various vaccine-preventable diseases. Fifth, vaccination actually contributes to the preservation of wealth. It is an extremely cost-effective intervention that makes logical sense in that it is always better to prevent a disease than to treat it and its resultant complications.[12] Hence, one is responsible to be vaccinated and to have one's children vaccinated against vaccine-preventable diseases.

DIRE NECESSITY AND ABORTION IN THE CASE OF RUBELLA CONTRACTED DURING PREGNANCY

A pregnant mother-to-be who contracts rubella during the first twelve weeks of pregnancy risks her baby's developing congenital rubella syndrome (CRS). Problems with CRS include deafness, eye defects (which may lead to blindness), heart malformations, and neurologic problems, such as intellectual disability. While some defects are detected at birth, other problems manifest later in infancy and childhood.[13] Hence, the decision that a mother-to-be faces is whether to risk her child's developing CRS or to proceed with an abortion. From an Islamic perspective, all schools of law concur that every effort ought to be made to protect the right to life of the unborn.[14] Yet Islamic theological views about ensoulment are important to consider. While some Muslim scholars hold that ensoulment of the fetus occurs forty days after fertilization of the ovum (about twelve weeks' gestation), the majority consider ensoulment to occur at 120 days based on their interpretation of statements from the Prophet Muhammad.[15] Because of this view, the Islamic Jurisprudence Council of the Muslim World League issued a *fatwā* in 1990 sanctioning abortion of a fetus that is less than 120 days' gestation and is grossly malformed with untreatable severe conditions.[16] This juridical decree is grounded in the concept of *ḍarūra* as the council noted it would be in the interest of the fetus (and the parent) for the child not to be born with such health hazards.

It is important to point out here that while CRS might not lead to the vaguely termed "grossly malformed fetus," it does include other disabilities. Moreover, it also implicates psychological trauma that the mother-to-be would face in rearing a potentially disabled child. A case may be made to justify her having the abortion on the grounds of *ḍarūra* for the sake of mental health in conformity with one of the objectives of Islamic law—preservation of her mind. There is precedent for such a rationale, as Islamic jurisconsults revisited the issue of termination of pregnancy after Muslim women were raped by "terrorists" in Algeria and by Serb soldiers in Bosnia in the 1990s.[17] They allowed for abortion on the grounds of *ḍarūra* as related to maternal mental health. For example, Shaykh Yūsuf al-Qaraḍāwī cautiously gave his approval for the termination of rape-related pregnancy:

> Undoubtedly raping a Muslim woman by an evil enemy is a strong reason for the victim and for her family to have an abortion, for she will hate this fetus, the result of this iniquitous attack and she will want to get rid of it. So, this dispensation is given on the basis of *ḍarūra* especially in the first days of pregnancy. But this case of dire necessity should be determined by religious scholars, doctors and people of wide experience and wisdom. Otherwise, the original rule (of prohibition) should be applied.[18]

For both cases analyzed, it is important to recognize that the theological construct of *ḍarūra* is bounded and contingent. For example, in the context of vaccines with porcine elements made licit for Muslims on the basis of *ḍarūra* for the preservation of life, this allowance will fall away once a viable substitute for porcine elements in such vaccines is available. Likewise, if a cure for CRS is found, there will be no need for abortion on the ground of dire necessity based on a credible threat to the mental health of the mother-to-be. Hence the rulings are predicated on knowledge of the viable alternatives present (or not present).

ḌARŪRA AND LIFE THREAT: INSIGHTS FROM A NATIONAL SURVEY OF MUSLIM PHYSICIANS IN THE UNITED STATES

Before moving on to discuss how jurists and physicians can work together to better clarify the application of *ḍarūra* in healthcare contexts, examining how physicians presently understand and apply the concept merits reflection.[19] One of us (A.I.P.) recently conducted a national survey of Muslim physicians in the United States and examined how these clinicians engaged with notions of medical necessity and *ḍarūra* when deliberating over cases of abortion, porcine-based vaccination, and other Islamically controversial medical procedures.[20] This survey of 255 Muslim clinicians yielded insight into the ways in which medically informed notions of necessity overlap with the juridical concept of *ḍarūra* as a life threat in the minds of practicing Muslim clinicians. Before sharing these views, it is important to recognize that the survey respondents where highly religious (89 percent indicated that their religion was the most important part of their lives or a very important part of them, 85 percent strictly performed Ramadan fasting, and 63 percent reported praying five times daily), and thus one might expect them to be careful and precise when invoking religious exemptions in medical practice.

When considering a hypothetical case scenario in which a pregnant Muslim cancer patient is debating whether to pursue abortion of her ensouled fetus because of complications of chemotherapy, physicians who viewed abortion as a medical necessity were more likely to recommend an abortion, as were those who believed continued pregnancy presented a life threat. Importantly, fewer than half of respondents (45 percent) believed a medical necessity existed, and similarly fewer than half (49 percent) considered there to be a life threat to the mother. In the hypothetical case in which a Muslim patient must decide whether to receive a porcine-based flu vaccine based on the recommendations of the Centers for Disease Control in the United States even though there have been no documented deaths from the flu for those vaccinated againt it, perceptions of medical necessity similarly correlated with Muslim physicians' recommending vaccination. The majority of respondents (61 percent) agreed that a medical necessity to be vaccinated existed. Although more than 60 percent of respondents also felt the flu represented a life threat, and thus the threshold needed to invoke *ḍarūra* existed, holding a life threat to exist was not associated with respondents' recommending that the patients receive the porcine-based vaccine.

While one of us (A.I.P.) will comment on these findings in greater detail in chapter 7, it is worth highlighting here that these data suggest that notions of medical necessity and *ḍarūra* may not overlap in the minds of Muslim clinicians. More importantly, when recommending that patients pursue therapies that are normatively prohibited but contingently permissible according to Islamic law, their views on whether the procedure is medically necessary may motivate their recommendations more than their belief that the life-threat threshold for *ḍarūra* exists. The survey findings point to the need to better understand the circumstances under which Muslim physicians use *ḍarūra* to ground their recommendations to patients, as well as what clinical markers meet the threshold for its application. In order to appropriately invoke *ḍarūra* in clinical practice, physicians and jurists need to build bridges of understanding between the clinical and the juridical to find where medical and juridical imaginaries meet.

ḌARŪRA AND THE INTERPLAY OF MEDICAL SCIENCES WITH LEGAL SCIENCES

As the above examples illustrate, the ethico-legal construct of *ḍarūra* is invoked in many Islamic bioethics rulings. Jurists use it to relax prohibitions when they deem that a sufficient threshold has been met in a clinical context, and Muslim clinicians may consider the concept of life threat when they make recommendations to patients. Classical jurists held that a life threat or harm to one's organs must be credible prior to invoking *ḍarūra* in the medical context; more modern scholars have expanded this view to include considerations of mental health and psychological trauma, and some invoke *ḍarūra* whenever any of the overarching interests/objectives of Islamic law might be at stake. This ambiguity about what threshold is needed is problematic, as it leads to confusion and a haphazard approach to Islamic bioethical assessment on the part of both Muslim clinicians and jurists.

Nonetheless, *ḍarūra* must be invoked based on knowledge of the clinical circumstances. If one holds that *ḍarūra* means that there is a life threat or a mental health risk, a clinician must provide evidence that a credible life threat or significant mental health risk is present. The jurist or team of jurists will then take this testimony as the foundation for invoking *ḍarūra*. Similarly, if a jurist contends that *ḍarūra* applies whenever any of the *maqāṣid* are at risk, scientists must confirm to what extent such values are threatened. It would thus seem that the *ḍarūra* construct needs a clearer definition and delineation so that clinicians and others can attest that the threshold for its applicability is present in a specific clinical context. Moreover, in order for the concept to be appropriately applied by doctors to advise Muslim patients, more specific thresholds need to be delineated.

Setting out the parameters for *ḍarūra* would appear to be a project that jurists and clinicians could undertake collaboratively. Jurists could reclassify *ḍarūra* based on risk probabilities for different sorts of harms or based on another rubric to measure threats to life and health that is provided by clinicians and medical scientists. In this way, knowledge of contemporary biomedicine would inform ethico-legal constructs and reasoning exercises within Islamic law. Alternatively, one could opt for the classical definition of dire necessity as a life threat, and epidemiologists and clinicians could provide insight into statistical probabilities and types of life threats that are present.[21]

CONCLUSION

It has been pointed out that within the practice of Muslims at the ground level (patients and clinicians) the trend has changed from relying on individual *fatāwā* to now relying on *qarārāt* (collective resolutions) for Islamic ethico-legal guidance. Collective resolutions involve collective *ijtihād*, where Islamic jurisconsults work with physicians to better understand biomedical contexts. However, what is needed is to widen the discourse to include not just clinicians but biomedical scientists and other researchers working at the intersection of Islam and medicine. This will enable all participants to be better informed about the biomedical science, the clinical context, and the Islamic ethical worldview. At present, the problem is that within many Muslim communities jurisconsults prematurely issue *fatāwā* on many of the innovative biomedical interventions without an in-depth understanding of the biomedical contexts. Greater collaboration between the scientists and Muslim jurisconsults and broadening the expertise at the deliberative table will enable Islamic jurisconsults to become better informed about the pros and cons of biomedical interventions. In the case of the principle of *ḍarūra*, such a holistic understanding is needed to move from theory to practice. Indeed, as outlined in chapter 3 in this volume, by Stodolsky and Kholwadia, clinicians must participate in *taḥqīq al-manāṭ* (actualization or certification that the criterion for invoking a juridical ruling is present) and determine when *ḍarūra* is applicable to a certain clinical context.

NOTES

The paper on which this chapter is based was presented in provisional and partial form at "Interfaces and Discourses: A Multidisciplinary Conference on Islamic Theology, Law, and Biomedicine," University of Chicago, April 15–17, 2019.

1. A. F. M. Ebrahim, *An Introduction to Islamic Medical Jurisprudence* (Durban: Islamic Medical Association of South Africa, 2008), 5.

2. Mansour Z. Al-Mutairi, "Necessity in Islamic Law" (University of Edinburg, 1997).

3. Al-Mā'idah 5:3, *Sahih International Qur'an*.

4. Muhammad Abu Zahrah, *Usul Al-Fiqh* (Cairo: Dar al-Fikr al-'Arabi, 1985), 299.

5. Sunan Abi Dawud, "Sunan Abi Dawud 4772," in *Book of Model Behavior of the Prophet* (*Kitab al-Sunnah*), English translation, Book 41, *Hadith* 4754 (Sunnah.com).

6. al-Mutairi, "Necessity in Islamic Law," 10–13.

7. Ibid., 27.

8. This view is in accord with the dominant Shafi'ī position. See A. I. Padela et al., "Dire Necessity and Transformation: Entry-Points for Modern Science in

Islamic Bioethical Assessment of Porcine Products in Vaccines," *Bioethics* 28, no. 2 (2014): 61.

9. There are multiple traditions that carry this meaning, including the following statement, "Allah has sent down both the disease and the cure, and He has appointed a cure for every disease, so treat yourselves medically, but use nothing unlawful" (Sunan Abi Dawud 3874), and his proscription of using wine for medicine (see Sunan Abi Dawud 3873). Jurists differ on their grading and interpretation of these narrations, with some categorically prohibiting the use of impure substances, e.g., wine and anything porcine, within medicine and others allowing it, citing the rule of dire necessity.

10. Padela et al., "Dire Necessity and Transformation," 61.

11. Ahmked Khaleel Babakr, "Second Declaration of the International Islamic *Fiqh* Academy on the Obligatory Nature of Polio Vaccination" (Jeddah: Organisation of Islamic Cooperation, International Islamic *Fiqh* Academy, 2013).

12. Abul Fadl Mohsin Ebrahim, *Islam and Vaccination* (Durban: Islamic Medical Association of South Africa, 2013), 67–68.

13. Baby Center L.L.C., 1997–2016. "Rubella (German Measles) in Pregnancy." https://www.babycenter.com.my/a536354/rubella-german-measles-in-pregnancy (accessed March 8, 2019).

14. Ebrahim, *An Introduction to Islamic Medical Jurisprudence*, 114.

15. It is beyond the scope of this chapter to detail Islamic juridical views on the permissibility of abortion, which hinge on views about ensoulment, whether or not the fetus takes on human shape, and the health risks to the mother-to-be. See, for example: Muhammad ibn Adam al-Kawthari, *Birth Control and Abortion in Islam* (Santa Barbara, CA: White Thread Press, 2006); M. Katz, "The Problem of Abortion in Medieval Fiqh," in *Islamic Ethics of Life: Abortion, War, and Euthanasia*, ed. John Brockopp (Columbia: University of South Carolina Press, 2003); Thomas Eich, "Induced Miscarriage in Early Mālikī and Ḥanafī Fiqh," *Islamic Law and Society* 16, nos. 3–4 (2009); D. Atighetchi, *Islamic Bioethics: Problems and Perspectives*, International Library of Ethics, Law, and the New Medicine vol. 31 (New York: Springer, 2007), 91–133.

16. Mohammad Ali Albar, *Human Development as Revealed in the Holy Qur'an and Hadith* (Jeddah: Saudi Publishing and Distributing, 2002), 628.

17. Ebrahim, *An Introduction to Islamic Medical Jurisprudence*, 125.

18. al-Qaraḍāwī, Yūsuf. Fatwa dated May 13, 2004.

19. Chapter 7 in this volume, "Muslim Doctors and Islamic Bioethics: Insights from a National Survey of Muslim Physicians in the United States," provides more details on survey methodology and respondent characteristics, as well as further analytic commentary on the relationship between these two concepts. This section is but a brief overview meant to foreshadow that discussion.

20. For more discussion and predictive analyses, see S. Mahdi et al., "Predictors of Physician Recommendation for Ethically Controversial Medical Procedures: Findings from an Exploratory National Survey of American Muslim Physicians," *Journal of Religion Health* 55, no. 2 (2016): 403–21.

21. O. Qureshi and A. I. Padela, "When Must a Patient Seek Healthcare? Bringing the Perspectives of Islamic Jurists and Clinicians into Dialogue," *Zygon* 51, no. 3 (2016).

REFERENCES

Abu Zahrah, Muhammad. *Usul Al-Fiqh.* Cairo: Dar al-Fikr al-'Arabi, 1985.

Albar, Mohammed Ali. *Human Development as Revealed in the Holy Qur'an and Hadith (Creation of Man between Medicine and the Qur'an).* Jeddah: Saudi Publishing and Distributing, 2002.

al-Kawthari, Muhammad ibn Adam. *Birth Control and Abortion in Islam.* Santa Barbara, CA: White Thread Press, 2006.

al-Mutairi, Mansour Z. "Necessity in Islamic Law." University of Edinburg, 1997.

al-Qaraḍāwī, Yūsuf. "Aborting a Fetus Resulting from Rape (Fatwa)." May 13, 2004. http://www.islamawareness.net/FamilyPlanning/Abortion/abo_fatwa003.html.

Atighetchi, D. *Islamic Bioethics: Problems and Perspectives.* International Library of Ethics, Law, and the New Medicine. Vol. 31. New York: Springer, 2007.

Babakr, Ahmked Khaleel. "Second Declaration of the International Islamic *Fiqh* Academy (IIFA) on the Obligatory Nature of Polio Vaccination." Jeddah: Organisation of Islamic Cooperation: International Islamic *Fiqh* Academy, 2013.

Baby Center L.L.C., 1997–2016. "Rubella (German Measles) in Pregnancy." https://www.babycenter.com.my/a536354/rubella-german-measles-in-pregnancy. Accessed March 8, 2019.

Dawud, Sunan Abi. "Sunan Abi Dawud 4772." In *Book of Model Behavior of the Prophet (Kitab al-Sunnah), English Translation.* Book 41, *Hadith* 4754. Sunnah.com.

Ebrahim, Abul Fadl Mohsin. *An Introduction to Islamic Medical Jurisprudence.* Durban: The Islamic Medical Association of South Africa, 2008.

———. *Islam and Vaccination.* Durban: Islamic Medical Association of South Africa, 2013.

Eich, Thomas. "Induced Miscarriage in Early Mālikī and Ḥanafī Fiqh." *Islamic Law and Society* 16, nos. 3–4 (2009): 302–36.

Katz, M. "The Problem of Abortion in Medieval Fiqh." In *Islamic Ethics of Life: Abortion, War, and Euthanasia*, ed. John Brockopp, 25–50. Columbia: University of South Carolina Press, 2003.

Mahdi, S., O. Ghannam, S. Watson, and A. I. Padela. "Predictors of Physician Recommendation for Ethically Controversial Medical Procedures: Findings from an Exploratory National Survey of American Muslim Physicians." *Journal of Religion and Health* 55, no. 2 (April 2016): 403–21.

Padela, A. I., S. W. Furber, M. A. Kholwadia, and E. Moosa. "Dire Necessity and Transformation: Entry-Points for Modern Science in Islamic Bioethical

Assessment of Porcine Products in Vaccines." *Bioethics* 28, no. 2 (February 2014): 59–66.

Qureshi, O., and A. I. Padela. "When Must a Patient Seek Healthcare? Bringing the Perspectives of Islamic Jurists and Clinicians into Dialogue." *Zygon* 51, no. 3 (September 2016): 592–625.

THREE

A Jurisprudential (*Uṣūlī*) Framework for Cooperation between Muslim Jurists and Physicians and Its Application to the Determination of Death

MUHAMMED VOLKAN YILDIRAN STODOLSKY
AND MOHAMMED AMIN KHOLWADIA

Contemporary medicine has developed unprecedented treatments. One of the aims of those who engage in Islamic bioethics is to assess these developments to ensure that medical treatments that are aimed to stop or prevent harm to the human body do not cause harm to a patient's eternal life after death by conveying Islamic norms to physicians. Therefore, Islamic bioethics requires cooperation between two often distinct sets of specialists: the *'ulamā'* and physicians, each with different skill sets and methodologies. The *'ulamā'* make up the body of Muslim scholars who know the Shariah and whom the previous generation of scholars have entrusted with explaining and applying its rulings, starting with the generation of the Companion of the Prophet Abū l-Qāsim Muḥammad b. 'Abd

Allāh, whom he authorized to teach the Shariah. The *'ulamā'* specialize in *fiqh*, which is the discipline of understanding and interpreting the revelation that the Prophet Muhammad taught to his Companions. The goal of *fiqh*, however, as it deals with divine revelation and the transmission of Prophetic knowledge, stands in contrast to modern medicine, which is based on empirical knowledge. Given this difference, there needs to be a conceptual framework that delineates the boundaries of this relationship and the individual roles of the jurists and the physicians in order for meaningful cooperation between the two groups. In this chapter we aim to present such a framework based on Islamic jurisprudence (*uṣūl al-fiqh*), taking the influential work of Abū Isḥāq Ibrāhīm b. Mūsā al-Shāṭibī (d. 790/1388), *al-Muwāfaqāt fī uṣūl al-Sharī'ah*, as a starting point.[1] Specifically, through the articulation of this conceptual framework, we reexamine the important ethico-legal issue of the criteria for determining death.

SHĀṬIBĪ'S MODEL

Shāṭibī defines *ijtihād* as doing one's utmost to obtain certain or probable knowledge of a ruling according to the Shariah.[2] According to Shāṭibī, there are two types of *ijtihād*: one that will continue as long as the legal obligation of humanity continues (in other words, until the day of resurrection), while the other is a type of *ijtihād* that may cease before then.[3] The first type consists of *taḥqīq al-manāṭ*, which is a legal cause in which there is an agreed-upon criterion of the Shariah, but it remains to be determined whether the criterion is met in daily life. Shāṭibī illustrates the concept with examples. The Qur'an requires two just eyewitnesses in litigation in a case in which there is an allegation that the legal rights of a human being are violated (Q 65:2). Shāṭibī writes that once we understand the meaning of justness in Shariah, we will still need to designate the individuals who have the quality of justness, something in which individuals differ greatly. There are people who have the highest degree of justness—such as Abū Bakr, the first Rightly Guided Caliph—those who cannot be considered just witnesses, and a whole spectrum of individuals between whom the judge must decide whether their testimonies should be considered legal proof. What Shāṭibī means is that the Shariah will not accept the testimony of someone who publicly commits grave sins, since such a person does not fit the qualification of being just, as is required in the statement of revelation, on the one hand; but, on the other hand, it will accept the testimony of someone who avoids major sins and does not intentionally commit minor sins. However, there are people who avoid major sins and at the same time intentionally commit minor sins, in which case the judge has to exercise his discretion in accepting their testimony. If the good deeds of such a person are deemed dominant, the testimony will be accepted; if the bad actions are deemed dominant, the testimony will not be considered legal proof.[4] Hence, although the Shariah identifies the criterion of justness as a requirement for the validity of testimony, the fulfillment of the criterion will be based in many cases on the judge's discretion.

The obligation of determining the actualization of the criterion is not limited to litigation but is a duty for every Muslim. As an example, Shāṭibī cites the issue of unnecessary movement in *salat* (prayer). The agreed-upon criterion in the Shariah is that excessive unnecessary movement invalidates the *salat*, whereas nonexcessive movement does not: the person performing the *salat* has to judge for himself whether his movement is excessive. It is clear from these examples that the actualization of the criterion in the way Shāṭibī articulates it is something that concerns every Muslim and is inescapable. Hence Shāṭibī states that there is a consensus in the Muslim community that this type of *ijtihād* is valid.

The second type of *ijtihād*, which may cease before the day of resurrection, consists of three categories. The first is *tanqīḥ al-manāṭ* (literally, the refinement of the pivot), for which the relevant criterion is mentioned with other attributes in the Qur'an or the *Sunnah*, so that the attributes have to be sifted to single out the applicable factor. Shāṭibī mentions an example that is often cited in works of jurisprudence in which a Bedouin relates to the Prophet that he had intercourse with his spouse in daylight hours during Ramadan. The Prophet responds by saying that he needs to emancipate a slave as expiation. Jurists eliminate the factors that are not relevant, such as the fact that the person was a Bedouin or that the female was his spouse to ascertain the relevant factor upon which the judgment rests. According to Abū 'Abd Allāh Muḥammad b. Idrīs al-Shāfi'ī (d. 204/820), this factor is intercourse while fasting in Ramadan, whereas, according to Abū Ḥanīfah Nu'mān b. Thābit (d. 150/767) and Mālik b.

Anas (d. 1797/795), it is intentionally doing something that breaks the fast in Ramadan.

The second category is *takhrīj al-manāṭ* (literally, the extraction of the pivot), in which the statement in the Qur'an or the *Sunnah* that is the basis of a ruling does not mention the applicable attribute at all. In such cases, the jurist has to investigate the issue to extract the legal cause. This constitutes legal analogy proper (*qiyās*). Examples include the prohibitions of drinking wine and exchanging a lower quantity of wheat with a higher quantity of wheat, in which the causes of the prohibitions are not explicitly stated. Jurists attempt to discover the causes of the prohibitions and conclude that the former is prohibited because it is an intoxicant and the latter is prohibited because of the unequal exchange of two commodities that are of the same kind and measured in the same way.[5] The extraction of the *ratio legis* allows its application to other cases in which the same cause exists.

The third category is a specific type of the actualization of the criterion (*taḥqīq khāṣṣ*), which is that the jurist attains a special discernment through fearing Allah that allows him to know how a general ruling relates to a specific individual and his personal traits. In this regard, Shāṭibī cites a verse of the Qur'an, "If you fear Allah, he will make for you a *furqān*" (Q 8:29), which means a criterion by which one distinguishes truth from error. For example, Shāṭibī states that the Prophet said to the Companion Abū Dharr Jundab b. Junādah al-Ghifārī, "Oh Abū Dharr, truly I see you are weak and truly I love for you what I love for myself. Verily do not become a commander over two people and do not be in charge of the wealth of an orphan." Although being a just ruler and taking care of orphans are among the best of deeds according to other statements of the Prophet, Shāṭibī observes that the Prophet told Abū Dharr not to engage in these because of what he discerned from his character.

It is clear from Shāṭibī's exposition of *ijtihād* that the first type of *ijtihād*, the general actualization of the criterion (*taḥqīq ʿām*), concerns all Muslims, whereas the second type of *ijtihād* is the domain of the Muslim jurist, since it requires reading revelation in its original language and processing it with technical legal thought and insight. According to the command of the Qur'an, in any disputed matter the criterion for determining its resolution must be based on revelation: "If you dispute something, return it to Allah and the Messenger if you believe in Allah and the last day" (Q 4:59). Once the applicable criterion for the issue is identified by the Muslim jurist based on revelation, one does not need to be a jurist to observe the realization of the relevant factor in daily life.

Here it should be noted that Shāṭibī uses the word *manāṭ* to refer to the specific criterion of the legal cause (*ʿillah*), while in this chapter we use the broader category of legal criteria because the normative elements of Islamic law that may be relevant for the physician are not restricted to legal causes. Statements of revelation establish either rulings (*al-ḥukm al-sharʿī*), such as permissibility or prohibition, or the factors upon which these rulings depend (*al-ḥukm al-waḍʿī*), such as legal occasions (*sabab*), causes (*ʿillah*), conditions (*sharṭ*), and signs (*ʿalāmah*), the details of which are discussed in works of Islamic jurisprudence (*uṣūl al-fiqh*).

The *mujtahid*, a Muslim jurist who is capable of doing *ijtiḥād*, directly derives both the rulings and the factors on which they depend from revelation. The jurist who is not a *mujtahid* uses, beyond the criteria the *mujtahid* identifies, additional normative criteria to address new issues. Through the legal process of *takhrīj*, which refers to the derivation of norms from the legal heritage of the school, jurists identify the specific maxims (*ḍābiṭ*) pertaining to each legal subject through an inductive analysis of the opinions of the *mujtahid* on related cases. The jurist then applies these specific maxims to new issues that resemble the issues in the repository of the school. Some jurists also use the criteria of general legal maxims (*al-qāʿidah al-kulliyyah*), although this is not agreed upon. The committee that wrote the *Majallah*, the Ottoman law of transactions that was the first codification of Islamic law in history and whose introduction became one of the most influential reference works for legal maxims, explicitly prohibited judges from using legal maxims to issue rulings in the absence of other legal proofs, stating that "Rulers of the Shariah" cannot rule by these [general maxims] without finding an explicit transmission." Ali Haydar Efendi also voiced the same opinion in his commentary on the *Majallah*.[6] However, other jurists have used general legal maxims as normative criteria in the absence of relevant statements of revelation and opinions transmitted from the *mujtahid*.[7] In sum, Muslim jurists use a number of normative criteria that may be relevant to the physician.

In the context of Islamic bioethics, then, the role of the Muslim jurist is to determine the pivotal criteria of bioethical issues based on revelation, while the role of the Muslim patient and physician is to determine whether the criteria are met in actual cases. For instance, Ḥanafī jurists, based on revelation, identify three criteria for the permissibility of the usage of prohibited substances in medicine: necessity (*ḍarūra*), which refers to danger to life or limb; the absence of a permissible alternative; and certain or satisfactory knowledge that the treatment is effective.[8] Once the jurists disclose the criteria, it is the role of the patient and the physician to determine whether the criteria are met in a certain illness.

To summarize the conceptual framework, Shāṭibī identifies two broad categories of *ijtihād*: (1) determining the applicable Islamic criteria based on revelation through specific jurisprudential methods, which is the duty of the Muslim jurist, and (2) applying the criteria, which is the responsibility of whoever is tested with a situation in which the criteria are applicable. If we apply Shāṭibī's framework to Islamic bioethics, jurists have to identify the criteria in bioethical issues based on revelation, and patients and physicians need to apply them in particular cases.

APPLICATION OF THE MODEL TO THE ISSUE OF DETERMINING DEATH

With this conceptual framework in mind, let us evaluate the disputed issue of determining death through what is popularly called brain death. To begin with, it has to be stated that the expression "brain death" is misleading since it leads to the misimpression that in this condition the brain is "dead," that is, it has irreversibly lost all functions. As Aasim Padela and Taha Abdul-Basser note, brain death is a misnomer given that certain functions of the brain may continue: "For example, the pituitary gland may continue to release hormones, the hypothalamus may continue to regulate body temperature, in response to surgery, blood regulation may be intact, and some brain dead patients have demonstrated a breathing response. Extreme examples include the ability of the brain dead women to undergo labor."[9] Others have observed that "brain-dead patients maintain residual vegetative functions; e.g. growth, reproduction, pregnancy, childbirth etc. that are mediated or coordinated by the brain or brainstem."[10] Hence, "irreversible coma," which is how the Ad Hoc Committee of the Harvard Medical School that popularized the concept referred to it, might be more accurate and less misleading to the public.[11] Nonetheless, in this chapter, "brain death" will be used to refer to this clinical state, since it is the designation that is more commonly used and was the one Muslim jurists contended with in juridical councils.

There is consensus among Muslim scholars that death is the separation of the soul from the body.[12] The Qur'an describes how the soul of a dying person comes up to the throat: "Then, when [the soul of the dying person] comes up to the throat while you are looking on at that moment, We are closer to him than you, but you do not perceive" (Q 56:83–85). Since the separation of the spirit is a metaphysical occurrence that living human beings cannot perceive through the senses, Muslim jurists consider the physical signs of life and death to infer that the spirit has separated from the body and the person is deceased. The disputed issue is whether one who is diagnosed with brain death but exhibits other signs of life, such as a heartbeat, breathing, and being warm to touch by means of life support equipment, is to be considered dead or alive. In other words, is the physician's determination of a neurologically compromised state (in common parlance, brain death) a sufficient threshold to meet the standards for legal death in Islamic law?

One of the consequences of considering brain death as death is that it makes possible the extraction of vital organs that cannot be recovered after clinical death when the heartbeat, blood circulation, and breathing stop. If brain death is not considered real death and the person is considered alive in this state, the extraction of these vital organs constitutes intentional killing of the patient. In fact, this was the opinion of the Majlis al-ʿUlamāʾ in Port Elizabeth, South Africa, which was issued in 1994.[13] The Majmaʿ al-Fiqhī—Islamic *Fiqh* (Legal) Academy (IFA)—of what was at the time the Organisation of Islamic Conference (OIC, currently the Organisation of Islamic Cooperation) decided in 1988 that whole-brain death is legal death even if the heart is still beating.[14] In contrast, the *fatwā* committee of the Ministry of Foundations of Kuwait in 1981 and the legal academy of the Muslim World League in 1987 decided that the death of the brain stem without cessation of the heartbeat is not considered death.[15] Their main argument was the universal Islamic legal principle "Certainty is not removed with doubt," as expressed in this verse of the Qur'an: "Verily speculation is of no avail against certainty" (Q 10:36).[16] Since it is certain that the patient was originally alive, and it is disputed whether he is really deceased when brain death takes place, the patient must be considered alive until there is certainty that he is deceased. The main argument of the Muslim proponents of brain death as legal death is that since there is no explicit statement in revelation that determines when death actually takes place, the judgment of physicians as experts in medicine that brain death is death has to be accepted.[17]

One of the problems with the argument of the proponents of considering brain death as legal death is that determination of death is a disputed issue that has not only medical but numerous religious and ethico-legal consequences, such as hastening of the burial, distributing the inheritance, executing bequests, and determining when the spouse can get remarried. In other words, given the religious and ethico-legal significance of the disputed issue, it is problematic to leave it to the judgment of the physicians as if it were a purely medical issue. Rather, the Muslim jurists must identify the solution based on the Shariah. Based on their claim that there is no explicit statement of revelation that determines the criterion for death, the proponents do not identify the pivotal criterion of the issue but rather refer and defer it to the physicians. However, even if one grants the claim, the search for criteria according to revelation should start, not end, precisely when there is no explicit statement in revelation. In identifying criteria according to the Shariah, *ijtihād* does not stop but rather starts when there is no *naṣṣ* (explicit statement in the Qur'an or the *Sunnah*). Even though the only type of *ijtihād* physicians are capable of doing is *taḥqīq al-manāṭ*, the proponents entrust them with *takhrīj al-manāṭ*, or, in other words, determining the criterion based not on the *Sunnah* of the Prophet and the Companions, but on medical practice. This is not in accordance with this command of Allah: "If you dispute something, return it to Allah and the Messenger if you believe in Allah and the last day" (Q 4:59). This is not to dismiss the value of expert testimony in Islamic law, which is obvious, but to state that experts cannot determine religious and ethico-legal criteria by adopting and transplanting non-Islamic standards and practices without referring to the Qur'an and the *Sunnah*. Rather it is the duty of the expert to establish whether criteria that are established based on the Shariah are fulfilled in their field of expertise.

Since Sunni legal thought is cumulative, similar to the principle of *stare decisis* in US law, in which precedence guides court decisions, we must first ask within the framework of Islamic jurisprudence whether Muslim jurists have determined the criterion by which death is established in cases where there is doubt. The answer is affirmative and, significantly, there seems to be consensus on the issue among the four Sunni schools. This criterion is certainty of death (*tayaqqun al-mawt*).

The Ḥanafī jurist Ḥasan b. ʿAmmār al-Shurunbulālī (d. 1069/1659), in *Marāqī al-falāḥ*, a widely taught work on the laws of worship, writes, "If one is certain of death, the funeral preparations are expedited." He brings two pieces of evidence for the necessity of certainty, one based on transmission, the other on the experimental knowledge of physicians. The transmitted evidence is no less than the passing away of the Prophet himself. Shurunbulālī writes, "The Prophet, may peace and blessings be upon him, died on Monday before noon and was buried late at night on Wednesday." While some scholars suggest that this delay in burial was due to the fact that the Companions were engaged in the important task of selecting the leader of the Muslim community, Shurunbulālī's extraction of the criterion is that the Companions delayed the burial to be certain that the Prophet had indeed passed away. The experimental evidence is a testimony from a physician who states that in certain sicknesses only the best of physicians can determine that death has taken place.[18] In other words, since even physicians who are the experts on human health make mistakes in diagnosing death, one must make sure no signs of life remain to declare death when there is any suspicion that the person may still be alive.

In *Bidāyat al-mujtahid*, the Mālikī jurist Abū l-Walīd Muḥammad b. Aḥmad Ibn Rushd (d. 595/1198), known in the West as Averroes, first notes that it is commendable to expedite the burial, except for one who dies from drowning. According to the Mālikī school, in this case it is commendable to delay the burial for fear that signs of life might not be recognized. Ibn Rushd observes, "If this is the case for drowning, it is all the more so for many other patients."[19] Al-Shāfiʿī, the founder of the Shāfiʿī school, addresses the issue in *al-Umm*, one of the earliest works of Islamic law. He states: "If the deceased has been struck by lightning, or dies from grief, or has been tortured, or due to burning or drowning, or he has an illness that hides like death [i.e., gives the impression of death], his burial is delayed and he is attended to until his death becomes certain ... even if it is a day, or two days, or three days, as long as death does not become clear-cut." Elsewhere he states, concerning the same conditions, "I like it that he is delayed until his decomposition is feared, even if that takes two or three days."[20] The prominent Shāfiʿī jurist Abū Zakariyyā Yaḥyā b. Sharaf al-Nawawī (d. 676/1277) echoes the same position, "If there is doubt [concerning death] due to the fact that there is no [observable] cause of death, or the probability of heart attack . . . or others, it is delayed until certainty."[21] The Ḥanbalī jurist Abū Muḥammad Muwaffaq al-Dīn 'Abd Allāh b. Aḥmad Ibn Qudāmah al-Maqdisī (d. 620/1223), whose *al-Mughnī* is arguably one of the most influential work of the Ḥanbalī school, also identifies certainty as the criterion for the determination of death: "If the matter of the deceased is ambiguous [i.e., if there is doubt concerning his death], the manifestation of the signs of death is considered. . . . One waits for these signs until his death becomes certain."[22] This survey shows that leading jurists of all four Sunni schools independently identified certainty as the pivotal criterion for the determination of death when there is doubt, in accordance with the verse of the Qur'an and the legal maxim mentioned above. This means that no sign of life should remain. Since there are obvious signs of life after the diagnosis of brain death, such as heartbeat, breathing, and being warm to touch, brain death cannot be considered legal death according to the criterion of certainty. Given that Muslim jurists of all four extant Sunni legal schools agreed upon certainty as the criterion for the determination of death when there is doubt, Muslim physicians can fulfill their role of applying this criterion in actual situations. Accordingly, the Muslim physician must not declare death until all signs of life cease and cannot be detected by available methods, whether by palpating a heartbeat or listening with a stethoscope or looking at the monitor of an electrocardiograph.

Proponents of brain death counter that classical jurists listed possible signs of death, such as the stopping of breathing, the becoming limp of the feet, the drooping of facial muscles, the sinking of the temples, and the body's becoming cold, and assert that since physicians consider different signs today, this shows that there is no problem with adopting new standards such as brain death. This overlooks the obvious fact that jurists searched for these signs only when there were no signs of life. No one advocated looking for signs of death when there were obvious signs of life, such as breathing. To the contrary, even when there were no signs of life, we have seen that the *'ulamā'* were so careful to preserve and protect human life that they were unanimous in advocating waiting until no doubt remains—even if that means waiting until the beginning of decomposition.

Let us consider how this jurisprudential exposition relates to the reality on the ground and whether it answers the questions of the clinicians and patients on the verge of death. The application of brain death as a criterion to determine legal death suffers from a number of important problems. First, proponents of brain death disagree on whether brain death should be determined through whole-brain, higher-brain, or brain-stem criteria.[23] Second, although the US government recognized whole-brain death as legal death, it did not determine the criteria to be used to ascertain it, and, as a result, there is wide variability of protocols.[24] According to recent research led by neurologist David Greer and published in the *Journal of the American Medical Association Neurology*, 66.9 percent of hospitals in the research did not require the determiner of brain death to be a neurologist or neurosurgeon, and 56.9 percent of the hospitals did not even require the determiner to be the attending physician. Most of the hospitals also did not test for hypothermia and hypotension, which can resemble brain death.[25] Third, there are documented cases in which patients diagnosed with brain death turned out to be brain-alive.[26] Physicians typically respond to such cases by saying that although mistakes are possible in diagnosis, brain death is reliable for prognosis, since no brain-dead patient who has been correctly diagnosed has survived. However, as one paper puts it, "these reports speak to difficulty of diagnosing brain death and the potential for misdiagnosis given the widespread variability in clinical criteria."[27] These data raise major questions about the reliability of brain death determination in the United States and corroborate the universal validity of the Islamic bioethical criterion of certainty to establish death when there is doubt.

As for clinical concerns, the popularity of brain death as a way of determining death is related to two clinical concerns: freeing hospital beds and harvesting organs. In fact, these concerns are openly stated in the abstract of the report of the Ad Hoc Committee of the Harvard Medical School, which reads, (1) "The burden is great on patients who suffer permanent loss of intellect, on their families, on the hospitals, and on those in need of hospital beds already occupied by these comatose patients. (2) Obsolete criteria for the definition of death can lead to controversy in obtaining organs for transplantation."[28] From the perspective of Islamic law, the question of freeing hospital beds is irrelevant, since according to Islamic law neither the patient nor the physician is legally obligated to continue any treatment that they consider futile, whether the patient is conscious or comatose.[29] Thus there is no need to accept brain death as a criterion for the determination of death to free hospital beds. As for organ transplant, the criterion of certainty this chapter and other writings advocate will prohibit the harvesting of vital organs in the state of brain death, since this will constitute intentional killing of the patient. The Shariah categorically forbids the killing of an innocent human being and equates the killing of a single innocent person with the killing of all humanity: "Whoever kills a soul not for a soul or for causing corruption in the land is as if he has killed all humanity" (Q 5:32). Hence no human being can be killed because of utilitarian concerns. As regards nonvital organs, for jurists who consider organ transplantation prohibited, like the majority of the Ḥanafī school, again this is a separate legal issue on which the brain-death criterion has no bearing, since they consider organ transplantation prohibited whether the patient is conscious or comatose or dead, based on this *hadith* of the Prophet: "Breaking the bones of the dead is like breaking them when he is alive."[30] On the other hand, jurists who do allow it for a conscious person will also allow it for a comatose person. Finally, the clinician does not have to struggle with different criteria and protocols of determining brain death, since cardiopulmonary manifestation of death will determine that the patient has passed away. Clinicians may object that there is no 100 percent certain test for any measure, which means that the criterion of certainty can never be applied. The response is that the criterion does not seek quantitative certainty but rather requires that, according to the physician, no signs of life remain.

In sum, according to the jurisprudential framework of *ijtihād* articulated by Shāṭibī, the domain of the jurist comprises identifying legal criteria, whereas the domain of the patient and the physician is their application. Jurists need to identify the applicable Islamic criteria based on revelation through jurisprudential methods, and Muslim patients and physicians need to judge whether the criteria are met in particular cases. In bioethical controversies the physician must not be assigned the duty of the jurist.

NOTES

The following chapter is based on a paper presented at "Interfaces and Discourses: A Multidisciplinary Conference on Islamic Theology, Law, and Biomedicine" at the University of Chicago, April 15–17, 2016.

1. Abū Isḥāq Ibrāhīm b. Mūsā al-Lakhmī al-Shāṭibī was a Mālikī jurist from Muslim Granada. His work *al-Muwāfaqāt* is perhaps the best-known work of

Maqāṣid al-Sharī'ah (the aims of the Shariah) and is one of the few works of Islamic law that is studied and taught by jurists of schools other than that of the author. See *Turkiye Diyanet Vakfi Islam Ansiklopedisi*, s.v. "Şâtibî, İbrâhim b. Mûsâ."

2. Abū Isḥāq Ibrāhīm b. Mūsā al-Lakhmī al-Shāṭibī, *al-Muwāfaqāt fī uṣūl al-Sharī'ah* (Beirut: Dār al-Kutub al-'Ilmiyya, 2009), 789. We refer to the Shariah as the rules that Allah ordains for competent beings to follow as a religion through revelation, which cannot be known without revelation, regardless of whether revelation decrees the rule itself or its like. 'Alī Ḥaydar Arsebuk, *Durar al-ḥukkām sharḥ majallat al-aḥkām* (Beirut: Dār al-Kutub al-'Ilmiyyah, 2010), 1:13.

3. Shāṭibī, *al-Muwāfaqāt fī uṣūl al-Sharī'ah*, 774 ff. Shāṭibī's discussion of *ijtihād* is based on and develops al-Ghazālī's earlier exposition of the same subject. al-Ghazālī, *al-Mustaṣfā* (Beirut: Dār al-Kutub al-'Ilmiyyah, 1993), 1:281 ff. We discussed Ghazālī's exposition and its relevance to the juristic role of the Muslim physician in Muhammed Volkan Stodolsky and Mohammed Amin Kholwadia, "Physician's Juristic Role," in *Encyclopedia of Islamic Bioethics*, ed. Ayman Shabana. *Oxford Islamic Studies Online*, http://www.oxfordislamicstudies.com/article/opr/t343/e0271 (accessed April 4, 2018).

4. Cf. 'Abd al-Ghanī b. Ṭālib Maydānī, *al-Lubāb fī sharḥ al-kitāb* (Damascus: Maktabat al-'Ilm al-Ḥadīth), 578.

5. This is the legal cause according to the Ḥanafī school; according to the Mālikī and Shāfi'ī schools, the legal cause is the unequal exchange of foodstuff of the same kind.

6. Necmettin Kizilkaya, *Hanefi Mezhebi Baglaminda Islam Hukukunda Kulli Kaideler* (Istanbul: Iz Yayincilik, 2013), 335 ff., 399.

7. Zayn al-Dīn Ibn Nujaym, *al-Ashbāh wa l-naẓā'ir* (Beirut: Dar al-Kutub al-'Ilmiyyah, 1999), 14.

8. Muḥammad Amīn Ibn 'Ābidīn, *Radd al-muḥtār 'alā al-durr al-mukhtār sharḥ tanwīr al-abṣār* (Beirut: Dar al-Fikr, 1992), 1:210.

9. A. I. Padela and T. A. Basser, "Brain Death: The Challenges of Translating Medical Science into Islamic Bioethical Discourse," *Medicine and Law* 31, no. 3 (2012): 441.

10. M. Y. Rady et al., "Islam and End-of-Life Practices in Organ Donation for Transplantation: New Questions and Serious Sociocultural Consequences," *HEC Forum* 21 (2009): 175–205, quoted in Aasim I. Padela, Ahsan Arozullah, and Ebrahim Moosa, "Brain Death in Islamic Ethico-Legal Deliberation: Challenges for Applied Islamic Bioethics," *Bioethics* 27, no. 3 (March 2013): 8.

11. "A Definition of Irreversible Coma," Report of the Ad Hoc Committee of the Harvard Medical School to Examine the Definition of Brain Death, *Journal of the American Medical Association* 205, no. 6 (1968): 337–340. http://jamanetwork.com/journals/jama/article-abstract/340177. Cf. Padela and Basser, "Brain Death," 436.

12. Padela, Arozullah, and Moosa, "Brain Death," 6.

13. Ibid., 3. On the same page, the authors provide a useful chart that notes the dates of Islamic verdicts issued on brain death.

14. Padela and Basser, "Brain Death," 439. Padela discusses the philosophical and clinical problems of this and other opinions in the articles cited in this paper.

15. Articles on the subject also mention a third position that they attribute to the Islamic Organization for Medical Sciences (IOMS). This position is that brain death is an intermediate state between life and death so that some rulings of death can be applied, such as those regarding the removal of life support, but not all, such that legal death will take effect according to the cardiopulmonary criteria. This chapter will not deal with this position, as we were not able to access the original documents in Arabic or to engage the arguments and the application of the position to related issues in detail. Articles that mention the position do so very briefly. See Padela and Basser, "Brain Death," 439, and Padela, Arozullah, and Moosa, "Brain Death," 3. For a brief discussion and rejection of the position in Arabic, see Sa'd b. 'Abd al-'Azīz al-Shuwayrikh, "Mawt al-dimāgh," *Majallat al-Jam'iyyah al-Fiqhiyyah al-Sa'ūdiyyah* 11 (2011): 310, who quotes the prominent classical jurist Ibn Ḥazm in saying, "No two experts on the Shariah or anyone else differ on the fact that one is either alive or dead."

16. Ibn Nujaym, *al-Ashbāh*, 6.

17. For a summary of the issue in Arabic with citation of sources and fatwās, see Ḥamd Muḥammad al-Hājirī, "Mawt al-dimāgh bayn al-fuqahā' wa l-aṭibbā,'" *Majallat Kulliyat al-Sharī'ah wa l-Dirāsāt al-Islāmiyyah*, Qatar University 24, 1427/2006, pp. 291–338; Sa'd b. 'Abd al-'Azīz al-Shuwayrikh, "Mawt al-dimāgh," 241–350; Aḥmad 'Abd al-Wahhāb Sālim Muḥammad, "'Alāmat al-mawt bayn al-fuqahā' wa l-aṭibbā'" (http://www.islam.gov.kw/eftaa/ControlPanel/ScientificResearchDocuments/1268209811.doc).

18. Aḥmad b. Muḥammad al-Ṭaḥṭāwī, *Ḥāshiyat al-Ṭaḥṭāwī 'alā marāqī al-falāḥ sharḥ nūr al-īḍāḥ lil-Shurunbulālī* (Beirut: Dār al-Kutub al-'Ilmiyyah, 1997), 565 ff.

19. Abū l-Walīd Muḥammad b. Aḥmad Ibn Rushd, *Bidāyat al-mujtahid wa nihāyat al-muqtaṣid* (Cairo: Dār al-Ḥadīth, 2004), 1:239.

20. Abū 'Abd Allāh Muḥammad b. Idrīs al-Shāfi'ī, *al-Umm* (Beirut: Dār al-Ma'rifah, 1990) 1:315, 322.

21. Abū Zakariyyā Yaḥyā b. Sharaf al-Nawawī, *Rawḍat al-ṭālibīn* (Beirut: al-Maktab al-Islāmī, 1991), 2:98.

22. Abū Muḥammad Muwaffaq al-Dīn 'Abd Allāh b. Aḥmad Ibn Qudāmah, *al-Mughnī* (Cairo: Maktabat al-Qāhira, 1968), 2:337.

23. Aasim I. Padela, Hasan Shanawani, and Ahsan Arozullah, "Medical Experts and Islamic Scholars Deliberating over Brain Death," *Muslim World* 101, no. 1 (2011): 66.

24. Padela and Basser, "Brain Death," 437.

25. David Greer, "Variability of Brain Death Policies in the United States," *Journal of the American Medical Association Neurology* 73, no. 2 (2016): 213–18, http://archneur.jamanetwork.com/article.aspx?articleid=2478467; Sarah Kaplan,

"When Are You Dead? It May Depend on Which Hospital Makes the Call," https://www.washingtonpost.com/news/morning-mix/wp/2015/12/29/when-are-you-dead-it-may-depend-on-which-hospital-makes-the-call/.

26. U.S. Centers for Medicare and Medicaid Services, "Report on St. Joseph Hospital's Handling of Patient Colleen Burns," http://www.scribd.com/doc/148583905/U-S-Centers-for-Medicare-and-Medicaid-Services-report-on-St-Joe-s.

27. Padela, Shanawani, and Arozullah, "Medical Experts," 68.

28. "A Definition of Irreversible Coma," 337–40.

29. Omar Qureshi and Aasim Padela, "When Must a Patient Seek Healthcare? Bringing the Perspective of Islamic Jurists and Clinicians into Dialogue," *Zygon* 51, no. 3 (September 2016).

30. ʿAbd al-Razzāq al-Ṣanʿānī, *al-Muṣannaf* (Beirut: al-Maktab al-Islāmī, 1403 AH), 3:444; Basser and Padela, "Brain Death," 448.

REFERENCES

al-Hājirī, Ḥamd Muḥammad. "Mawt al-dimāgh bayn al-fuqahā' wa l-aṭibbā'." *Majallat Kulliyat al-Sharīʿah wa l-Dirāsāt al-Islāmiyyah*, Qatar University 24, 1427/2006.

al-Nawawī, Abū Zakariyyā Yaḥyā b. Sharaf. *Rawḍat al-ṭālibīn*. Beirut: al-Maktab al-Islāmī, 1991.

al-Ṣanʿānī, Abd al-Razzāq. *al-Muṣannaf*. Beirut: al-Maktab al-Islāmī, 1403 AH.

al-Shāfiʿī, Abū ʿAbd Allāh Muḥammad b. Idrīs. *al-Umm*. Beirut: Dār al-Maʿrifah, 1990.

al-Shuwayrikh, Saʿd b. ʿAbd al-ʿAzīz. "Mawt al-dimāgh." *Majallat al-Jamʿiyyah al-Fiqhiyyah al-Saʿūdiyyah* 11 (2011).

al-Ṭaḥṭāwī, Aḥmad b. Muḥammad. *Ḥāshiyat al-Ṭaḥṭāwī ʿalā marāqī al-falāḥ sharḥ nūr al-īḍāḥ lil-Shurunbulālī*. Beirut: Dār al-Kutub al-ʿIlmiyyah, 1997.

Arsebuk, ʿAlī Ḥaydar. *Durar al-ḥukkām sharḥ majallat al-aḥkām*. Beirut: Dār al-Kutub al-ʿIlmiyyah, 2010.

"A Definition of Irreversible Coma." Report of the Ad Hoc Committee of the Harvard Medical School to Examine the Definition of Brain Death. *Journal of the American Medical Assocaition* 205, no. 6 (1968): 337–40.

Greer, David. "Variability of Brain Death Policies in the United States." *Journal of the American Medical Association Neurology* 73, no. 2 (2016): 213–218. http://archneur.jamanetwork.com/article.aspx?articleid=2478467.

Ibn ʿĀbidīn, Muḥammad Amīn. *Radd al-muḥtār ʿalā al-durr al-mukhtār sharḥ tanwīr al-abṣār*. Beirut: Dar al-Fikr, 1992.

Ibn Nujaym, Zayn al-Dīn b. Ibrāhīm. *al-Ashbāh wa l-naẓā'ir*. Beirut: Dar al-Kutub al-ʿIlmiyyah, 1999.

Ibn Qudāmah, Abū Muḥammad Muwaffaq al-Dīn 'Abd Allāh b. Aḥmad. *al-Mughnī*. Cairo: Maktabat al-Qāhira, 1968.

Ibn Rushd, Abū l-Walīd Muḥammad b. Aḥmad. *Bidāyat al-mujtahid wa nihāyat al-muqtaṣid*. Cairo: Dār al-Ḥadīth, 2004.

Kaplan, Sarah. "When Are You Dead? It May Depend on Which Hospital Makes the Call." https://www.washingtonpost.com/news/morning-mix/wp/2015/12/29/when-are-you-dead-it-may-depend-on-which-hospital-makes-the-call/.

Kizilkaya, Necmettin. *Hanefi Mezhebi Baglaminda Islam Hukukunda Kulli Kaideler*. Istanbul: Iz Yayincilik, 2013.

Maydānī, 'Abd al-Ghanī b. Ṭālib. *al-Lubāb fī sharḥ al-kitāb*. Damascus: Maktabat al-'Ilm al-Ḥadīth.

Padela, Aasim, and Taha Abdul-Basser. "Brain Death: The Challenges of Translating Medical Science into Islamic Bioethical Discourse." *Medicine and Law* 31, no. 3 (September 2012): 433–50.

Padela, Aasim, Ahsan Arozullah, and Ebrahim Moosa. "Brain Death in Islamic Ethico-Legal Deliberation." *Bioethics* 27, no. 3 (March 2013).

Padela, Aasim, Hasan Shanawani, and Ahsan Arozullah. "Medical Experts and Islamic Scholars Deliberating over Brain Death." *Muslim World* 101, no. 1 (2011): 53–72.

Qureshi, Omar, and Aasim Padela. "When Must a Patient Seek Healthcare? Bringing the Perspective of Islamic Jurists and Clinicians into Dialogue." *Zygon* 51, no. 3 (September 2016).

Rady, M.Y., et al. "Islam and End-of-Life Practices in Organ Donation for Transplantation: New Questions and Serious Sociocultural Consequences." *HEC Forum* 21 (2009): 175–205.

Shāṭibī, Abū Isḥāq Ibrāhīm b. Mūsā. *al-Muwāfaqāt fī uṣūl al-Sharī'ah*. Beirut: Dār al-Kutub al-'Ilmiyya, 2009.

Stodolsky, Muhammed Volkan, and Mohammed Amin Kholwadia. "Physician's Juristic Role." In *Encyclopedia of Islamic Bioethics*, ed. Ayman Shabana, *Oxford Islamic Studies Online*. Forthcoming. http://www.oxfordislamicstudies.com/article/opr/t343/e0271. Accessed April 4, 2018.

U.S. Centers for Medicare and Medicaid Services. "Report on St. Joseph Hospital's Handling of Patient Colleen Burns." http://www.scribd.com/doc/148583905/U-S-Centers-for-Medicare-and-Medicaid-Services-report-on-St-Joe-s.

FOUR

Considering Being and Knowing in an Age of Techno-Science

EBRAHIM MOOSA

A philosopher, whose brother recently died, was asked: "What ailment caused your brother to die?" He replied: "His being *in the world (*kaynūnatuhu fī l-dunyā*)."*

—'Alī ibn Muḥammad Abū Ḥayyān al-Tawḥīdī,
Al-Baṣā'ir Wa-Al-Dhakhā'ir

A brain-dead patient is no longer alive in the eyes of the mainstream medical profession. Yet the moral and theological status of a person on a respirator remains contested in multiple religious traditions. This also holds true for some tendencies in Islamic juristic theology. Some Muslim jurists and ethical councils around the world declare brain-dead persons to be "dead" in terms of Muslim ethics and Islamic law, while some with other perspectives contest their claims. The drama plays out at hospitals and emergency rooms when families, especially Muslim families, struggle to make crucial decisions about organ donation or ending life support for seriously injured dependents.

Why does this happen? In my view, the juridical and ethical reasoning does not supply a convincing juro-ethical literacy to make clear the difference between what is a functioning human being and what is the status of a body or organism with an irreversibly damaged brain. The juro-ethical teachings that yield a simple "Yes" or "No," permissible or impermissible, are clearly insufficient for many laypersons and professionals.

Can one draw on a more sophisticated and complex Islamic literacy, one that informs both laypersons and experts on the conceptions of personhood associated with those who are medically deemed to suffer irreversible brain death and irreparable damage? To engage that complex literacy involves revisiting arguments of ontology, epistemology, and theology in the archives of Muslim thought and their contemporary invocation, if at all, by Muslim ethicists.

ONTOLOGY, EPISTEMOLOGY, AND THEOLOGY

"Metaphysics" might sound like a complex and mystifying word, but it has a very lucid, if not obvious, sense if we ponder it. Think of the complex ways of thinking you will deploy when you, as a physician, next of kin, or a healthcare surrogate, have to decide to switch off a ventilator for someone with cerebral death and no consciousness. Or think of a scenario in which you refuse to do so. In each case you have relied on a range of metaphysical decisions, knowingly or unknowingly, things that are not palpable but have informed your decision-making either way. If you think that death has occurred in a person in such a condition, you have reached certain conclusions on that patient's personhood, human biology, and the limits of science and medicine. And if you reached the opposite conclusion, you have reached different decisions about each of these complex issues. Whatever decisions you reached, there is a complex story of existence or being-in-the-world to which you subscribe that grounds your arguments and views. Whether you believe these conceptions are immaterial, for "the tendency to overlook metaphysical dependencies," writes Susan Neiman, "only makes them deeper."[1]

Early Muslim philosophers and philosophically minded theologians in the medieval world took metaphysics seriously. Metaphysics forms the foundation of philosophical thinking and gives us a sense of what the world truly is in terms of the best cognitive and scientific tools at our disposal. The prominent political philosopher Abū Naṣr al-Fārābī (d. 950–51), the metaphysician par excellence Abū Alī Ibn Sīnā (d. 1037), and the jurist-theologian and polymath Abū Ḥāmid al-Ghazālī (d. 1111) valued metaphysics as integral to their thinking about matters of science, faith, morals and values.[2] It goes without saying that the absence of metaphysical thinking, or, rather, the paucity of complex modes of philosophical and moral thinking, has resulted in the impoverishment of contemporary Muslim thought, especially ethical thought.

Medieval Muslim thinkers friendly toward philosophy engaged with the Greek legacy, especially that of Aristotle and Plato, whose insights shaped large areas of Muslim religious thought from theology, mysticism, and law to ethics. Ghazālī, for instance, repeats the claim made by Aristotle to explain that each theoretical science (*al-'ilm al-naẓarī*), such as physics, mathematics, and metaphysics, is a way of understanding being or what exists.[3] As a theologian, Ghazālī gives priority to metaphysics, which Muslim thinkers translated as "divine knowledge" (*al-'ilm al-ilāhī*) and he describes as "first philosophy" (*al-falsafa-t al-ūlā*), repeating Aristotle's phrase for metaphysics.[4] For Aristotle, first philosophy means that "all causes must be eternal . . . that operate on so much of the divine as appears to us," a proposition Ghazālī heartily endorsed.[5] Metaphysics enjoys priority because the science of "an *immovable substance*" (italics mine), as Aristotle puts it, must be prior to the immovable substance, by which it then becomes a first philosophy. In other words, in this scheme metaphysics becomes universal, namely, a way of reasoning about the divine, which is what "theology" means. Its purpose is to comprehend the immovable Creator. [6] Apart from Muslim philosophers, many Muslim metaphysicians, and most theologians, will not describe the "immovable" as a "substance" since, as Ghazālī reminds us, "God the Sublime is neither a substance (*jawhar*) nor an accident (*'araḍ*)."[7] So any discussion about God will be at the beginning of a metaphysical conversation to consider being as we know it as a condition initiated by God.[8]

Ontology, the total view of what exists or the study of what there is, lies at the center of metaphysics.[9] Today a large part of what exists is made known to us by science, especially physics, chemistry, cosmology, and astrophysics. But, as Alvin Toffler reminds us, science is not an "independent variable" and does not develop in splendid isolation from the world around it. Many scientific hypotheses, including those about medicine, as well as theories, metaphors, and models, are shaped by economic, cultural, and political forces operating outside of science.[10] Yet a recognition of human finitude and a surprising postmodern modesty has cast doubt on whether it is even feasible to aspire to attain a coherent understanding of all that exists. The hostility to metaphysics of positivism in the early twentieth century has been replaced by a new turn in favor of metaphysics, but with a difference, thanks to our altered picture of science itself. Ilya Prigogine and Isabelle Stengers explain that notions of traditional science that tended to emphasize stability, order, uniformity, and equilibrium were associated with a closed system and with linear relationships in physics and science more broadly. The Prigoginian paradigm makes us shift our attention to an age of acceleration where disorder, instability, diversity, disequilibrium, nonlinear relationships in which "small inputs can trigger massive consequences," and temporality related to the flows of time are the important features. The ontological shift occasioned by an open and accelerated cosmological order also impacts our epistemological categories. The concept of certainty, for instance, especially when dealing with levels of complexity introduced by techno-science, is the first casualty. The certainty produced by Aristotelian theoretical reason is very different from the notion of reason produced by the "manipulative" effect of techno-science that inhabits us.[11] While closed systems are still evident in some small parts of the universe, we now admit that most of our universe is made up of open systems where energy, matter, and information are constantly exchanged with the environment. Hence, mechanistic systems and modes of thinking provide us with a limited view.[12] Now there is a more "pluralistic" and "exuberant metaphysics of the explorers of possible worlds," writes the philosopher Anthony Kenny.[13] Divergences and disagreements between philosophers, metaphysicians, and theologians bear witness to the "complexity of the epistemological configuration" with which we view the universe and how we perceive it.[14]

At an earlier time, someone like Ghazālī provided the answer to ontology in a closed system. Nevertheless, we turn to him today, for he allows us to enter the conversation held several centuries back, aspects of which still make sense at a fundamental level. Existence/being (*wujūd*), he explained, at its most elementary level, consists of two categories, a substance (*jawhar*) and an accident (*'araḍ*).[15] Atoms are substances, but redness in apples is an example of an accident. All things temporal are designated either as a substance or as an accident. If we think of God as a necessary being, such a being "is intelligible in itself, without reference to any external thing," explains Lenn Goodman with accuracy. "A contingent being's existence," he explains, "is not intelligible in itself."[16] Realizing how the conditions of existence impact our thinking, Ghazālī made it a requirement for serious theologians to study the big picture of the universe in order to examine "the most general of things, namely, reality or existence (*mawjūd*)."[17] While Ghazālī was thinking of mental categories, he would not be opposed to considering empirical categories of what exists.

In metaphysics, writes Ghazālī, one expends "thinking in the causes of being in its totality."[18] A simple reason animates thinking and reflection in order to configure the grounds of what exists, namely, "a cause and its effect" and the discursive search for the "singular cause, the necessary existent (*wājib al-wujūd*)" God.[19] More pertinent is the need to decipher the attributes of the divine as well as the "connection of all existing things with the Divine and the mode of how things stem from God."[20] For Ghazālī the connection between the world and metaphysics was indispensable and thus places him in a unique category of jurist-theologians who genuinely valued aspects of philosophy. Once a theologian grasps the big picture of the world, there is a coherent relationship with the micro realm of morality, which, he writes, "as a consequence establishes the foundations of knowledge of good conduct (religion) (*al-'ulūm al-dīnīya*) derived from the [revealed] Book, the *Sunnah* and the truthfulness of the messenger."[21]

Establishing the necessity of prophecy with the authority of reason, Ghazālī reminds himself, follows from the ontological question of God as first philosophy. Once the authority of God is ontologically supported, from that point onward all the dependent teachings follow with some metaphysical backing. These include, among others, teachings about how to establish the credentials of divinely sent emissaries—how to secure relationships of trust between prophets and the communities to which they were sent and the details of how to make the world a place where the moral good can flourish. The authority of reason, Ghazālī concedes, as an Ash'arī theologian, might not be able to validate the totality of the teachings the prophets received from God. Reason can neither conceive of such matters nor provide compelling arguments in support, since the authority for such matters comes from an authority outside of the autonomous self. Philosophers call this heteronomy: action that is required by a force outside the individual. Reason, for example, says Ghazālī, cannot confirm or justify why obedience to God will be the cause of happiness in the hereafter or why disobedience will be the cause of suffering in the hereafter.[22] And reason is also unable to declare why it is impossible to enjoy happiness or suffering in the hereafter.[23] What reason can do is to provide plausible structures and explanations as to how obedience and disobedience, compliance and noncompliance to ethical imperatives, can result in happiness or suffering in the material world.

Ghazālī clearly identifies the Muslim knowledge framework as a force field that combines intellect or reason and revealed teachings. In a well-known discussion, Ghazālī describes obedience to God as consisting of the duality of knowledge (*ʿilm*) and practice (*ʿamal*).[24] Knowledge is not separated from a practice, he explains. Indeed, the very act of knowing involves a certain kind of work that takes place in the heart. In short, to know and to possess knowledge are always-already practices, in his view. The heart, literally and figuratively, enjoys a pre-eminence among all human organs as the most crucial physical organ as well as the most revered and relevant spiritual organ, Ghazālī explains.[25] As the locus of the soul and the spirit, the heart plays an intimate role in human subjectivity, identity, and the complex ways we understand the world, ourselves, and others. Understanding is associated with the intellect, which Ghazālī describes as the "vehicle for commitment to the salvation practices—*markab al-diyāna*"—and as the "carrier of the covenant of responsibility—*ḥāmil al-amāna*."[26]

Knowledge is derived from two sources, intellect or reason and revelation, explains Ghazālī.[27] Some forms of rational knowledge are innate to us, and others are acquired. Revealed knowledge reaches us via the prophets, especially the scriptures they received and the exemplary lives they led. People acquire revealed knowledge by way of authoritative teaching (*taqlīd*), but this teaching cannot be fully understood and appreciated without the help of the intellect. Revelation serves primarily as a remedy and a healer for the condition of the heart and soul by relying on reason. As Ghazālī explicitly writes:

> The intellect cannot entirely dispense with revealed authority (*samā'*), nor can revealed authority dispense with the intellect. The proponent who relies exclusively on authoritative teaching and entirely dismisses the intellect is an ignoramus. The one who is solely content with intellect by neglecting the illumination provided by the Qur'an and the *Sunnah* is an arrogant person. So, beware that you do not fall into one of these two camps, but rather combine both sources instead. For the intellectual sciences are like nutrition and revealed knowledge is like medication.[28]

We need a multiplicity of resources, Ghazālī says, in order to know ourselves and the world we live in.

Medieval theologians like Ghazālī or early modern scholars like 'Abd al-Raḥmān Ibn Khaldūn (d. 1406) were sanguine about grasping reality. It may well be that they were constrained by their Ash'arī theological lenses and dispositions. Despite urging us to be intimately familiar with reality, Ghazālī issues a damper on any optimistic effort to grasp reality. To define reality is an extremely complex matter, he warns. "Most sensory perceptible things (*al-mudrakāt al-ḥissīya*) are challenging to define," he writes. "For instance," he continues, "if we were required to define the smell of musk or the taste of honey, we will be hard pressed to do so. So, if we are challenged to define sensory perceptible things, then it will be even more impossible to define perceptions (*idrākāt*)."[29] Reality is very much the picture on the inside of our minds for a soft idealist like Ghazālī. And if there is inner uncertainty, of course it will impact the view of external reality. His attitude was not an isolated one in Muslim thought and was characteristic of ideas espoused by Ash'arī theologians. It might be precisely this theological imagination that lends itself to uncertainty that finds echoes and resonance with the open systems of contemporary science.

MODERN BEING AND KNOWING

Since Ghazālī's time, much has changed in our perceptions of nature and the universe, and also of our understanding of the self and the body. Nature itself has been revolutionized by technology, and we can apprehend matter and the cosmos in ways that were previously impossible to grasp.

We might continue to talk about substances and accidents, but how substances perform under different conditions now results in an understanding of physics unimagined by our forebears. "Mathematics, ontology, and metaphysics," writes the novelist and thinker Marilynne Robinson, "have become one thing," given the breakthrough discoveries of modern science.[30] How the physical world operates and functions is now empirically verifiable. And, in the view of many materialists, "metaphysics is philosophy masquerading as natural science."[31] Materialists have pursued a reductionist line of inquiry that has alarmed many. Robinson has identified neuroscience as one field in which mental function can be explained as casually as a game of billiards.[32] Philosopher Anthony Kenny also cautions, saying: "It is a metaphysical error to think, for instance, that exploration of the brain will help us to understand what is going on in our minds when we think and understand."[33] There is no need to be overly confident about the resources of science, and hence humility is useful. Yuval Noah Harari, the noted historian and philosopher, writes: "After centuries of extensive scientific research, biologists admit that they still don't have any good explanation for how brains produce consciousness."[34]

Both Robinson and Kenny draw our attention to the sciences that are "entangled" with ontology, the question of being. Quantum entanglement raises questions about time and space and ultimately about causality. Particles that are entangled, no matter how distant from each other, do indeed undergo the same changes simultaneously.[35] So, if the basic question ontology asks is "What exists?," the question that metaontology asks is "Are there objective answers to the basic question of ontology?" Put differently, "Can we clearly and coherently spell out what exists?" Ontological realists reply, "Yes," and anti-realists more cautiously say, "No."[36] But if you are an advocate of the theory that there is not only a universe but rather a multiverse, the question will be met with another question: "Which world are you talking about?" Robinson writes with clarity: "However pervasive and robust entanglement is or is not, it implies a cosmos that unfolds or emerges on principles that bear scant analogy to the universe of common sense. It is abetted in this by string theory, which adds seven unexpressed dimensions to our familiar four. And, of course, those four seem suddenly tenuous when the fundamental character of time and space is being called into question."[37]

Yes, the meaning of the constantly expanding cosmos in human consciousness and the story of the cosmos itself is a constantly shifting and open one, varying with our knowledge of the self in relation to the world. Is there "something" beyond the physical universe that gives us meaning? How metaphysics relates to other branches of philosophy might require us to agree with Wittgenstein that philosophy was not a house, nor a tree, but a web.[38] And a web constantly intersects to create a certain oneness with difference.

Knowledge itself, or the theory of knowledge (epistemology) for non-nominalist interpreters of Islam, always had some form of metaphysical backing. Let's think of metaphysics as the hidden backstory against which our assumptions about the world and our identities or selves are measured. In short, metaphysics is the meta-theory of meaning-making that also shapes our knowledge frameworks. Meaning, in the broadest sense, is the question that metaphysicians try to address. Philosophers give that something a name, "being," or "be-ing," to be in the world or how to exist in the world. Except that being-in-the-world or existence per se is not separate from us; rather, we already *are*, we exist and are already embedded in the world. In short, we make sense to ourselves or we make meaning of our lives in relation to others and in relation to sacred and secular orders.

But Wittgenstein promptly disturbs our comfort zone and has a way to make us question our assumptions. "Where in the world is a metaphysical subject to be found?," he asks. Then he adds, "You will say that this is exactly like the case of the eye and the visual field. But really you do *not* see the eye. And nothing *in the visual field* allows you to infer that it is seen by the eye."[39] So even if we do not *see* certain aspects of being, in the same way that we do not see our own eye when we look, experientially we do indeed concede that things exist, even if we do not see the instrument with which we are seeing.

Metaphysicians, philosophers, and theologians have for centuries puzzled over what exists and what is known. Why? For the simple reason that humans devised and discovered a multitude of ways of knowing what exists, and also multiple ways of giving meaning to these known realities. In other words, human experiences culminated in some ways of knowing and made other modes of knowing ambiguous over time. Cultural and civilizational power also has a role in making some ways of being and knowing visible and makes other modes of knowing invisible.

Philosopher Owen Flanagan possibly describes this realization best when he writes: "All actual differences across cultures and across individuals make a difference and not just for the descriptive side of ethics. Goods—moral, aesthetic, epistemic—are often internal to practices and tradition and possibly intermixed in unfamiliar ways. . . . Almost everyone will think that some practices are good, bad, right, or wrong depending on how they are situated in a complex normative web that is partly up to the people who live inside or abide the normative web in question."[40]

So we have to agree that there are multiple narratives to explain being or ontology, as well as a multitude of languages of knowing. The differences are located at the theoretical level where presumptions, understandings, and feelings about being and knowing are expressed. But in practice, being and knowing are the ways Flanagan describes them to be.

Ethical and moral answers are determined by the perspective of reality adopted by individuals, communities, or experts in terms of scholars or views held by a discursive community. For a time, the term "worldview" made sense, meaning "a system of beliefs that are *interconnected* in something like the way the pieces of a jigsaw puzzle are interconnected."[41] In its simple form, a worldview approach involves figuring out how to abbreviate a complex set of views in a reductive form without isolating the relationship between being-in-the-world and knowledge and knowing. There are instances when a more complex understanding of a worldview can also reveal how being-in-the-world and knowledge are separated and operate on different planes. So one might still adhere to such a task, but it requires a historical account, an experiential account, followed by a normative ontological account based on metaphysics. For someone like Ghazālī, metaphysics was grounded in the Divine.

The preceding conceptions of the relationship between metaphysics and theology are clearly inadequate. Thinking about God in relationship to an ever-expanding cosmos today intimately ties our theological conceptions to the precepts of metaphysics based in part on a mechanistic view of science and an ever-growing open view. The relationships become more complex and interdependent than previously thought. If ontology intersects with theology, clearly the shape of being will also have implications for knowing the self and the world.

MODERN MUSLIM METAPHYSICS

Modern Muslim metaphysics is a hybrid of pre-modern constructions of ontology and epistemology that grapples with modern technology and modern ethical practices. Contemporary Muslim jurist-theologians in particular, together with Muslim bioethicists and ethicists in general, hardly attempt to outline their ontological commitments and premises in a systematic manner. Instead, their metaphysical claims are implicit in their judgments without clear elaboration.

They deploy juridical methods premised on an Aristotelian metaphysical order that has lost much of its efficacy in practical terms. The juridical thinking is linear as part of a closed ontological and epistemological order. Terms used by Muslim jurists today, such as certainty, truth, cause, effect, ratio, and reality, are wedded to a very different order of things. While they are used rhetorically, there is very little indication on the part of the users that these categories resonate with a contemporary metaphysics.

Often Muslim jurists today find answers derived from pre-existing rules that were made over the centuries in order to settle contemporary ethical questions and dilemmas. Often the rhetoric used by the jurists is the application of aphoristic rules and certain dicta that either approve or disapprove of practices by saying they are permissible (*mubāḥ/jā'iz*) or prohibited (*maḥdhūr/ḥarām*). Often the judgment of permissible or prohibited for an action, the use of a substance, or the utterance of a thought is arrived at on the basis of whether the new question resembles an earlier one or whether it meets a standard of public interest. While the latter is an improvement, it remains randomly utilitarian without a complex process of assessment of how the public interest (*maṣlaḥa*) is assessed and what personal, social, and public harms its use might inflict. Unlike Ghazālī, who took the ontology and metaphysical premises of his world seriously, with some criticism, today there is little indication that contemporary metaphysics resonates integrally with the juridical and ethical enterprise of Muslim jurists. The chasm between science and medicine, on the one hand, and ethical enterprise, on the other, symbolizes two very different languages that are often mechanically tethered but not integrally and organically resonant.

Of the methods used to fill the requirements for ethical and moral deliberation, two are prevalent today: a scriptural approach and a canonical discursive approach. Often a scriptural approach is deployed in broad brushstrokes. The scriptural approach reaches for selective teachings from the Qur'an and the prophetic tradition (*Sunnah*) as the ultimate fonts of moral and ethical norms. This approach often relies on the hermeneutical harvest of the past while making some adjustments in order to apply it to issues in the present. But it is best characterized as an approach whereby interpreters assert what revelation promises and pledges, and this is followed by pronouncements as to what revelation authorizes and commands by way of norms. There is an assumed expectation that the Qur'an and the *Sunnah* contain stipulated truths in such perfect symmetry as to match the "world-to-word" need of the interpreter, only to assert the "word-to-world" solution by invoking scriptural sources.[42] All the virtues are assumed to be self-evident and defined in the truth structures of the two forms of revelation, the scriptures of God and the normative authority of the Prophet Muhammad.

The other method used to fill the requirements for ethical and moral deliberation is the complex discursive approach in historical Muslim hermeneutics, composed of a canon of writings and dizzyingly complex hermeneutical frameworks that defy easy summation. This method is wedded to a strong sensibility of tradition—broadly conceived—with primacy given to understanding the world with the help of a variety of knowledge practices ranging from the ontological and epistemological concerns embedded in theology, philosophy, and moral judgment to a reading of the history of the formative society of revelation and the place of prophecy. Historically, the various Muslim law schools, *Sunni* and *Shīʿa*, adopted versions of this approach, and they still exist in some form today when elements of these hermeneutical traditions (*madhhab*, pl. *madhāhib*) are invoked. These schools consist of a hermeneutic that functions "simultaneously as a constructive interpretive method and as a justification of preconceived views."[43] The canonical law schools acknowledge a certain historical sensibility of context and interpretation with the application of meticulous hermeneutics. While they treat the authority of the text with due reverence, it is the authority and practices generated by the hermeneutical traditions in their multiplicity that carry the day in this schema, not so much the authority of sacralized texts and laws.[44] The canonical approaches draw on a long tradition of understanding and interpretation that had been authorized over the centuries. Thus, tradition has evolved up to some point and is still invoked by practitioners in the present who recognize such authority.

Practitioners in the present who combine the scripturalist and canonical approaches, or hybrids thereof, tacitly and mechanistically acknowledge the prevalence of a modern scientific cosmology and ontology. Yet both systems, as I previously pointed out, hardly account for the ontological premises of contemporary science and its engagement with the ontologies of tradition in a bid to foment new ontological and epistemological coherence in the present. The absence of a systematic account of contemporary ontology often leads to incoherence, paradox, contradiction, and anachronism in moral and theological claims.

A contemporary Muslim ethicist has to grapple with a fairly large set of questions posed by modern ontologies that in themselves are hardly settled. Modern metaphysicians in the simplest presentation are divided into idealists and realists. Idealists believe that the material world does not exist independent of our perceptions of it and that we do *not* have direct perceptual knowledge of the world. Realists say just the opposite. In their view, a real world exists "that is totally independent of human beings and what they [humans] think and say about it," and they claim things are true or false to the extent that these things are the way we say or describe them to be.[45] It is not that the world has become unintelligible in "some exciting and apocalyptic way," says the philosopher John R. Searle, but that the world "is a lot harder to understand for the rather boring and unexciting reason that you have to be smarter and you have to know a lot more."[46]

Even if Searle is not an ardent defender of an idealist metaphysics, he does show some understanding of the metaphysical dilemma religious people face in an age of science. In an age of Newtonian mechanics and Darwin's theory of evolution, the claim that the universe has an intelligibility makes sense to some educated and religious people. There are at least two metaphysical spheres: a spiritual and mental metaphysical sphere and a material metaphysical sphere. The spiritual and mental sphere, Searle explains, is owned by religion. The material metaphysical realm, he argues, is owned by science.[47] Many dimensions of ontology are becoming more accessible through the steady growth of our knowledge and understanding of science in conversation with religion, metaphysics, and philosophy.[48] In the Muslim sphere, this conversation is in its infancy with respect to contemporary ethics.

But would a scientific naturalist metaphysics be determinative or even sufficient within the Islamic tradition? Scientific naturalism implies that only natural laws and forces operate in the world and constitute our metaphysics. In my view, it remains insufficient. Why? The question of consciousness as a first-person ontology will certainly rear its head and contradict scientific naturalism. The more dominant forms of naturalism would not always square with a belief in God, since there is a possibility of reducing nature and the body to the material.

Today, the situation has become more challenging since, in addition to the mental or spiritual realms owned by religion, what are dominant are the material and physical realms owned by science; the latter dominates and determines the ontological game.[49] Even if one admits that the history of metaphysics in the Islamic tradition is replete with complexity, providing us with ample discourses about the material, physical, mental, imaginal, and spiritual dimensions of the world, there is still a difference between these. They were closed systems with notions of comforting certainty. In the age of techno-science, uncertainty, and contingency, the open ontology of science requires new theological and moral categories. Many religious people find an open and contingent scientific ontology extremely threatening since it invites revisiting moral and ethical norms that once appeared settled. Death is no longer univocal, meaning one thing. We can now, with reasonable certainty, determine cerebral death while an organism can simulate life.

A POSSIBLE WAY FORWARD

Philosophical concepts have a "becoming"—a constant transmutation—in relationship to concepts and ideas in the same order and plane.[50] Since contemporary Muslim ontology is in search of new concepts, we will do well to heed the words of Gilles Deleuze and Félix Guattari when they say, "New concepts must relate to our problems, to our history, and, above all, to our becomings."[51] Recall that one sense of being a Platonist, an Aristotelian, an Avicennian, a Ghazālian, a Ṣadrian, or a Kantian is that one finds oneself justified "in thinking their concepts can be reactivated in our problems,"[52] but, even more, that it might not be as easy a task to accomplish. What is crucial is that, by engaging the ideas of past thinkers, they will, in turn, "inspire those concepts that need to be created."[53] We repeat certain things they said to show a sense of continuity with our present, or we identify an age-old problem, but the task remains "*to do what they did*" and create concepts for problems and challenges that necessarily change.[54] In short, in the Muslim realm there is a need to revitalize the Muslim ethical tradition with fresh insights drawing on the experiences of Muslims living in the present. This tradition assumes that life and experience are not static and therefore being is not static but rather always-already in a state of becoming. Our constant becoming resonates with the open scientific universe we are now accustomed to.

Brought back into our philosophical thinking by figures like Martin Heidegger, the idea of "becoming" is not unfamiliar to the history of Muslim philosophy, albeit in a different key. Critical philosophers like Shihāb al-Dīn al-Suhrawardī (d. 587/1191) and especially Ṣadr al-Dīn al-Shīrāzī (d. 1050/1640),[55] better known as Mulla Ṣadrā, whose perceptive ideas were revived by Mulla Hādī Sabzawārī (d. 1295, 1298/1878, or 1881), among others eagerly engaged with notions of dynamism and becoming.

Ṣadrā identifies a genre of metaphysical knowledge linked to the constitution and generative qualities of persons, which he describes the "learning of human beings (*'ilm al-insān*) and their cognitive and practical powers."[56] Philosophy, in Ṣadrā's view, has two parts. One is to understand (*ma'rifa*) and thereby acquire knowledge of things as they truly exist by reaching a decision (*ḥukm*) with the help of demonstrative evidence (*barāhīn*) and by shunning conjecture (*ẓann*) and arguments from authority (*taqlīd*) in one's methodology.[57] The other aspect of philosophy is to put such knowledge in the service of the "perfection of the human soul (*istikmāl al-nafs al-insānīya*)," by which he means the body and mind or psyche.[58] Nevertheless, theologians, moral philosophers, and ethicists past and present do work within a framework of what exists, namely, they have an ontological framework. Early Muslim philosophers and theologians often staked out their positions with regard to the topic of "existence" (*wujūd*).

Ṣadrā writes that knowledge and intellection (*ta'aqqul*) are forms of existence. And existence is united to its essence (*māhīya*); similarly, knowing is united to the known. Some really existing things (*wujūdāt*) are inferior, and others are superior.[59] Really existing things transcend matter through intensification in existence.[60] In my view, Ṣadrā deserves a great deal of attention since he might be our best ally of past Muslim philosophers whose ideas avail contemporary Islamic thought best in order to navigate the waters of philosophy in the twenty-first century. Ṣadrā took the position that existence (*wujūd*) is the foundation of all philosophical principles.[61] For him, all of existence "is in truth a single substance having a single identity, while possessing multiple stations as well as degrees, high and low."[62]

Ṣadrā's ontology allowed him to say that

> bodies and potentialities (*ṭabā'i'*) are always subject to fluidity or flow (*sayalān*), to change (*tabaddul*) and to perish (*inqiḍā'*), hence they cannot enjoy permanence (*baqā'*) in two separate moments. For [bodies and potentialities] resemble movement, which has a graduated existence (*tadrījīya-t al-wujūd*). All those substances (*jawāhir*) when they change in their essence (ipseity), demonstrate a type of movement. Not in the sense that this movement affects substances as accidents, when substances are viewed as passive (*sākina*). Substances are identical to all movements occurring in other contingent categories. Following this line of reasoning, these [bodies and potentialities] are not permanent, just as no single thing consisting of multiple movements is permanent.[63]

Elaborating Ṣadrā's ideas and dwelling on the theme of the above citation, Christian Jambet writes: "The act of being is animated by a movement that robs it of all permanence in each of the ranks or degrees of existence that it traverses or instantiates. It thus places in doubt the reality of these provisional stations to which its impetus has carried it. . . . This skepticism of being places into doubt the truth in and for itself, the separate, fixed, and definitive reality of each degree of its expression."[64] Each expressed degree of reality, Jambet writes, explaining Ṣadrā's position, then becomes "consolidated in a reality distinct from the unique act of being that has its source and truth in God alone."[65] It was Henri Corbin who described the movement of being as the "restlessness" of being, which manifests "the very freedom of being, always producing, beyond any one of its expressions, a more intense expression, ceaselessly surpassing the finite in its infinite perseverance."[66]

In Ṣadrā, human understanding is linked to the divine source of all things: being as truth. Revelation enunciates God to the world. God is the subject of the enunciation but is also the subject of the statements of revelation along with humans. The subject of revelation is both God and human. Therefore, prophecy becomes possible in the human form. And because the proto-human in the form of the prophet is always in need of revelation and speech from the divine speaker, revelation is the truth of being. In this sense, writes Jambet, "Islam is the bearer of an immanent ontology."[67] For Ṣadrā, the age-old duel between transcendence, or distance (*tanzīh*) from God and presence to God, immanence, or closeness (*tashbīh*) is resolved by saying that we see God through both eyes of transcendence and immanence with a singular vision, not a dual one.[68] Nature is constantly invested with dynamism according to this model. It may well be possible to also bring human experience and culture along with nature to a more meaningful fruition. Henri Corbin describes a whole range of personal acts, such as diverse forms of expression from garden art, calligraphy, and painting to mystical intuition as a "philosophical founding."[69] One witnesses the significance in action of a motif with the possibility of leading the past back into the present. "It is essentially a *hermeneutic*—by *understanding* it, the interpreter implicitly takes on responsibility for what he understands."[70] As Lenn Goodman aptly reminds us: "A preoccupation with efficient causes is the mark of materialism, but metaphysics seeks the ultimate ground or the basis of the existence of all things."[71]

THE METAPHYSICS OF DEATH

The metaphysical perspective has often been absent from modern Muslim discourses of death, since contemporary jurist-theologians do not sufficiently elaborate their metaphysical claims. Talk of death is often focused on the idea of the heart, especially the physical heart, as well as the figurative heart, as the seat of identity and personhood and the reference point for the spirit (*rūḥ*) and the soul (*nafs*). It is perhaps better to talk about the spirit-soul-heart complex, since each is distinct, but also integrated in their functioning.

A description of death by an eighteenth-century Indian Muslim thinker, sage, and mystic, Shāh Walīyullāh (d. 1762), is perhaps a good place to begin. Death from Walīyullāh's perspective is when the spirit (*rūḥ*) parts from the body. And how do we know the spirit has parted? When the body ceases to spontaneously generate (*tawlīd*) itself.[72] The explanation will follow later; first let's deal with some of the issues Walīyullāh himself addresses.

First, he responds to a nominal reading of a passage of the Qur'ān that at first blush appears to say that Muslims are prevented from making inquiries about the spirit. Verse 17:85 reads: "They ask you [Muḥammad] about the spirit, *rūḥ*. Say! the spirit, *rūḥ*, comes from the order of my Lord and you have been given very little knowledge of it." Walīyullāh explains that this Qur'ānic reply was in response to what appeared to be a vexatious question posed to the Prophet Muḥammad. So the verse was the kind of response needed to silence the questioner, but it does not mean that one cannot speak intelligently about the spirit. Walīyullāh's reply deserves quotation in full since it is also a model lesson in the hermeneutics of a complex learned and canonical tradition of Islam, not a nominalist, scripturalist one. Walīyullāh writes:

> The verse is not a univocal or an explicit text (*naṣṣ*) stating that no one from the community, on whom is God's mercy, will acquire knowledge pertaining to the reality of the spirit as it is assumed. For it does not mean that everything on which the revelation (*shar'*) is silent, therefore it is absolutely impossible to have knowledge of such a matter. Rather, many of the things about which the revelation is silent actually require sophisticated knowledge. And it is not appropriate to share this knowledge with the entire multitude, while it is possible to share it with some of them.[73]

Then Walīyullāh explains that the spirit is the source of life, which becomes evident in any living creature (*ḥayawān*). He has a two-step process to explain the workings of the spirit. First, according to the science of Walīyullāh's time, the quintessence as well as the combination of the four humors—black bile, yellow bile, blood, and phlegm—generate a subtle vapor in the heart. This vapor also carries the faculties of perception, movement, and the distribution of nutrition in the body, based on the principles of medicine.[74] Altering states of the vapor, in terms of its density, light, purity, or opaqueness—have a commensurate effect on the various faculties and their functions. The existence of this vapor signifies life, and its dissolution indicates death. Hence, the vapor is often superficially identified and equated with the spirit, *rūḥ*. On closer inspection it becomes clear that this vapor is the lowest rung of the spirit, call it an elementary spirit. It provides the matter for the heavenly spirit to be attached to the body. Another way to think of the spirit and the body is to think of them as the aromatic oil in the petals of the rose or the potential of coal to combust. We can, for practical purposes, replace Walīyullāh's vapors with our biological knowledge of embryology. What he is saying is that some kind of biological spirit first inheres in the fetus.

The second step of the process to explain the workings of the spirit is the animation of a living creature by the in-breathing of the heavenly spirit into the body. It is this heavenly spirit that gives particularity and identity, in Walīyullāh's view. The characteristics of the carrier of the spirit can differ. It can be a young person or an old person, a learned one or an ignorant one, but the person remains the same person in all these stages. If we assume these changing attributes for argument's sake, Walīyullāh says, the adult person is the very infant of decades ago. And, of course, we cannot be certain that the characteristics of the person will permanently remain in the same condition, but we can be certain about one thing, he says, namely, that the person will remain the same. We might have to concede, says Walīyullāh, that the person is something different from all these changing attributes. Here Walīyullāh is possibly invoking Ibn Sīnā's position to say that the soul is closely identified with our bodies:

> The thing by which a person becomes what one is (haecceity—*huwa bihi huwa*) is not the spirit, nor the body or the individuation that is seen at the first instance. The spirit in all truth is a unique individuating essence (*ḥaqīqa fardānīya*) and a luminous point. The condition of the spirit (luminous light) is elevated from the other altering and contrasting conditions of [the body]: some of these conditions are made up of substances and some others of accidents. The spirit with the young is exactly like it is with old, with a black person as it is with a white person, as it is with similar opposites. And this luminous spirit has a special relation with the pneumatic spirit (lit. airy spirit) firstly, and the body secondly, in so far as the body is the substrate (lit. mount) for the pneuma (*nasama-spirit*). The luminous spirit is an aperture [of light] from the Sanctified World (*'ālam al-quds*). From [that sanctified world] descends everything which equips the pneuma. As to the changing conditions to the

> [embodied] spirit, its changes stem from the earthly dispositions. It is similar to the different effects of the heat of the sun: it bleaches [colored] garment, but darkens (or tans) the person doing the bleaching [assuming the work is done in the open].[75]

Walīyullāh spends some time explaining how an infant's attributes might change as he or she becomes an adult, but he or she remains the same person. Of course, the child's *embodied* spirit undergoes numerous changes, but identity is attached to a separate/individuating essence (*ḥaqīqa fardānīya*) that we also call the spirit. But recall that the pneuma (*nasama*) also plays an important role in Walīyullāh's schema and plays a significant role as an indicator of death. The *nasama* also plays an important intermediary role between the divine soul and the earthly body. Hence, it plays a critical role in the transition of the body to the afterlife at the point of death.

So, what is death? His metaphysical and mystical intuitions, Walīyullah explains, lead him to understand that death is the separation of the life-giving breath (*nasama*) from the body. How do we know this separation has taken place? He gives an interesting answer: When the body loses the ability to be generative and spontaneously generate itself. Importantly, he says, death is not the separation of the sanctified spirit (*al-rūḥ al-qudsī*) from the life-giving breath (pneuma/*nasama*). What happens is that the life-giving breath (*nasama*) deteriorates as a result of serious and life-threatening illness in the body. As part of God's wisdom, most of the *nasama* leaves the body, but a residual component of the life-giving breath remains in the body.[76] This residual *nasama* makes it possible for the divine spirit (*al-rūḥ al-ilāhī*) to connect to the body of the deceased person as part of the transition to the afterlife. That residual life-giving breath now generates a *sensus communis* within the person in the afterlife. What is the *sensus communis*? It is that plane between the tangible world and the intangible world. In this shared world we acquire a faculty to hear, see, and speak with the help of the "world of images," *ʿālam al-mithāl*. Obviously, the means of communication will be different from the way we experienced it in the world, but the worldly sensibility allows for an approximation.

Walīyullāh further explains that at the time of death the life-giving breath (*nasama*) might be wrapped up in a garment of light or of darkness thanks to the effects of the world of images. Then the person begins to experience either the wonders or the horrors of the intermediary world, *barzakh*, depending on one's salvific status, which is based on one's moral performance in this world.

The pneuma, in turn, has two aspects: It is the screen between the divine spirit and the earthly body. One side is holy or sacred, and the other side is animalistic. Now, on resurrection day the holy side of this screen is activated and the emanation of the divine spirit enables the life-giving breath, *nasama* (pneuma), to take on a bodily form on judgment day.

CONCLUSION: ALTERATION IN KNOWING AND BEING—HOW TO TALK ABOUT DEATH IN THE AGE OF TECHNO-SCIENCE

A vexing question in Muslim bioethics is how can we determine the status of a person who is declared to be brain dead based on a medical determination of irreversible brain-stem damage. Muslim theologians have applied a variety of criteria based on historical Islamic legal and ethical strictures to determine if a person in such a condition can for all intents and purposes be declared to be dead.[77] Several Muslim jurisdictions accept the idea of brain death, but their decisions are insufficiently grounded in both the metaphysical and the scientific literature, with the result that some people view their conclusions to uncritically veer to the medical status quo. Some clinicians, too, have raised doubts, claiming that the criteria for brain-death determinations differ around the world.[78] One should at least point out that clinical criteria for any judgment is as variable as are ethical criteria in judgment, and therefore variation and a plurality of responses are to be expected. A good number of Muslim ethicists have accepted the idea of brain death following the expertise of medical experts, but their judgments have not satisfied everyone. However, few have addressed this question on the basis of metaphysics and hence personhood.

From an Islamic perspective of personhood, I view a patient diagnosed as cerebrally dead, what is called brain dead by any of the three international clinical criteria, as an individual who has reached the stage of an embodied biological organism. The individual and embodied organism once had personhood, but the irreversible nature of the damage to the person's vital body has permanently and irreversibly erased consciousness, the key criterion for personhood. One could make an argument for the residual personhood of the biological organism drawing on Walīyullāh's idea of the remnant *nasama* or pneuma in the body of the organism that can no longer spontaneously regenerate. The availability of the remnant *nasama* can at least metaphysically account for the features of residual and biological life in the organism, on Walīyullāh's reading. It is precisely because the organism once was a locus of personhood that we continue to sustain the dignity of the corpse or, in the case of a cerebrally dead organism, the externally supported body/corpse, just as we honor the memories of the dead as persons. We provide the dead with a proper burial and take care with the dignified handling of the corpse. We also refer to persons long dead as "persons" who existed, acknowledging their vital being as persons as well as their personhood.

However, when medical certainty predicts that a patient cannot recover consciousness, in my view, personhood is extinguished. Ghazālī explained the beginning of life as the spirit-soul entering the body and saw it as analogous to the lighting of a wick. As Ghazālī, Walīyullāh, and other Muslim theologians will concur, consciousness is diminished with the exit of the spirit-soul.

Jeff McMahan has argued that the cessation of cerebral function and consciousness, which is usually seen as the criterion for death, means that to be a human being is to be a mind. Once one can determine that the mind is absent, there is no longer an embodied mind, only an organism called the body.[79] In this case, with the help of techno-science, it is possible for the biological organism to show signs of breathing and therefore resemble—or, rather, more accurately, simulate cardio-pulmonary "life." Other forms of vegetative life, we already know, continue even in a corpse, as when hair and nails might continue to grow. So forms of organic life are no indicators of personhood. In an irreversibly damaged brain stem there could be other forms of minimal expression of life or even residual brain function, but we can say with a high degree of certainty that consciousness, for a viable human existence, is irreversibly diminished.

The quandary arises over the dominance of the cardiopulmonary definition of death as a standard measure of the end of life and, under normal circumstances, an index of the exit of the soul from the body. For this reason, it is extremely difficult for laypersons and families to conclude that cerebral death has occurred when the body still simulates life due to the use of externally assisted breathing techniques. But if families and relatives realize that an organism is now merely a vessel for oxygenation for a limited time, it could help them to process what they see to have a different meaning. If we correct our vocabulary and identify the person as an individual and a human organism supported by techno-science, it is a step in the right direction.

In my view, the spirit-soul complex serves a body or physical organism that has full integrity. When the body is irreversibly damaged, experiencing irreparable cerebral damage with growing unfavorable conditions for the physical organism, it is no longer tenable to conclude that the soul subsists and can still perform its functions in the body. We have to switch to the mind-dependency field as our guide. In other words, death is determined not by the onset of the end of normal breathing but by indicators of brain function. A brain-dead organism is in essence identical to a corpse except that techno-science allows us to simulate life in the organism.

To begin with, a severely damaged organism has no intentional states, nor does it have a capacity for a first-person perspective. For these complex indications of brain death, techno-science's intervention requires us to revisit our conceptions of mind-body dualism. We now have to admit that the brain and the mind play significant roles as indicators of the presence of the spirit-soul. Furthermore, we have to admit that the mind is far more dependent on the brain than was previously acknowledged by pre-modern traditionalists.

Recall that personhood is highly dependent on the spirit-soul-heart-mind complex in pre-modern Islamic accounts. But we can glean something from the insights of Fakhr al-Din al-Rāzī, who wrote: "The human soul is endowed with a special property, the cognitive property to perceive the reality of things as they are. Cognition is the property or vessel through which the light of divine knowledge becomes manifest and in it radiates the light of His majesty, and it is cognition that is privy to the secrets of the material and nonmaterial world."[80] Rāzī opened the door for us to think about the connection between the spirit-soul and our cognitive abilities and the significance of these abilities for personhood.[81]

The current state of science makes us even more aware of the neuronal dimension of our bodily constitution. The philosopher Catherine Malabou helpfully writes:

> The current state of research and observation allows cognitive scientists to conclude that thought, knowledge, desires, and affects all proceed on a neuronal, that is to say, biological, basis, and that the mental images constituting the life of the mind are indeed formed in the brain. This chief affirmation, which is the basis for all "reductions" (in other words, the basis for assimilating the mind to a natural datum), is at once the strongest and the weakest point of neuroscientific discourse in general.[82]

The current state of science is at its "strongest," explains Malabou, when the neuroscientific discourse is an advance insofar as these inquiries have allowed us to understand memory, learning, and psychic and behavioral problems more precisely and objectively. It is at its "weakest" in that the "certainty of continuity" between the neuronal and the mental can never strictly be a scientific postulate.[83] It is precisely here, in this absence of certainty or the space of uncertainty as to what happens between the neuronal and spiritual/mental realms—as pointed out by Kenney, Robinson, and Malabou—that theological and philosophical accounts, in short, metaphysics, can play a role. Walīyullāh's metaphysical deliberations discussed above help a contemporary Muslim physician and theologian to consider whether it is still meaningful to call a cerebrally dead person supported by a ventilator and other external aids "living." Muslim metaphysics of both the past and the present cannot be immune to scientific inquiry merely to devalue it on the basis of a mechanistic understanding of both human physiology and the tenets of Islamic law and ethics.

Collaboration between neuroscientists, philosophers, theologians, and ethicists is reaching a point at which there is a recognition of the indispensable "proto-self" consisting of the "state of the internal milieu, viscera, vestibular system, and musculoskeletal frame" to which we attribute the notion of consciousness.[84] Neurobiologists treat the brain as the mysterious link between what we call our personality and the nervous system, or what is also called the synaptic self. Muslim bioethics cannot ignore the undeniable results of neuroscience. Body-soul dualism or substance dualism in Islam, and possibly other traditions, is subject to revision.

I would align myself with "soft dualism," where there is no abyssal separation between body and mind (soul) since our bodies are part of our integral personhood.[85] Yet strict dualism "can't connect the soul to its neural template," as a recent study noted.[86] Unfortunately, the distorted reception of Cartesian dualism has created the wrong impression, as if the brain is not part of the body and embodiment, when in fact the brain is integral to the body and, as a result, gives rise to something called the mind, a faculty vital to personhood. Soft dualism should be coupled with emergence, the notion that a human being is always-already formed in relation to both material and immaterial conditions.[87] William Hasker explains emergent dualism as a view that states that the "mind (or soul) is an individual that is *generated by* the functioning of the biological body, specifically the brain and nervous system, and yet is *distinct from* the physical body."[88] In the words of Kelly James Clark, the mental emerges from the physical: "Consciousness and mental properties appear when body and brain have evolved to the appropriate level of complexity."[89]

Omar Sultan Haque has argued for Muslims to adopt the corporeal monist position of the human person.[90] Corporeal monism holds that there is one ontologically distinct substance, the material body. Haque is agnostic as to whether the soul is material or immaterial. If the former, it squares with his preference for corporeal monism, which he believes is compatible with modern intellectual life. But his proposal is inattentive to the refinements and sophistication of the body-mind dualist position and a range of traditional views demonstrating a much more complex relationship between the body and incorporeal aspects of the self, such as the spirit, soul, and the heart in Muslim metaphysics. Despite a robust advocacy, Haque's position takes us away from the conceptual understanding of the body-soul or person-mind relationship in the tradition, and there is no good reason why a complex position should be abandoned in favor of a reductionist view. One of the salient advantages of the body-soul dualism is precisely the advantage that it serves as a shield against reductionist understandings of personhood.

A plethora of pre-modern Muslim insights on metaphysics couple being and knowing in sophisticated discourses. Attention to that complex Islamic metaphysical literacy in conversation with contemporary philosophy opens the door to understanding the human being as a "unique individuating essence" (*ḥaqīqa fardānīya*) of the relationship between the spirit-soul complex and the mind as being at the center of human personhood and the question of being in a modern Muslim metaphysics. I am fully aware that the debate is an ongoing one, with ample room for refinement and development.

NOTES

1. Susan Neiman, *Moral Clarity: A Guide for Grown-up Idealists*, rev. ed. (Princeton, NJ: Princeton University Press, 2009), 29.

2. See Jon McGinnis and David C. Reisman, *Classical Arabic Philosophy: An Anthology of Sources* (Indianapolis: Hackett, 2007).

3. Abū Ḥāmid Muḥammad b. Muḥammad al-Ghazālī and Aḥmad Farīd Mazīdī, *Maqāṣid Al-Falāsifa Wa Yalīhi Iljām Al-ʿawām Min ʿilm Al-Kalām Wa Al-Fuṣūl Fī Al-As'ila Wa Ajwibatihā* (Beirut: Dār al-Kutub al-ʿIlmīya, 2003), 64–67.

4. Aristotle, "Metaphysica (Metaphysics)," trans. W. D. Ross, in *The Basic Works of Aristotle*, ed. Richard McKeon (New York: Modern Library, 2001), 1026a 24, 31, 778; al-Ghazālī and Mazīdī, *Maqāṣid*, 64.

5. Aristotle, "Metaphysica (Metaphysics)," 1026a 16–18, 779.

6. Ibid., 1026a, 19, 29–33, 779.

7. Abū Ḥāmid Muḥammad b. Muḥammad al-Ghazālī, *Iḥyā' ʿulūm Al-Dīn*, 5 vols. (Beirut: Dār al-Kutub al- ʿIlmīya, 1421/2001), "Kitāb sharḥ ʿajā'ib al-qalb," 3:16. For philosophers designating God a substance (*jawhar*), see Abū al-Baqā' Ayyūb b. Mūsā al-Ḥusaynī al-Kafawī, *Al-Kulliyāt: Muʿjam Fī Al-Muṣṭalaḥāt Wa Al-Furūq Al-Lughawīya*, edited and annoted by ʿAdnān Darwīsh and Muḥammad al-Maṣrī, 2nd ed. (Beirut: Mu'assasa al-Risāla, 1419/1998), 345.

8. See Hussein Ali Abdulsater, *Shi'i Doctrine, Muʿtazili Theology: Al-Sharīf Al-Murtaḍā and Imami Discourse* (Edinburgh: Edinburgh University Press, 2017), 70.

9. Thomas Hofweber, "Logic and Ontology," in *The Stanford Encyclopedia of Philosophy*, ed. Edward N. Zalta (Stanford, CA: Metaphysics Research Lab, Stanford University, 2017), 9/30.

10. Ilya Prigogine, Isabelle Stengers, and Alvin Toffler, foreword to *Order Out of Chaos: Man's New Dialogue with Nature* (Toronto and New York: Bantam Books, 1984), xii.

11. Hans Jonas, *The Imperative of Responsibility: In Search of an Ethics for the Technological Age* (Chicago and London: University of Chicago Press, 1984), 138.

12. Prigogine, Stengers, and Toffler, foreword to *Order Out of Chaos*, xiv–xv.

13. Anthony Kenny, *Philosophy in the Modern World*, vol. 4, *A New History of Western Philosophy* (Oxford and New York: Clarendon Press, Oxford University Press, 2007), 191.

14. Michel Foucault, *The Order of Things: An Archaeology of the Human Sciences* (New York: Vintage Books, 1973), 348.

15. al-Ghazālī and Mazīdī, *Maqāṣid*, 67.

16. Lenn E. Goodman, *Avicenna* (London and New York: Routledge, 1992), 66.

17. Abū Ḥāmid Muḥammad b. Muḥammad al-Ghazālī, *Al-Mustaṣfā Min 'ilm Al-Uṣūl*, ed. Muḥammad Sulaymān al-Ashqar, 2 vols. (Beirut: Mu'assasa al-Risāla, 1417/1997), 1:37; Muḥammad b. 'Abd al-Karīm Shahrastānī, *Kitāb Al-Milal Wa Al-Niḥal*, ed. Muḥammad Sayyid Kīlānī, 2 vols. (Cairo: Dār al-Ma'rifa, 1402/1982), 2:173.

18. al-Ghazālī and Mazīdī, *Maqāṣid*, 67.

19. Ibid.

20. Ibid.

21. al-Ghazālī, *Mustaṣfā*, 1:37.

22. Ibid.

23. Ibid.

24. Ibid., 1:32.

25. al-Ghazālī, *Iḥyā'*, "Kitāb sharḥ 'ajā'ib al-qalb," 3:12.

26. al-Ghazālī, *Mustaṣfā*, 1:32.

27. al-Ghazālī, *Iḥyā'*, "Kitāb sharḥ 'ajā'ib al-qalb," 3:16–17.

28. Ibid., 3:17.

29. al-Ghazālī, *Mustaṣfā*, 1:67.

30. Marilynne Robinson, *The Givenness of Things: Essays* (New York: Farrar, Straus, and Giroux, 2015), 5. Kindle edition.

31. Kenny, *Philosophy in the Modern World*, 188.

32. Robinson, *The Givenness of Things*, 5–6.

33. Kenny, *Philosophy in the Modern World.*

34. Yuval Noah Harari, *Sapiens: A Brief History of Humankind* (New York: HarperCollins, 2015), Kindle locations 4022–23.

35. Robinson, *The Givenness of Things*, 5.

36. David Chalmers, "Ontological Anti-Realism," chap. 3 in *Metametaphysics: New Essays on the Foundations of Ontology*, ed. David Chalmers, David Manley, and Ryan Wasserman (Oxford: Clarendon, 2009), 77.

37. Robinson, *The Givenness of Things*, 5.

38. Kenny, *Philosophy in the Modern World*, 188.

39. Ludwig Wittgenstein, *Tractatus Logico-Philosophicus*, trans. D. F. Pears and B. F. McGuinness (New York and London: Routledge, 2001), 69, S 5.633.

40. Owen J. Flanagan, *The Geography of Morals: Varieties of Moral Possibility* (New York: Oxford University Press, 2016), 7.

41. Richard DeWitt, *Worldviews: An Introduction to the History and Philosophy of Science*, 2nd ed., World Views (Chichester, UK, and Malden, MA: Wiley-Blackwell, 2010), 7; emphasis mine.

42. Anthony C. Thiselton, *New Horizons in Hermeneutics* (Grand Rapids, MI: Zondervan, 1992), 298.

43. David Vishanoff, *The Formation of Islamic Hermeneutics: How Sunni Legal Theorists Imagined a Revealed Law*, ed. Stephanie Jamison, Peri Bearman, and Gary M. Beckman, vol. 93, American Oriental Series (Ann Arbor, MI: American Oriental Society, 2010), 264.

44. Ibid. I respectfully disagree with Vishanoff, who, in my view, makes too strong a case for the sacralized nature of Islamic law, viewing it as analogous to Goodrich's claim about religious law in the Christian tradition, where the law is closely hewed to the sacred. See Peter Goodrich, "Law, Religion, and Critical Theory," in *Encyclopedia of Religion*, ed. Lindsay Jones (Detroit: Macmillan Reference USA, 2005), 5359. It might well be that many modern Muslim authors sacralize the law, perhaps more fervently than, say, premodern interpreters. There is no denial that that law is related to revealed texts, but to claim that the interpretation of these texts turn them into sacred icons of the divine might be a stretch. There is a difference between a reverential approach and a sacred approach.

45. John R. Searle, *Mind, Language and Society: Philosophy in the Real World* (New York: Basic Books, 1998), 13.

46. Ibid., 4.

47. Ibid., 1–2.

48. Ibid., 1.

49. Ibid., 1–2.

50. Gilles Deleuze and Félix Guattari, *What Is Philosophy?* (New York: Columbia University Press, 1994), 18.

51. Ibid., 27.

52. Ibid., 28.

53. Ibid.

54. Ibid., emphasis in original.

55. The year of his death is also said to be around 1045/1635–36.

56. Muḥammad b. Ibrāhīm Ṣadr al-Dīn al-Shīrāzī and Muḥammad Riḍā al-Muẓaffar, *al-Ḥikma al-Muta'āliya fī Al-Asfār al-'aqlīya al-Arba'a*, 9 vols. (Beirut: Dār Iḥyā al-Turāth al-'Arabī, c. 1387/1967), 1:47.

57. See full translation in Sajjad H. Rizvi, *Mullā Ṣadrā and Metaphysics: Modulation of Being* (London and New York: Routledge, 2009), 21.

58. Ṣadr al-Dīn al-Shīrāzī and al-Muẓaffar, *Asfār*, 1:47.

59. Ibid., 3:297.

60. İbrahim Kalın, *Mullā Sadrā* (New Delhi: Oxford University Press, 2014), 84.

61. Muḥammad ibn Ibrāhīm Ṣadr al-Dīn Shīrāzī, *The Book of Metaphysical Penetrations: A Parallel English-Arabic Text*, ed. Seyyed Hossein Nasr and İbrahim Kalın (Provo, Utah: Brigham Young University, 2014), 3.

62. Ibid., 4, with stylistic amendments to the translation.

63. Ṣadr al-Dīn Muḥammad ibn Ibrāhīm Shīrāzī, *Majmū'at Rasā'il Falsafīya* (Beirut: Dār Iḥyā' al-Turāth al-'Arabī, 2001), 178.

64. Christian Jambet, *The Act of Being: The Philosophy of Revelation in Mullā Sadrā*, trans. Jeff Fort (New York and Cambridge, MA: Zone Books, distributed by MIT Press, 2006), 174.

65. Ibid.

66. Ibid. Ṣadrā offers a tantalizing idea of how to think of being. First, he introduces us to the idea of the skepticism and gradation (*tashkīk*) of being. What Ṣadrā implies is that our relation to being involves both skepticism, or a suspension of belief, on the one hand, and the gradation and a susceptibility of being to the possibilities of modulation, on the other hand. See Jambet, *The Act of Being*, 174.

67. Ibid., 21.

68. Kalın, *Mullā Sadrā*, 78.

69. Henry Corbin, *The Voyage and the Messenger: Iran and Philosophy*, trans. Joseph Rowe (Berkeley: North Atlantic Books, 1998), 58.

70. Ibid.

71. Goodman, *Avicenna*, 66.

72. Aḥmad bin 'Abd al-Raḥīm and Shāh Walī Allāh al-Dihlawī, *Ḥujjat Allāh Al-Bāligha*, 2 vols., ed. al-Bālanbūrī (Pālanpūrī) Sa'īd Aḥmad bin Yūsuf (Deoband, India: Maktaba Ḥijāz, 1426AH/2005), 1:76; see Shāh Walī Allāh al-Dihlawī, *The Conclusive Argument of God: Shāh Walī Allāh of Delhi's Ḥujjat Allāh Al-Bāligha*, trans. Marcia K. Hermansen (Islamabad: Islamic Research Institute, 2003), 53–59.

73. al-Dihlawī, *Ḥujjat Allāh Al-Bāligha*, 1:74.

74. Ibid.

75. Ibid., 1:75–76; al-Dihlawī, *The Conclusive Argument of God*, 54.

76. Walīyullah gives an interesting explanation as to why the body does not collapse with the extraction of the *nasama*. It is like sucking out all of the air from a bottle and creating a perfect vacuum. But if the pressure inside the bottle decreases more than the exterior pressure, it could crack. What prevents a normal body from collapsing is the residual *nasama*, in his view.

77. See my "Languages of Change in Islamic Law: Redefining Death in Modernity," *Islamic Studies* 38, no. 3 (1999).

78. Aasim I. Padela, Ahsan Arozullah, and Ebrahim Moosa, "Brain Death in Islamic Ethico-Legal Deliberation: Challenges for Applied Islamic Bioethics," *Bioethics* 27, no. 3 (2013); Aasim I. Padela and Taha A. Basser, "Brain Death: The Challenges of Translating Medical Science into Islamic Bioethical Discourse," *Medicine and Law* 31 (2012).

79. Jeff McMahan, "An Alternative to Brain Death," *Journal of Law, Medicine, and Ethics* 34, no. 1 (2006).

80. Fakhr al-Dīn Muḥammad ibn 'Umar Rāzī, *al-Tafsīr al-Kabīr*, 32 vols. (Damascus: Dār al-Fikr, 1401/1981), 21:13 The terms and translations are as follows:

"composite substance" is *jawhar murakkab*; "vital spirit" is *nafs*; "body" is *badan*; "fundamental properties or drives" are *quwāhā al-aṣlīya thalāth*; "animal spirit" is *al-nafs al-ḥaywānīya*; "sentience" is *ḥassāsa*; and "nonmaterial world" is *'ālam al-khalq wa al-amr*.

81. Ibid. Rāzī's observation would be helpful to ponder. "Know that the human being is a composite substance consisting of the vital soul and body," he writes. "The human soul is the most noble of existing souls in the lower world. The human body is among the most noble of bodies in the lower world. The reason for assigning this excellence to the human soul is due to the fact that the human soul consists of three fundamental properties or drives, namely nutrition, growth, and reproduction. Whereas the animal soul consists of two properties or drives: sentience, irrespective whether it is internal or external perception, and voluntary movement. . . . Then the human soul is endowed with a special property, the cognitive property to perceive the reality of things as they are. Cognition is the property or vessel through which the light of divine knowledge becomes manifest and in it radiates the light of His majesty, and it is cognition that is privy to the secrets of the material and nonmaterial world." http://library.islamweb.net/newlibrary/display_book.php?idfrom=3429&idto=3430&bk_no=132&ID=1461.

82. Catherine Malabou, *What Should We Do with Our Brain?* (New York: Fordham University Press, 2008), 55–56.

83. Ibid., 56.

84. Ibid., 59.

85. Richard Swinburne, *The Evolution of the Soul*, rev. ed. (Oxford: Clarendon, 1997), 11.

86. Lenn E. Goodman and D. Gregory Caramenico, *Coming to Mind: The Soul and Its Body* (Chicago and London: University of Chicago Press, 2013), 17.

87. Christian Smith, *What Is a Person? Rethinking Humanity, Social Life, and the Moral Good from the Person Up* (Chicago: University of Chicago Press, 2010), 25–42.

88. William Hasker, "The Constitution View of Persons: A Critique," *International Philosophical Quarterly* 44, no. 1 (2004): 34. Emphasis in original.

89. Kelly James Clark, *Religion and the Sciences of Origins: Historical and Contemporary Discussions* (Basingstoke, UK: Palgrave Macmillan, 2014), 176.

90. Omar Sultan Haque, "Brain Death and Its Entanglements: A Redefinition of Personhood for Islamic Ethics," *Journal of Religious Ethics* 36, no. 1 (2008): 23.

REFERENCES

Abdulsater, Hussein Ali. *Shi'i Doctrine, Mu'tazili Theology: Al-Sharīf Al-Murtaḍā and Imami Discourse.* Edinburgh: Edinburgh University Press, 2017.

al-Dihlawī, Aḥmad bin ʿAbd al-Raḥīm, Shāh Walī Allāh (Walīyullāh), al-Bālanbūrī (Pālanpūrī), and Saʿīd Aḥmad bin Yūsuf, eds. *Ḥujjat Allāh Al-Bāligha.* 2 vols. Deoband, India: Maktaba Ḥijāz, 1426AH/2005.

al-Dihlawī, Shāh Walī Allāh (Walīyullāh). *The Conclusive Argument of God: Shāh Walī Allāh of Delhi's Ḥujjat Allāh Al-Bāligha.* Trans. Marcia K. Hermansen. Islamabad: Islamic Research Institute, 1996, 2003.

al-Ghazālī, Abū Ḥāmid Muḥammad b. Muḥammad. *Al-Mustaṣfā Min ʿilm Al-Uṣūl.* Ed. Muḥammad Sulaymān al-Ashqar. 2 vols. Beirut: Mu'assasa al-Risāla, 1417/1997.

———. *Iḥyāʾʿulūm Al-Dīn.* 5 vols. Beirut: Dār al-Kutub al-ʿIlmīya, 1421/2001.

al-Ghazālī, Abū Ḥāmid Muḥammad b. Muḥammad, and Aḥmad Farīd Mazīdī. *Maqāṣid Al-Falāsifa Wa Yalīhi Iljām Al-ʿawām Min ʿilm Al-Kalām Wa Al-Fuṣūl Fī Al-As'ila Wa Ajwibatihā.* Beirut: Dār al-Kutub al-ʿIlmīya, 2003.

al-Kafawī, Abū al-Baqā' Ayyūb b. Mūsā al-Ḥusaynī. *Al-Kulliyāt: Muʿjam Fī Al-Muṣṭalaḥāt Wa Al-Furūq Al-Lughawīya.* Ed. and annotated by Adnān Darwīsh al-Maṣrī, Muḥammad. 2nd ed. Beirut: Mu'assasa al-Risāla, 1419/1998.

al-Rāzī, Fakhr al-Dīn Muḥammad ibn ʿUmar. *Al-Tafsīr Al-Kabīr.* 32 vols. Damascus: Dār al-Fikr, 1401/1981.

Aristotle. "Metaphysica (Metaphysics)." Trans. W. D. Ross. In *The Basic Works of Aristotle,* ed. Richard Mc Keon, 681–926. New York: Modern Library, 2001.

Chalmers, David. "Ontological Anti-Realism." Chap. 3 in *Metametaphysics: New Essays on the Foundations of Ontology,* ed. David Chalmers, David Manley, and Ryan Wasserman, 77–129. Oxford: Clarendon Press, 2009.

Clark, Kelly James. *Religion and the Sciences of Origins: Historical and Contemporary Discussions.* Basingstoke, UK: Palgrave Macmillan, 2014.

Corbin, Henry. *The Voyage and the Messenger: Iran and Philosophy.* Trans. by Joseph Rowe. Berkeley: North Atlantic Books, 1998.

Deleuze, Gilles, and Félix Guattari. *What Is Philosophy?* New York: Columbia University Press, 1994.

DeWitt, Richard. *Worldviews: An Introduction to the History and Philosophy of Science.* 2nd ed. World Views. Chichester, UK, and Malden, MA: Wiley-Blackwell, 2010.

Flanagan, Owen J. *The Geography of Morals: Varieties of Moral Possibility.* New York: Oxford University Press, 2016.

Foucault, Michel. *The Order of Things: An Archaeology of the Human Sciences.* New York: Vintage Books, 1973.

Goodman, Lenn E. *Avicenna.* London and New York: Routledge, 1992.

Goodman, Lenn E., and D. Gregory Caramenico. *Coming to Mind: The Soul and Its Body.* Chicago and London: University of Chicago Press, 2013.

Goodrich, Peter. "Law, Religion, and Critical Theory." In *Encyclopedia of Religion,* ed. Lindsay Jones, 5358–61. Detroit: Macmillan Reference USA, 2005.

Haque, Omar Sultan. "Brain Death and Its Entanglements: A Redefinition of Personhood for Islamic Ethics." *Journal of Religious Ethics* 36, no. 1 (2008): 13–36.

Harari, Yuval Noah. *Sapiens: A Brief History of Humankind.* New York: HarperCollins, 2015.

Hasker, William. "The Constitution View of Persons: A Critique." *International Philosophical Quarterly* 44, no. 1 (2004).

Hofweber, Thomas. "Logic and Ontology." In *The Stanford Encyclopedia of Philosophy*, ed. Edward N. Zalta. Stanford, CA: Metaphysics Research Lab, Stanford University, 2017.

Jambet, Christian. *The Act of Being: The Philosophy of Revelation in Mullā Sadrā.* Trans. Jeff Fort. New York and Cambridge, MA: Zone Books, distributed by MIT Press, 2006.

Jonas, Hans. *The Imperative of Responsibility: In Search of an Ethics for the Technological Age.* Chicago and London: University of Chicago Press, 1984.

Kalın, İbrahim. *Mullā Sadrā.* New Delhi: Oxford University Press, 2014.

Kenny, Anthony. *Philosophy in the Modern World.* Vol. 4: *A New History of Western Philosophy.* Oxford; New York: Clarendon Press; Oxford University Press, 2007.

Malabou, Catherine. *What Should We Do with Our Brain?* New York: Fordham University Press, 2008.

McGinnis, Jon, and David C. Reisman. *Classical Arabic Philosophy: An Anthology of Sources.* Indianapolis: Hackett, 2007.

McMahan, Jeff. "An Alternative to Brain Death." *Journal of Law, Medicine and Ethics* 34, no. 1 (2006): 44–48.

Moosa, Ebrahim. "Languages of Change in Islamic Law: Redefining Death in Modernity." *Islamic Studies* 38, no. 3 (Autumn 1999): 305–42.

Neiman, Susan. *Moral Clarity: A Guide for Grown-up Idealists.* Rev. ed. Princeton, NJ: Princeton University Press, 2009.

Padela, Aasim I., Ahsan Arozullah, and Ebrahim Moosa. "Brain Death in Islamic Ethico-Legal Deliberation: Challenges for Applied Islamic Bioethics." *Bioethics* 27, no. 3 (2013): 132–39.

Padela, Aasim I., and Taha A. Basser. "Brain Death: The Challenges of Translating Medical Science into Islamic Bioethical Discourse Islamic Law." *Medicine and Law* 31 (2012): 433–50.

Prigogine, Ilya, Isabelle Stengers, and Alvin Toffler. Foreword to *Order Out of Chaos: Man's New Dialogue with Nature.* Toronto and New York: Bantam Books, 1984.

Rizvi, Sajjad H. *Mullā Ṣadrā and Metaphysics Modulation of Being.* London and New York: Routledge, 2009.

Robinson, Marilynne. *The Givenness of Things: Essays.* New York: Farrar, Straus, and Giroux, 2015. Kindle edition.

Ṣadr al-Dīn al-Shīrāzī, Muḥammad b. Ibrāhīm, and Muḥammad Riḍā al-Muẓaffar. *Al-Ḥikma Al-Muta'āLiya Fī Al-Asfār Al-'aqlīya Al-Arba'a.* 9 vols. Beirut: Dār Iḥyā al-Turāth al-'Arabī, c. 1387/1967.

Searle, John R. *Mind, Language and Society: Philosophy in the Real World.* New York: Basic Books, 1998.

Shahrastānī, Muḥammad b. ʿAbd al-Karīm. *Kitāb Al-Milal Wa Al-Niḥal.* Ed. Muḥammad Sayyid Kīlānī. 2 vols. Cairo: Dār al-Maʿrifa, 1402/1982.

Shīrāzī, Muḥammad ibn Ibrāhīm Ṣadr al-Dīn. *The Book of Metaphysical Penetrations: A Parallel English-Arabic Text.* Ed. Seyyed Hossein Nasr and İbrahim Kalın. Provo, Utah: Brigham Young University, 2014.

———. *Majmūʿat Rasāʾil Falsafīya.* Beirut: Dār Iḥyāʾ al-Turāth al-ʿArabī, 2001.

Smith, Christian. *What Is a Person? Rethinking Humanity, Social Life, and the Moral Good from the Person Up.* Chicago: University of Chicago Press, 2010.

Swinburne, Richard. *The Evolution of the Soul.* Rev. ed. Oxford: Clarendon, 1997.

Thiselton, Anthony C. *New Horizons in Hermeneutics.* Grand Rapids, MI: Zondervan, 1992.

Vishanoff, David. *The Formation of Islamic Hermeneutics: How Sunni Legal Theorists Imagined a Revealed Law.* Vol. 93 of the American Oriental Series. Ed. Stephanie Jamison, Peri Bearman, and Gary M. Beckman. Ann Arbor, MI: American Oriental Society, 2010.

Wittgenstein, Ludwig *Tractatus Logico-Philosophicus.* Trans. D. F. Pears and B. F. McGuinness. New York and London: Routledge, 2001.

FIVE

Exploring the Role of Mental Status and Expert Testimony in the Islamic Judicial Process

HOOMAN KESHAVARZI AND BILAL ALI

The sheer size and continued growth of the global Muslim population calls for a comprehensive understanding of Muslim cultural perspectives and practices by international law makers, academics, researchers, judges, and forensic experts. Muslims make up approximately 23 percent of the world's population, and there are more than fifty countries across the world with Muslim-majority populations.[1] Additionally, nearly a third of the world's Muslims live as minorities in non-Muslim states.[2] Furthermore, an estimated 3.3 million Muslims live in the United States of America,[3] and Islam is the fastest growing religion both in the world and in the United States.[4]

Needless to say, a central part of Muslim culture is shaped by Islamic values, which, in turn, are influenced by Islamic law. In theory, Islamic law informs the permissions, limitations, and sanctions of the state, society, the community, and individuals—and even the religious conduct of its adherents. Thus, Islamic law is of great relevance to the daily lives of a large segment of the global Muslim population, whether through state regulations in countries that adopt Islamic law for their legal system or as part of the pastoral advice they receive from Islamic clergy in countries not governed by Islamic law. Despite the in-group variability represented by Muslim customs and practices, the Islamic tradition serves to unify cultural mores and sensibilities across the population. And, arguably, at the heart of these unifying norms is the motivation to live a life in adherence to Islamic ethics as well as personal, ritual, and civil law.

Islamic law or jurisprudence is the human endeavor to understand and apply divine injunctions, sourced in the Qur'an, prophetic traditions (*Sunnah*), juristic consensus (*ijmā'*), and analytical reasoning (*qiyās*).[5] Well over one-third of the countries with Muslim majorities across Africa and Asia have some form of governance derived from the Islamic law, or Shariah. Additionally, a study by the Pew Research Center has found that the overwhelming majority of Muslims in the world believe that the Shariah should be the legal system enforced on Muslims in their respective countries.[6] Though the Shariah is an ancient system, its application is tied to context, as Islamic law demonstrates flexibility in addressing the nuances of contemporary societies. Part of the reason for such flexibility is that the Islamic legal system incorporates a wide range of legal reasoning instruments, permits differences of opinion, and allows for a diversity of legal precedent, thereby affording jurists the capacity and room to maneuver through and derive multiple legal rulings/decisions.

Traditional Islamic law recognizes mental illness and thereby institutes differential rights and obligations for people based on their mental capacities. These mental-status considerations focus largely on the determination of an individual's mental competence (*ahliyya*) and capacity (*idrāk*). Such determinations were never clear-cut in the past; however, they have become more complex because of the finer gradations of mental status made possible by contemporary mental health and behavioral sciences. Given the growth of the field of clinical psychology and psychiatry, these developing sciences of human behavior may significantly aid Islamic jurists in their legal reasoning and issuances of verdicts. In particular, the subfield of forensic psychology/psychiatry can be invaluable in updating both Islamic bioethics and biolaw.

Forensic psychology, as defined by the American Board of Forensic Psychology, is "the application of the science and profession of law to questions and issues relating to psychology and the legal system."[7] Current practices in most secular legal systems allow for the expert testimony of a clinical psychologist/psychiatrist in cases in which the psychological statuses of the defendants or the victims are relevant to the legal decisions. These can include criminal liability, custody evaluations, and insurance claims, among other legal issues.[8] The utility of considering the psychological states of subjects of law prior to issuing legal penalties or outlining ethical duties is self-evident. Although past precedent demonstrates that Islamic jurists afforded the mental statuses of the subjects roles to play in the judicial process, modern understandings of gradations within mental disease and of mental capacities as attested to by forensic psychologists/psychiatrists can assist jurists in making more nuanced ethico-legal judgements.

Certainly, legal implications are often high-stakes, and exploring the psychological conditions of subjects when relevant is critical to the administration of justice, rehabilitation, and the well-being of members of society. For example, the fear of loss of mental capacity (*khawf dhahāb al-ʿaql*) is a classical legal consideration in lifting normative legal restrictions in Islamic law, such as in the case of a widow who is mandated to pass her mourning period (*ʿidda*) in her marital home unless she finds herself in such solitude that it is feared she will lose her mind (*dhahāb al-ʿaql*), in which case she may choose a separate residence.[9] By analogy, the permissibility of abortion may be sought within Islamic law for a woman who may endure overwhelming psychological harm by pregnancy or birth. It follows, then, that the Islamic jurist could be assisted by an expert in gathering the necessary psychological variables and in performing psychological assessments—which is the role of a forensic psychologist—to prove overwhelming psychological harm (*ḍarar*) or the likelihood of the loss of mental capacity (*dhahāb al-ʿaql*), thereby providing more objective indicators for predicting the potential for significant mental health risk and psychological distress.

Studies of the legal decision-making processes of modern Islamic jurists have not been documented in the Islamic bioethics literature, thus it is unknown how much practicing jurists engage with specialized mental health expertise. Additionally, mental health experts administering such assessments in order to inform jurists may be unaware of the traditional Islamic legal categories of insanity and their accompanying ethico-legal implications, such as the effects mental illness can have on the distribution of inheritances, the validity of marriages, and child custody.[10] Thus, there appears to be a knowledge and literature gap that needs to be filled in.

Accordingly, this chapter presents an exploratory qualitative study aimed at understanding the process of the judicial reasoning of a sample of jurists in hypothetical cases involving mental-status concerns, their views on the role of the expert and the science of psychiatry/psychology in aiding the determination of mental status in Islamic jurisprudence, and their recommendations for improving the adjudication of cases with mental-status concerns. In essence, this study seeks to explore what judicial process a sample of jurists employ in cases where the subject's mental status is in question. We aim to describe the current practices and attitudes of practicing Islamic jurists, thereby presenting lived experiences rather than canvassing the Islamic judicial process (*uṣūl al-iftā*) as articulated by the Islamic legal literature for theoretical purposes. Our interviews provide phenomenological data based on the lived experiences and ideas of participants that may or may not converge with Islamic legal theory or categories that are illustrated in the corpus of Islamic legal literature. In other words, interview data provides an illustration of current practices, gaps between the textual Islamic legal process and actually applied methodologies, and jurists' willingness to use psychological expert testimony and their professional experiences. The researchers who performed this study were acutely interested in exploring the actual processes and experiences of jurists in the field in order to inform seminary curriculum reform, facilitate collaboration between mental health experts, and identify potential discursive gaps between jurists and mental health professionals.

METHODS

Participants

Purposive sampling of Muslim clergy was conducted with the following inclusion criteria: (1) having completed training in Islamic jurisprudence during the course of their seminary degrees and (2) having at least one year of either a formal appointment as a legal expert/judge or engagement in providing official written legal decisions (*iftāʾ*) to the polity. Furthermore, the respondent pool was targeted for diversity in training backgrounds and judicial experiences.

Respondents were recruited through convenience sampling by inquiring into the academic faculties of Islamic institutions and seminaries in the United States and overseas that were readily available to the researchers. Convenience sampling entails the recruitment of participants for a study through the enlistment of readily accessible individuals available to the principal investigator, that is, the first author of this chapter. Individuals were approached for interviews after contact information was obtained, and sampling continued until thematic saturation was achieved. Approval from an institutional review board (IRB) at the Illinois School of Professional Psychology was obtained for this study.

Measures

An initial demographic questionnaire was administered to participants to obtain basic information about each participant and to ensure that they met the listed inclusion criteria. Items on the demographic questionnaire included age, ethnicity, education, number of years of experience in Islamic legal practice, and religious affiliation.

The second measure used in this study was a qualitative semi-structured interview designed by the researcher and a research assistant. Questions were designed to elicit an exploration of all jurists' conception of mental status and its role in Islamic law, their reported process for assessing the potential existence of one of the categories of legal insanity, their attitudes toward and methods of using psychological expertise, potential challenges in the field as practitioners, and resultant recommendations for improving the adjudication of legal cases with mental-status aspects. Questions prepared and posed to participants in the semi-structured interview included the following:

- Tell me about yourself and your current work within the framework of *iftāʾ* (giving *fatwā*).
- What is the role of mental status in the Shariah?

- Are there categories of mental status in the Shariah?
  - To what extent are these categories considered while issuing a *fatwā*?
- What are the legal implications of mental status upon an individual?
- How is a subject assessed as to the appropriate application of these categories to him/her?
- In your knowledge, what is the current process of issuing a *fatwā* on cases that involve compromised mental status? Can you provide some examples?
- Within the field of *iftā'* and the judicial process, what is the role of an expert witness?
- Do you utilize forensic psychological experts to do evaluations?
- How might you utilize these mental-status evaluations in arriving at a legal decision? Is there a methodology you utilize or do you know of any established precedents for doing so?
- What do you think is lacking in the current procedures in bridging the relationship between psychological assessment and *iftā'*?
- What areas do you think need improvement?

Data Collection

Data was collected via interviews that lasted between 30 and 70 minutes and were conducted in person or via phone.

Data Analysis

Using conventions of grounded theory as adapted by Charmez,[11] interview transcripts were coded in the following stages:

Phase 1: Although Charmez recommends line-by-line coding, the researchers used Glaser's original style of coding, whereby researchers produce as many ideas as they can inductively from early data as opposed to strictly coding each line of data.[12] As data was collected, it was inserted into QSR NVivo 10 computer software to be organized and categorized. After each interview, the researchers wrote a case memo entry outlining the interviewer's impressions of the participant's experiences and the researcher's reactions.

Phase 2: The second phase involved focused coding. During focused coding, analysts selected a set of central codes throughout the entire dataset. This included decision-making regarding identification and inclusion of the most salient and dominant themes to help the researchers form the emerging theory. The results section detailed the identified themes gathered during phase two.

Phase 3: In theoretical coding, the researchers refined the final categories in the development of the theory and then compared them. This stage entails a conceptualization of how the identified themes relate to one another. Specifically, in this study, the researchers related themes to one another to capture the process of legal reasoning, their approach to mental-status data in forensic settings, agreement regarding legal maxims, and the process of decision-making. These themes formed the emergent theory to be discussed below.

In practice, the steps of analysis were not strictly sequential. Rather, the authors revisited codes, categories, and the model iteratively. In the following section, the process model will be described first, followed by a discussion of its parts. The reason for this order is that the parts receive their meaning when understood in relation to the whole model

RESULTS

Sample Characteristics

A total of fourteen jurists were approached, twelve of whom ultimately agreed to participate in interviews. (See table 5.1 below.) Despite our hope to obtain gender diversity, the sample referred to us was all male. These individuals were of diverse national backgrounds and work experiences, and half of the sample was between the ages of 30 and 39 and were Southeast Asian. In terms of legal school, seven of them adhered to the Ḥanafī school of law, three to the Mālikī school, and two to the Shāfiʿī school. Most jurists served in multiple roles across different occupations, such as being both *imāms* and teachers at seminaries. Their predominant roles are listed and the designation of "academic/research + institutional *iftā*'" was used to denote their primary roles as both researchers at an academic institution and as *muftīs*

TABLE 5.1 Demographic Profiles of Jurists Interviewed

Age	*No.*	*Ethnic Background*	*No.*
30–39	6	Southeast Asian	6
40–49	3	Arab	3
50–59	1	Turkish	1
60–69	1	Mixed	2
70+	1	Mixed	2
Seminary Affiliation	*No.*	*Legal Framework/Training*	*No.*
Dars Niẓāmī/Deobandi	5	Ḥanafī	7
Mauritania (*Maḥḍara*)	2	Mālikī	3
Azhar	3	Shāfiʿī	2
Ottoman	1		
Syria	1		
Predominant Roles	*No.*	*Experience (Years)*	*No.*
Imām	4	2–5	2
Academic/Research+	8	5–10	5
Institutional *Iftā*	5	20+	5
Country of Training/Education	*No.*		*No.*
United States of America	5	Egypt	2
South Africa	2	Turkey	1
Mauritania	1	India	1

Source: Authors' compilation.

involved in issuing legal verdicts (*fatwā*) in an unofficial legal tribunal/body for their respective institutions of employment. None of the participants served in the role of *qāḍī*, an official judge in a court, despite the fact that three out of the twelve participants had formally received training to serve as *qāḍīs*. Their seminary affiliations identify the scholastic methodology of training of the jurists. For example, the one Turkish participant formally studied in a traditional seminary (*madrasa*) that was erected during the Ottoman era and followed the Ottoman curriculum of seminary training. Two of the participants studied and officiated in South Africa in institutions adherent to the Deobandi seminary tradition. The countries of their practice are listed not by their current places of residence or practice but rather by the majority of their legal/employment experience.

During qualitative analyses, four domains containing multiple themes emerged: (1) the processes of judicial reasoning in cases with mental-status considerations, (2) the role of expert testimony in the judicial process, (3) the role of mental status in Islamic law, and (4) jurists' recommendations for improving the assessment of mental status in contemporary Islamic bioethical deliberation.

The first two domains yielded the process model used by jurists for assessing mental status in the judicial process and included the collaboration and usage of expert testimony in the process. The final two domains provided information for the categories and themes of mental status in Islamic law, as well as respondents' recommendations for better execution of the outlined judicial model.

Domain 1: The Processes of Judicial Reasoning Regarding Cases with Mental-Status Concerns

Before examining the participants' reports regarding the role of mental status in Islamic law, it is important to address how they understood the protocols used by Islamic jurists in deliberating about cases involving mental-status concerns. The emergent themes from the interviews were consolidated into a process model mapping the reported best practices of Islamic reasoning (see figure 5.1). Each of the stages of the process model illustrated by figure 5.1 is elaborated in the first two themes of the first domain in respective order.

This process model is a hierarchical outlining of the levels of reasoning required in considering such cases. Notably, interviewees (n = ten out of twelve) felt that the ideal judicial reasoning process would involve assessing the psychological state of the subject. In the words of one respondent, "A *muftī* has to really keep in mind the mental and the psychological background of the person who is asking the question." Given that mental status seems to be an important element of decision-making in all judicial

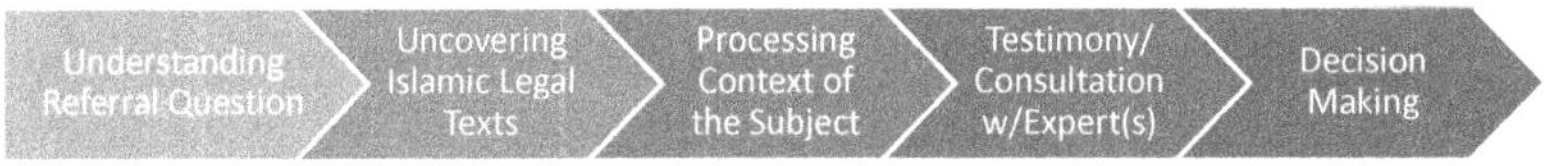

FIGURE 5.1 A Judicial Process Model for Assessing Mental Status within an Islamic Forensic Psychiatric Context

proceedings, understanding the overall judicial process can frame the discussion of the role of mental status and the expert's function in this process.

Theme 1. Determining the scope and context of their own practice

According to the participants, among the first steps in judicial reasoning is determining both the context and the role of the jurist. In other words, though legally trained, the jurist might actually be called on to play a different role in responding to the question-asker. Respondents outlined multiple potential roles that they could occupy and briefly elucidated how the methodology of legal reasoning potentially varies based on their role and the context. Based on their descriptions, it is possible to categorize the duties, positions, and responsibilities they identified into four broad roles: as (a) *mutakallims* (discursive theologians), (b) *murshids* (spiritual guides), (c) *qāḍīs* (judges), and (4) *muftīs* (private jurisconsults). For each of these designations the methodologies, authorities, responsibilities, and procedures explained would differ. The bearing of each role would be based on the nature of the question or the demands of their context. Participants emphasized that the roles of the *mutakallim* and the *murshid* are not necessarily to adjudicate according the sacred law. Rather, in a diverse cosmopolitan city, for example, the nature of questions put forward to the participant may primarily involve issues of Islamic creed and its tenants rather than ethico-legal concerns. One respondent emphasized their need to first thoroughly understand the nature of the question and identify their appropriate role prior to delving into any judicial reasoning: "Is this considered a legal issue according to our conception of law, or is it considered a theological (i.e., creedal) issue? That's the first thing (to identify): what type of issue is this?" He confined legal judgments to matters in which there is a scope for legal reasoning and defined the role of a jurist accordingly: "What they do is *ijtihād*, which is where a jurist expends all of his or her resources and talents and skills towards finding out what the will of God, or the will of Allah, is on this particular issue. Now that only takes place in the context where there is no clear definitive text (scripture)."

According to the participants, a *murshid* is someone who serves primarily in a position of spiritual leadership, guidance, and facilitation of spiritual growth. A *murshid* may function as an *imām*, chaplain, or spiritual guide in the community. Though he may also have received Islamic judicial training, this individual may answer ethico-legal questions in a manner that might be more consistent with the concept of harm reduction and gradual facilitation of spiritual growth. Therefore, he may choose to defer providing immediate legal verdicts in favor of focusing more on the facilitation of spiritual progression. This inclination may be toward the purpose of strengthening faith and eventually leading the congregant toward a stricter adherence to the standard legal expectations of a Muslim. One respondent characterized this role as such: "In the *imām* capacity there is often an ongoing relationship with that individual, their family, and their relationship to the community, so there is a lot more *irshād* (spiritual and behavioral counseling) involved. There is a lot more pastoral guidance involved than just giving a particular answer—I mean less *fatwā* and more *da'wa* (proselytizing)."

Participants were able to clearly distinguish between the above role and that of a *qāḍī* or *muftī*, both of whom are traditional legal practitioners in the truest sense. A significant difference between the *muftī* and *qāḍī* is the *qāḍī*'s power of enforceability, that is, their ability to make legal decisions that are both morally and practically binding. Additionally, the *qāḍī* bases his ruling on clear and apparent evidence and does not judge based merely on the subjective self-report of a subject. As one of the respondents mentioned, "The *qāḍī* has an official position. He has an office (post) where people go to him and he gives a judgment. The other thing is that the *qāḍī* can enforce that ruling."

A *muftī*, on the other hand, does not possess such an authority of enforcement. Instead, he is more of an informer of the law. As one respondent explained: "The *muftī* in that case will ask the person and answer according to his questions. He'll ask him: What was your state? What was going on? Here is the *fatwā* based on your question. He's just giving the answer based on the information provided." The *muftī* is thus not procedurally bound to investigate the circumstances or the evidence of a case to the degree of a judge. He is often at liberty to issue a ruling based simply on the report of the circumstances and details provided by an enquirer. At the same time, the *muftī* is described as not possessing the powers of enforcement. In certain circumstances, participants explained that the role of the *muftī* is expanded, such as in the case of the absence of Islamic courts and judges and the formulation of a legal council or tribunal that, in a limited capacity and with the agreement of all parties, will possess some power of enforceability.

In such a circumstance, one respondent explains: "A group of *muftīs* together will act like a *qāḍī*, so the rulings of the *qāḍī* apply [to] that. In the absence of a *qāḍī*, the council of *muftīs* together will act in that role, and in that case they have the same responsibilities of a *qāḍī* as well."

*Theme 2. Selecting a legal framework for the issuing of ethico-legal rulings (*fatāwā*)*

Respondents (n = ten out of twelve) provided a brief outline of a classical theoretical framework for the derivation of legal rulings. This section outlines the general approach they claimed that jurists classically employ. Participants explained that in determining the application of any ruling (obligation, dispensation, prohibition, and so on) to a specific case, jurists will seek to identify the existence of authoritative religious statements mentioned in the classical legal manuals that speak to the issue and can form the basis for a ruling. If such relevant texts do not explicitly provide an applicable attribute for the identification of a relevant legal criterion, or legal "pivot" (*manāṭ*), the jurist is required to investigate the issue further and extract a legal cause (*takhrīj al-manāṭ*), which is then used to analyze the case at hand. When, however, the text provides a variety of possible legal criteria due to the presence of several potentially relevant attributes, the jurist must sift through the attributes and identify the sole factor applicable (*tanqīḥ al-manāṭ*) to the ruling. In either case, once the legally applicable criterion (*manāṭ*) is identified through either its "extraction" (*takhrīj*) or its "refinement" (*tanqīḥ*), what remains is the question of its application to and actualization (*taḥqīq al-manāṭ*) of the case at hand. This requires an analysis by *both* the jurist and the mental health specialist to determine if the legally applicable criterion is satisfied by the scenario in question. One jurist described this process:

> So there is this realm of the *ḥukm* (legal injunction) where you're saying, "Okay, this is the ruling according to jurists—and that's not taking into consideration any type of contingent factors, such as the time, place, questioner, or situation the person may be in. At that level, this is simply called *takhrīj al-manāṭ*, where you're looking at a ruling in the texts and you're trying to say that this is possibly what the legal basis of that ruling is. In *tanqīḥ al-manāṭ*, you are kind of taking away any excluding factors that could influence the ruling. So

the jurist at this stage wants to determine the *ḥukm*. He's trying to really get to what's the legal basis for this particular ruling.

Theme 3. Judicial processing of the context and role of the expert

A salient theme that emerged at least twelve times across interviews was the need for judicial processing of the context prior to issuance of the legal verdict. Most respondents (*n* = ten out of twelve) reiterated this, and there was agreement across interviewees in this study. Participants mentioned that after scouring through texts and attempting to uncover the direct legal criterion relevant to the case in question, they would consider the actual context or application of the ruling (*ḥukm*) to the subject. For example, if a questioner asked whether a sick patient is ethically obliged to ingest medications that may potentially save his or her life, the answer would be contingent on the efficacy of the intervention. This ruling (*ḥukm*) of the patient's obligation to ingest medications is based on legal principles derived from some of the schools of law. However, in determining the efficacy of treatment and the application of a ruling of dispensation or obligation to receive treatment, the respondents would require expert testimony or analysis to determine efficacy and need. A medical expert would be required to help determine the real-life applicability of the ruling. One respondent describes this as follows:

> The area of *taḥqīq al-manāṭ* is not necessarily only the area of a *faqīh* or jurist. For example, when is a Muslim required or obligated to undertake medical treatment? No jurist, no school of law, says it's *wājib* or necessary at all times. Rather, it is based off of multiple factors. One of them is the certainty of the efficacy of treatment [which can be ascertained only by the clinician].

It is interesting to note here that what the participants describe as the realization of the legal pivot of an issue (*taḥqīq al-manāṭ*) is perhaps more properly described as the realization of a need (*taḥqīq al-ḍarūra*) that does not require any original and independent legal reasoning (*ijtihād*).

One respondent spoke about how the field of psychology has provided more avenues for the jurist to take to investigate the potential implications of mental status in legal cases, whereas in the past this may have been limited due to limitations in scientific advancement. He states, "Before the *qāḍī* was restricted to going based off of what was very apparent, whereas now there is a lot more scope for trying to prove what's apparent."

Other types of expert consultations that three jurists mentioned included the use of peer consultation during the legal extraction phase to ensure that they would not miss any potential precedents or legal considerations that could be employed. One respondent described their process as follows: "I would also consult other *imāms*. So, generally my policy is that if there's a question that's a little more complicated or a little more controversial, then I try to take the counsel of other *imāms* as well so that I can feel more confident of the decision." Perhaps such indications that jurists should seek consultations may occur in circumstances in which they needed affirmation as to whether their legal reasoning was sound or whether they felt unsure about their decisions. It appeared that this was more of an informal process rather than one necessarily indicated procedurally by their training. It is also unclear as to whether such consultations were intended to use the expertise of peers who were more experienced or better trained in the subject related to the issue in question.

Domain 2: The Use of Expert Testimony

In addition to the role of clinicians noted above, all respondents (n = twelve out of twelve) endorsed the use of expert consultation with a psychiatrist, psychologist, or other mental health specialist when the mental status of the subject was a concern. All respondents also professed their usage of expert testimony in the past, although the credentials of such experts were not provided. As mentioned previously, after a jurist uncovers the relevant legal rulings and realizes that such rulings are contingent on the mental status of the subject, a psychological expert may be called upon to clarify the applicability of the ruling to the subject. Specifically, the expert may ascertain whether the subject's psychological functioning or clinical symptomology implicates the relevant legal criterion, and the expert will then judge whether the subject is legally insane or otherwise psychologically impaired. A respondent said: "In the field of determining whether someone is *majnūn*, or any one of the other subcategories of being insane, or not being able to function mentally to the full extent, you need to get expert testimony or an expert witness for what this person is actually dealing with before you can give a ruling." It is noteworthy that respondents didn't necessarily exhibit knowledge of the distinctions between different types of allied mental health professionals and tended to lump medical professionals into one category. Additionally, it seemed that seeking expert consultation was contingent on the resources available to them in their communities and usually included more informal consults with a physician or professional without distinction between their academic and clinical expertise. Another respondent stated: "If I don't know whether the person is mentally well or not, I would probably send him for some sort of psychological evaluation."

Some respondents noted that clinical terminologies may or may not implicate legal categories. Therefore, it is necessary for the jurist to translate these expert findings or assessments into Islamic legal terms. One respondent gave an example of an instance in which psychological harm is a factor in ruling whether an abortion can be permitted. The expert will play a role in assessing the potential for a woman to develop severe postpartum depression, justifying an abortion. Such a predictive prognostic assessment is typically done by assessing the woman's current pre-existing clinical mental health conditions and/or the nature and severity of any postpartum depression she experienced following previous pregnancies, if applicable. He stated: "Is depression enough reason to abort a child? That's the issue. [The expectant mother] could bring medical data saying that, yes, I do have this. Now it's the *muftī*'s job to see whether [the depression] is grave enough to abort the child. That is, if it is one life being harmed for another life, how significant is the harm compared to the other harm?" Here the respondent is illustrating a situation in which psychological factors are important considerations and is alluding to this scenario as one that indicates the need to use expert evaluation for a prognostic assessment.

Theme 1. Expert prerequisites

More than two-thirds of the respondents (n = nine out of twelve) spoke about the prerequisite traits of the mental health expert. In general, two basic contexts emerged, and the two had different prerequisites. One setting is that in which the expert educates the jurist regarding human psychology and the consensus of the profession/field on a particular issue. The expert is not applying the knowledge or conducting a case assessment but rather providing psychoeducation. In this instance, the only prerequisite for such a testimony is that the expert be an established authority in the field. A jurist described this by saying, "If you have enough research from various people, even non-Muslim sources, and they are confirming something, then we can take that as *tawātur* information (information whose truth is established as certain through the massive and widespread transmission of its sources)."

Alternatively, if the expert is to discuss a specific case, conduct an assessment, or provide a psychological report regarding the subject and offer recommendations, it would be necessary for the expert to be an upright/God-conscious Muslim. One respondent stated that the primary reason is that a Muslim expert has an appreciation of Islamic law and will not be biased in favor of the client: "The reason is that a practicing Muslim knows the importance of Shariah and how grave it is to be excused." Three of the interviewees listed two experts as a minimum number to provide such consultation to the court.

Domain 3: Mental Status in Islamic Law

In Islamic law, information on mental status is necessary in establishing the rules and responsibilities that are normally required of Muslims. *Taklīf*, or legal responsibility, in Islamic law requires that a Muslim be sane and post-pubescent before holding him responsible to execute the normative demands made on him. The right of autonomous functioning and ability to execute legal and financial contracts is afforded to the *mukallaf*, that is, the legally responsible individual. As one of the jurists explained, "The ruling for an *'āqil* person, a sane person, is that he is *mukallaf*, and is responsible for the Shariah and his actions. The ruling for the *majnūn* person is that he is not responsible."

All respondents made mention of the concept of accountability, and eleven of them specifically mentioned the concept of *taklīf*. Therefore, if one is demonstrated to possess a loss of one's complete mental capacities, that is, legal insanity, such an individual is no longer accountable under the law.

Theme I. Categories of recognized mental statuses in Islamic law

As mentioned earlier, *taklīf*, or legal liability, in Islamic law often centers around mental-status considerations and the identification of an individual as *majnūn*. Simply put by one respondent, "A person who is *majnūn* is not considered *mukallaf*."

There are, however, many gradients between complete legal liability and no legal liability. If a subject's psychological status does not meet the threshold of *junūn*, other legal implications, such as partial accountability or legal interdiction (*ḥajr*), based on the degree of severity may still apply. Even in the case of *junūn*, the *majnūn* may have either acute or chronic subtypes of insanity, as one of the interviewees mentioned: "*Junūn muṭbiq* is a category of absolute insanity that makes the person not accountable in Islamic law and can also be divided into different categories, such as permanent and intermittent."

Another type of mental illness was mentioned by a respondent: "The *mubarsam* in Islamic *fiqh* is a person who is not psychologically sound. He is a person who has a psychological or mental condition that affects his perception and understanding of his surroundings. He might be a sane person but his perception and understanding of his surroundings is not fully intact."

Additionally, the *maʿtūh* was also mentioned by a respondent. "*ʿAtah*, which is not absolute insanity, is also a term used in *fiqh*. We have absolute *junūn*, and then we have *ʿatah*. *ʿAtah* might be considered like a mental retardation of some sort."

One of the respondents in the study also spoke about *waswasa*, what may be known as obsessive-compulsive disorder (OCD) or scrupulosity in modern clinical terminology. Individuals with this disorder may be preoccupied with verbal pronouncements of divorce or be obsessed with ritual cleansing. The verbal pronouncement of such an individual, according to a respondent, will not count. He stated, "The Ḥanafī *madhhab* does recognize, for example, if a person is *muwaswas*, that he has *waswasa* all the time, which we call OCD probably in today's time."

The respondent attempts to demonstrate that a clinical category such as OCD scrupulosity can remove legal liability in instances that would otherwise lead to the consequentiality of speech or actions, such as pronouncements of divorce. This seems to be consistent with the position of the Ḥanafīs and Mālikīs.[13]

The *safīh* was also mentioned by four of the jurists. As one put it, "There is a status in the Shariah known as *safāha*, which is basically foolishness, which is recognizing that the person is not [absolutely] mentally [incapacitated] yet they are . . . impulsive in dealing with their money."

Another category mentioned was *dhū-l-ghafla al-shadīda*, which means literally a person afflicted by severe heedlessness. A respondent described this category as follows: "Another category is that of the *dhū-l-ghafla al-shadīda*. This person has some psychological problems that affect his understanding and comprehension; the major impact of this (mental) condition, from the Islamic perspective, has to do with the person's ability to memorize reports and convey them (properly)."

Finally, some respondents spoke about intense emotional states that need to be considered in giving rulings. One respondent mentioned the prophetic tradition regarding the protocols of issuing judgments, in that a judge shall not preside over cases while in a state of anger. An interviewee stated that this could also be generalized for other emotional states, such as depression:

> Other conditions or states of mind that are taken into consideration when assessing the person's responsibility—and some of these are more like emotional conditions—are emotional states rather than mental disorders. For example, anger is an emotional state that can affect a person's mental capacity. Also, hunger is a physical condition that has some associated emotional and psychological impact. That's why in the sayings of the Prophet he said that a judge should not pass his judgment in a state of anger, and similarly the scholars explain that anything that would affect that judge's ability or capacity to pass sound and correct judgments is similar to anger in this condition, such as severe hunger, severe fear, and others.

Theme 2. Defining legal insanity or compromised functioning

Many respondents in the sample mentioned that a severe loss of normative functioning and an inability to make distinctions between opposites (*tamyīz*) was a major criterion for determining legal insanity. Two respondents described it nearly identically, with one proffering: "The *majnūn* is a person who has lost their *ʿaql*, their intellect, and is somebody who does things that don't make sense to a normal person." Another interviewee described it as "loss of *tamyīz*, which is the ability to differentiate between things. If [such] a person is spoken to with a logical question, [it affects] their ability to respond appropriately. That's the defining question in whether or not a person has intellect."

Other potential indicators of compromised legal mental status included compromised functionality, inability to manage finances, loss of self-control, poor decision-making, incoherent speech, low intelligence, and potential developmental delay.

TABLE 5.2 Mental-Status Categories in Islamic Law (Jurist Interview Reports)

Category	*Descriptions of Categories by Jurists Interviewed*
Majnūn	"A person who is *majnūn* is not considered *mukallaf* (legally responsible)."
	"*Junūn muṭbiq* is a category of absolute insanity which makes the person not accountable in Islamic law and can be divided into different categories, such as permanent and intermittent."
Mubarsam	"The *mubarsam* in Islamic *fiqh* is a person who is not psychologically sound. He is a person who has a psychological condition that affects his perception and understanding of his surroundings. He might be a sane person but his perception and understanding of his surroundings is not fully intact."
Ma'tūh	"*'Atah*, which is not absolute insanity, is also a term used in *fiqh*. We have absolute *junūn* and then we have *'atah*. *'Atah* might be considered like a mental retardation of some sort."
	"So the *ma'tūh* is a person who is not aware of his surroundings or aware of his speech. In other words he's *maghlūb* (mentally overcome or incapacitated), which means that his intellect has been covered. He's not able to distinguish. So, he's not responsible for Shariah (Islamic law). It's not 100% *junūn*, like, total insanity; neither is he 100% an *'āqil* or sane, maybe [just] a person that has very low IQ. His *shu'ūr* (perception) is mixed and his understanding is little. His sentences sometimes make sense, sometimes they do not make sense."
Waswasa	"The Ḥanafī *madhhab* (legal school) does recognize . . . if a person is *muwaswas* (afflicted with *waswasa*), that he has *waswasa* all the time, which we call OCD probably in today's time."

(*continues*)

TABLE 5.2 *Continued*

Category	*Descriptions of Categories by Jurists Interviewed*
Safāha	"You might have a person that has basic *tamyīz* (cognition of a level to be able to differentiate between a mule and a horse according to some jurists) but he could be considered a *safīḥ*, a person who is, in the literal translation is a foolish person. So he has *tamyiz*, he has his *'aql* (rational faculties), but he doesn't have *rushd*, which is soundness in making decisions. So, they can't make a sound decision."
Dhū-l-Ghafla Shadīda	"This person has some psychological problems that affect his understanding and comprehension. The major impact of this condition, from the Islamic perspective, has to do with the person's ability to memorize reports and convey them (properly)."
Emotional States or Psychotic Breaks	"Other conditions or states of mind that are taken into consideration when assessing the person's responsibility—and some of these are more of emotional conditions—are emotional states rather than mental disorders. For example, anger is an emotional state that can affect a person's mental capacity. Also, hunger is a physical condition that has some associated emotional and psychological impact. That's why in the sayings of the Prophet he said that a judge should not pass his judgment in a state of anger."

Sources: This table captures quotations from jurists participating in the qualitative interviews, who were anonymous.

Theme 3. Legal assessment of mental status

Most participants elected to rely on expert testimony to help them determine the presence of mental-status indicators that may fit into one of the legal categories. They mentioned that conventional assessment procedures laid out in Islamic legal manuals were not designed to offer sophisticated mental-status assessments and that these categories are not fixed and could be further refined. One participant stated, "How do you determine who is *majnūn*, that's not a procedure that is detailed within the Shariah, within the *fiqh* literature? That is where [psychological] experts will come in and help."

Respondents in the sample listed some of the methodologies that were used in the Islamic legal texts as well as their own personal practices. These included conducting interviews with the subjects, detailing their personal behavioral histories through corroborating reports, and attempting to analyze their psychological status. A respondent stated that the goal of the interview is to "test his memory, his orientation, his perception, his maturity, and so on." Another highlighted the utility of naturalistic observation, saying: "Through observation and spending time with them, you can tell that you know a person is, maybe, impaired."

Domain 4: Recommendations for Improvement of the Judicial Process Regarding Mental Status

Several interviewees (n = seven out of twelve) felt strongly about the need for improvement in this arena. Among the recommendations, four were the most salient and common across interviewees. First, many felt that it was necessary to create a coalition or committee of collaborating mental health experts and jurists. A respondent characterized this potential platform of discussion as a big achievement: "I think one of the ways of doing that is by just getting people together just to talk from different fields. I think you have something for the *imāms*, having some expert come in and that itself is such an important step. It's a huge step. It's a major significant step in breaking down these barriers and saying, 'Okay, this is information that we need and we need these people.'" One major objective for such a committee would be to help identify the symptoms of disorders that potentially impact and fall into traditional legal categories of insanity and thereby create guidelines for jurists to follow. For example, one respondent stated, "In the future, we need to have scholars, well-researched, well-established, Muslim psychologists/psychiatrists who will develop these categories and say that this falls into insanity, this will not."

Interviewees mentioned the need not only for a committee and a platform to discuss the intersection between psychology and mental health but also for a collaboration of parties in these fields to help one another in their respective domains of expertise in specific cases. Knowledge transfer is important not only to refine and delineate traditional mental health categories within Islamic law but also to understand how to identify them in practice. In sum, respondents pushed for increased collaborative care for the service of the global Muslim community (*umma*).

Another recommendation posited by interviewees was that jurists should undergo training in the sciences that would impact their capacity to function as jurists. Given the high-stakes positions that jurists occupy and the degree of power they possess, the interviewees felt that jurists should have exposure to humanistic sciences. One participant said: "Yes, I believe that as they're doing their Shariah studies and *iftā'* (studies), they must be exposed to at least one lecture on these sciences that exist in universities: anthropology, psychology, sociology, economics, finance, what have you, so they can know what happens in the world." Another agreed with this sentiment and went further to recommend a shift in the training of clergy in general to include psychological-status assessment, stating: "My recommendation is to change the system of training to include that type of understanding where different people and more investigation is involved when giving an answer, to include an understanding of the psychological state of the person, where they are coming from, as well as involving other experts."

A final recommendation included the formation of unofficial Islamic tribunals that could deal with civil cases of personal law. The recommendation was not listed with the state recognition of such a court in mind but rather to create a more unofficial space in which cases could be handled with more religious authority in the issuances of legal decisions. A respondent stated: "There (already) are certain Shariah boards and Shariah courts where people can go to for divorce-related issues and such. The group of *muftis* there can act (in the function of) the *qāḍī* and issue a ruling on a case, like a *fatwā* that annuls a *nikāḥ* (religious marriage contract)."

DISCUSSION

It is clear that Islamic law plays a central role in the lives of Muslims globally. In fact, all participants in this study resided in countries that did not officiate according to Islamic law, yet their community-based roles involved meeting the Islamic law needs of Muslim publics. It is important to consider that the lack of official judicial appointments of the participants may impact the quality of the data obtained in studies like this on account of the absence of extensive experience in adjudicating cases in an official capacity. However, this study identified numerous traditional mental health categories within Islamic law that are relevant to the practice of contemporary jurists.[14] Interviews of jurists further demonstrated a significant openness to mental health expertise and collaboration in determining whether moral subjects fit into these categories. The sample of jurists also outlined their reported best practices for the *fatwā*-making process. The applicability of this process model should be compared to the theoretical principles of issuing legal edicts (*uṣūl al- iftāʾ*) to explore the convergence of theory with practice.

Although there was significant diversity in the sample of jurists we studied (exemplified by their diverse backgrounds and locations of training and practice), all of them enthusiastically voiced the need for clinical experts to weigh in on Islamic bioethical deliberations and, in cases in which mental health concerns feature prominently, agreed that their rulings would be influenced by the reports of, or consultation with, mental health experts. This was a very interesting finding, as the attitudes of these jurists clearly demonstrated a willingness to collaborate and use psychological expertise in forensic practice. The interviewees included mental health experts as part of the judicial processing of cases with mental health implications. They viewed the experts as individuals who would decipher the actual context of the legal ruling (*ḥukm*) and help the jurists identify whether any of the clinical indicators of psychopathology fit one of the legal categories of insanity and its subtypes. Given the high-stakes decisions that jurists are required to make and the authoritative moral role that they play, all jurists emphasized the need to take into consideration all of the appropriate contextual variables as well as the psychological implications their legal decisions would have on the subjects, their families, and the larger society.

Some respondents also commented on the relative underuse of forensic experts by colleagues. It is interesting that despite their reporting widespread underuse of psychological expertise, all participants in this study reported its usage. This could be due to a social desirability–confounding variable in their desire to present themselves in a positive light, causing them to overrepresent their actual frequency of usage. Alternatively, it could point to the fact that this was an exceptional group of jurists. Respondents in the sample also offered numerous recommendations to close the gap of this underuse and the collaboration between mental health experts and the clergy. They suggested that a committee, coalition, or task force be charged with developing guidelines and standards of practice for other jurists and help further elaborate on the implications of mental status within Islamic ethico-legal deliberation. Other recommendations included increased training opportunities for jurists in psychology and the humanities, increasing collaboration between mental health providers and clergy on cases, and setting up an unofficial Islamic legislative council for the hearing of civil cases that include content experts. This demonstrated their epistemic humility in recognizing mental-status categories and expresses their desire to have avenues of growth in this area.

Additionally, Muslims often turn to Islamic clergy when they're experiencing psychological distress in non-Muslim countries. The roles of *imāms* in Western countries are multifaceted. They not only serve the spiritual and congregational service needs of the community but are also often charged with legal mediation and counseling demands.[15] Ali, Marzuk, and Milstein have also found that *imāms* often serve as first responders to mental health disorders.[16] An important problem emerges for the assessment of mental competence in regard to civil matters such as marriage, divorce, custody, and inheritance for Muslims. Muslims may turn to Shariah committees or individual jurists to get a verdict regarding their situation or that of a family member. The lack of professional psychological representation in these unofficial legislative groups may ignore underlying psychopathology that, if undetected, may have devastating implications in the religious verdict given. This is magnified by the fact that many Muslims, as mentioned above, opt out of mental health treatment, seeking religious alternatives instead. Religious practitioners may not be accustomed to detecting psychopathology that, under Islamic law, raises important considerations for verdicts issued. The novelty of advanced forensic medicine necessitates a more comprehensive examination of Islamic law and of contemporary medical literature in order to offer more systematic approaches to assessing mental status in such settings. Adherents to the Islamic tradition often turn to clergy to answer bioethics questions, yet a comprehensive approach to dealing with clinical pathology in such settings has not been developed.

Similarly, Islamic jurists and Muslim clinicians need to join together in order to devise international guidelines for determination of mental capacity. Currently, most Muslim countries lack sufficient mental healthcare legislation to address such nuances.[17] The application of such guidelines would not be limited to countries that apply Islamic law at a state level, but jurists or Muslim councils in the non-Muslim countries or secularized Muslim countries may also depend on such guidelines for the unofficial adjudication of civil cases.

Regarding forensic psychiatry/psychology more specifically, additional work is needed to further explore the legal categories identified by participants, with attention possibly given to the category of temporary insanity. Due to the wide scope of ramifications for the temporarily insane (*majnūn ghayr muṭbiq*) and the numerous categories of mental illnesses that fall into this category, further work is needed to create a more standardized synthesis of terms that integrates knowledge from clinical psychology/psychiatry and Islamic theology and law. The possibility of developing subcategories of the *ghayr muṭbiq* to assist Muslim clinical psychologists/psychiatrists in suggesting legal courses of action for patients can also be explored. For example, some types of ritual forms of worship or civil cases may likely be affected by bipolar manic episodes with psychotic features or any other *DSM* disorder with psychotic features. These guidelines may provide answers to important questions such as the stage of dementia where a patient may be considered *maʿtūh* or *majnūn*; when an individual enduring a psychotic break can be involuntarily hospitalized; and other such concerns. It may also be useful to further investigate emotional states that can compromise objectivity, as the jurists cited precedents to demonstrate that those in positions of authority are not to be charged with those responsibilities if emotional states impact their performance. This could potentially open up discussions regarding screenings of authorities in various domains, as is typically done with police officers in the United States.

Finally, our work demonstrates the importance of mental-status considerations in contemporary Islamic ethico-legal deliberations. It highlights an openness to and a desire for collaboration between experts in forensic psychiatry/psychology and experts in Islamic jurisprudence for their mutual benefit. Our work also anticipates the need for further research on forensic psychiatry and its potential relationship within Islamic bioethics discourses and on the specialized curricula needed by jurists to better equip them to use tools and categories from contemporary mental health and behavioral science when making decisions about the mental status of moral subjects. Therefore, we hope our study serves as a catalyst to the development of collaborations between mental health practitioners and jurists and that such collaborations can model the type of mutual learning needed in Islamic bioethical deliberations more broadly.

LIMITATIONS

Our study did not extensively explore the corpus of historical writings or Islamic legal literature that speak to the role of expert testimony in Islamic law, nor did it explore contemporary medical literature on competency assessment. Certainly, writings in classical Islamic law and in contemporary medicine will need to be mined to create nuanced curricular interventions and develop assessment tools for mental status that are relevant to Islamic jurists.

Limitations of our study also include the challenge of translating some interviewees' responses from the Arabic language, as well as the challenges encountered with interviewees for whom English is a second language. While these issues were small, it is possible that they contained information that could have improved the findings we report. Additionally, the small sample size and somewhat diminished diversity of respondents' characteristics detracts from the broad generalizability of our findings. This applies most notably to the underrepresentation of female jurists in our sample as well as jurists representing the Ḥanbalī school of law. Furthermore, as our sample did not contain Islamic jurists working in official legislative capacities in the Muslim world, our respondents' views may differ from those we might have received from those who can benefit from fully functional state systems in which mental health experts might be more accessible. Despite these shortcomings, our exploratory and first-of-its-kind work presents avenues for collaboration between clinicians and jurists in the making of Islamic bioethical guidelines.

NOTES

The material in this chapter was presented in partial form at "Interfaces and Discourses: A Multidisciplinary Conference on Islamic Theology, Law, and Biomedicine," University of Chicago, April 15–17, 2016.

1. Pew Research Center, *Mapping the Global Muslim Population: A Report on the Size and Distribution of the World's Muslim Population*, ed. Tracy Miller (Washington, DC, 2009).

2. Muhammad Anwar, "Muslims in Western States: The British Experience and the Way Forward," *Journal of Muslim Minority Affairs* 28, no. 1 (April 1, 2008).

3. Pew Research Center, *The Future of World Religions: Population Growth Projections, 2010–2050*, ed. Michael Lipka (Washington, DC, 2015).

4. S. R. Ali, W. M. Liu, and Majeda Humedian, "Islam 101: Understanding the Religion and Therapy Implications," *Professional Psychology: Research and Practice* 35, no. 6 (2004).

5. Mohammad Hashim Kamali, *Shari"ah Law: An Introduction*, The Foundations of Islam (Oxford: Oneworld, 2008).

6. Pew Research Center, "The World's Muslims: Religion, Politics and Society," in *The Pew Forum on Religion and Public Life*, Washington, DC, 2013.

7. A. M. Goldstein, *Comprehensive Handbook of Psychology: Forensic Psychology*, vol. 11 (Hoboken, NJ: John Wiley and Sons, 2003).

8. Ibid.

9. Qāḍī Khān and Ḥasan b. Manṣūr b. Maḥmūd al-Ūzajandī al-Farghānī, *Fatāwā Qāḍī Khān* (also known as *al-Fatāwā al-Khāniyya*), in *al-Fatāwā al-ʿĀlamgīriyya* (also known as *al-Fatāwā al-Hindiyya*) (Cairo: al-Maktaba al-Kubrā al-Amīriyya, 1310/1892).

10. K. S. Chaleby, "Issues in Forensic Psychiatry in Islamic Jurisprudence," *Bulletin of the American Academy of Psychiatry Law* 24, no. 1 (1996); Chaleby, *Forensic Psychiatry in Islamic Jurisprudence* (London: International Institute of Islamic Thought, 2001).

11. K. Charmez, *Constructing Grounded Theory: A Practical Guide through Qualitative Analysis* (London: Sage, 2006).

12. B. G. Glaser and A. L. Strauss, *The Discovery of Grounded Theory: Strategies for Qualitative Research* (Chicago: Aldine, 1967).

13. Zayn al-Dīn Ibn Nujaym, *al-Baḥr al-Rāʾiq* (Beirut: Dār al-Maʿrifa, 1983), 79; A. W. Ibn Rushd, *al-Bayān wa-l-Taḥṣīl* (Beirut: Dār al-Gharb, 1984), 161; A. A. Malik, *al-Mudawwana al-Kubrā* (Beirut: Dār Ṣādir, 1984), 83; M. A. Ibn ʿĀbidīn, *Radd al-Muḥtār* (Beirut: Dar al-Fikr, 2000), 409.

14. K. Bint Abdur-Rahman, *Aḥkām al-Marīḍ al-Nafsī fī al-Fiqh al-Islāmī* (Riyāḍ: Dar al-Somaie, 2013).

15. A. N. Kobeisy, *Counseling American Muslims: Understanding the Faith and Helping the People* (Westport, CT: Praeger, 2004).

16. Osman M. Ali, Glen Milstein, and Peter M. Marzuk, "The Imam's Role in Meeting the Counseling Needs of Muslim Communities in the United States." *Psychiatric Services* 56, no. 2 (February 1, 2005): 202–5.

17. Yasser A. Elsayed, Mohamed Al-Zahrani, and Mahmoud M. Rashad, "Characteristics of Mentally Ill Offenders from 100 Psychiatric Court Reports," *Annals of General Psychiatry* 9, no. 4 (2010).

REFERENCES

Ali, Osman M., Glen Milstein, and Peter M. Marzuk. "The Imam's Role in Meeting the Counseling Needs of Muslim Communities in the United States." *Psychiatric Services* 56, no. 2 (February 1, 2005): 202–5.

Ali, S. R., W. M. Liu, and Majeda Humedian. "Islam 101: Understanding the Religion and Therapy Implications." *Professional Psychology: Research and Practice* 35, no. 6 (2004). doi:10.1037/0735-7028.35.6.635.

Bint Abdur-Rahman, K. *Aḥkām al-Marīḍ al-Nafsī fī al-Fiqh al-Islāmī*. Riyāḍ: Dar al-Somaie, 2013.

Chaleby, K. S. *Forensic Psychiatry in Islamic Jurisprudence.* London: International Institute of Islamic Thought, 2001.

———. "Issues in Forensic Psychiatry in Islamic Jurisprudence." *Bulletin of the American Academy of Psychiatry Law* 24, no. 1 (1996): 117–24.

Charmez, K. *Constructing Grounded Theory: A Practical Guide through Qualitative Analysis.* London: Sage, 2006.

Elsayed, Yasser A., Mohamed Al-Zahrani, and Mahmoud M. Rashad. "Characteristics of Mentally Ill Offenders from 100 Psychiatric Court Reports." *Annals of General Psychiatry* 9, no. 4 (2010).

Glaser, B. G., and A. L. Strauss. *The Discovery of Grounded Theory: Strategies for Qualitative Research.* Chicago: Aldine, 1967.

Goldstein, A. M. *Comprehensive Handbook of Psychology: Forensic Psychology.* Vol. 11. Hoboken, NJ: John Wiley and Sons, 2003.

Ibn ʿĀbidīn, M. A. *Radd al-Muḥtār.* Beirut: Dār al-Fikr, 2000.

Ibn Nujaym, Zayn al-Dīn. *al-Baḥr al-Rāʾiq.* Beirut: Dār al-Maʿrifa, 1983.

Ibn Rushd, A. W. *al-Bayān wa-l-Taḥṣīl.* Beirut: Dār al-Gharb, 1984.

Jana-Masri, Asma, and Paul E Priester. "The Development and Validation of a Qur'an-Based Instrument to Assess Islamic Religiosity: The Religiosity of Islam Scale." *Journal of Muslim Mental Health* 2, no. 2 (2007): 177–88.

Kamali, Mohammad Hashim. *Shari'ah Law: An Introduction.* The Foundations of Islam. Oxford: Oneworld, 2008.

Khān, Qāḍī, and Ḥasan b. Manṣūr b. Maḥmūd al-Ūzajandī al-Farghānī. *Fatāwā Qāḍī Khān* (also known as *al-Fatāwā al-Khāniyya*). In *al-Fatāwā al-ʿĀlamgīriyya* (also known as *al-Fatāwā al-Hindiyya*), 554. Cairo: al-Maktaba al-Kubrā al-Amīriyya, 1310/1892.

Kobeisy, A. N. *Counseling American Muslims: Understanding the Faith and Helping the People.* Westport, CT: Praeger, 2004.

Pew Research Center. *The Future of World Religions: Population Growth Projections, 2010–2050.* Ed. Michael Lipka. Washington, DC, 2015.

———. *Mapping the Global Muslim Population: A Report on the Size and Distribution of the World's Muslim Population.* Ed. Tracy Miller. Washington, DC, 2009.

———. "The World's Muslims: Religion, Politics and Society." In *The Pew Forum on Religion and Public Life.* Washington, DC, 2013.

SIX

Muslim Perspectives on the American Healthcare System

The Discursive Framing of Islamic Bioethical Discourse

AASIM I. PADELA

As I noted in the introduction to this book, Islamic bioethics remains a field under construction as scholars debate its content, scope, and research methods. Ambiguities regarding the contours of an Islamic bioethics do not stem from the lack of a moral theology outlined by scripture,[1] nor from a dearth of ethico-legal judgments pertaining to medicine and healthcare formulated by Islamic jurists. Rather, the challenge is to devise a comprehensive bioethical theory, rooted in Islamic moral theology and attentive to those juridical assessments, that can serve healthcare stakeholders (patients, health professionals, religious leaders, and others) both in pluralistic Muslim-minority contexts and in Muslim-majority contexts where Islamic law may operate.

There is ample research evidence that Islamic ethical notions impact the decisions made by patients, medical professionals, policymakers, and other healthcare actors across the world.[2] While the influence of Islamic ethics and law on decision-making varies and the sources of Islamic ethical guidance are multiple, the extant Islamic bioethics literature often lacks conceptual rigor and leaves critical questions unaddressed such that it provides insufficient actionable guidance for those in the trenches.[3] I contend with these challenges on a daily basis in each aspect of my career; as a clinician I view my practice of medicine as part of a religious vocation and at times find the juridical rulings unclear; as a clinical ethicist I provide healthcare providers and patients in the United States (both Muslim and non-Muslim) with ethical advice and find that Muslim ethical positions are based on misrepresentations of the social, clinical, and legal contexts; and as an Islamic bioethics researcher I find that many writings lack rigor.

To be sure, an Islamic bioethics that accounts for the theological and ethico-legal frameworks of Islam could, for instance, enable the composition of Islamic bioethics manuals similar to the *Encyclopedia of Jewish Medical Ethics*.[4] Just like this Jewish encyclopedia, an Islamic encyclopedia could provide a comprehensive review of classical ethico-legal deliberations over, as well as modern perspectives on, pressing bioethical dilemmas.[5] Such a resource would, from my perspective, meet the needs of patients and healthcare providers seeking actionable guidance. More than that, however, such a manual would also provide an invaluable starting point for academic research into the field and enable the generation of a comprehensive bioethical theory that provides an "Islamic" *telos* for modern biomedicine. Moreover, a comprehensive, consistent, and cogent theoretical framework for Islamic bioethics would empower both the producers and the consumers of this field to address the multilayered ethical questions resulting from technological advancements that provide humans with increasing mastery over the body. It would also help them to consider the proper organization and prioritization of our increasingly complex array of different healthcare services and treatment modalities.[6]

Yet, prior to developing such resources and deriving such a theory, it is necessary for us to clarify the nature of what makes Islamic bioethics "Islamic." Indeed, the choice of methods applied to Islamic bioethics and the selection of sources for the study of it arguably depend on an a priori definition of what Islamic bioethics is. The present study works toward this end by examining divergent constructions of the "Islamic" in the bioethics-related discourse produced by two Islamic bioethics producers in the American context. As we will see, identifying what makes "Islamic bioethics" distinctively Islamic is not as straightforward as it might at first appear to be.

This project of constructing the field and discipline of Islamic bioethics faces a variety of challenges emerging from the respective disciplines invoked by each of the two terms "Islamic" and "bioethics." Beginning with the latter, Islamic bioethics as a subfield of bioethics faces the same challenge of multidisciplinarity and interdisciplinarity that modern bioethics faces. While bioethical discussions were originally the domain of religious experts and clinicians, the field has grown to involve secular philosophers, sociologists, anthropologists, policy experts, and lawyers.[7] As the expertise brought to bear upon bioethics has multiplied, so, too, have the measures and contents of the ethical. The nature of modern bioethical inquiry feeds into the epistemic and legitimacy crises confronting the field, and these crises are made more acute because of the purported religious claims the field makes.

For example, it is not clear how much weight should be accorded to the reality on the ground (what is) when considering the moral ordering of society (what should be). Hence, an overstated, but nevertheless pertinent, tension exists between religious authorities and philosophers, on the one hand, who consider moral reasoning to have normative value independent of social reality, and social scientists on, the other, who describe contextually driven human ethical decision-making. These debates bleed over into the realm of religious studies because Islamic bioethics claims to draw from the font of the religious tradition. As the academic study of religion has come to deploy social science–based methods for examining the lived experiences and meaning-making activities of religious communities, the primacy of the analysis of religious texts for understanding religion has become contested.[8] This methodological divide has at its root an epistemic quandary similar to the "is" and "ought" divide mentioned above. Finally, the contestations over what comprises the "Islamic" component of Islamic bioethics run deeper still to include debates surrounding the applicability and authority of the inherited Islamic legal canon and its juridical devices in addressing modern-day concerns.[9]

Suffice it to say that a demarcation of the posited content of Islamic bioethics and a delineation of its "Islamic" aspects is necessary to generate methodological guides and practical resources that facilitate both scholarly engagement and healthcare stakeholders' input into the emerging field. The present study works toward this end by examining the divergent constructions of the "Islamic" in Islamic bioethics discourse in a certain context, that of the United States, and by commenting on the social considerations that may influence such conceptions.

Using critical discourse analysis (CDA) approaches as an inspiration,[10] I apply both sociological and Islamic ethico-legal lenses to examine select writings of two kinds of producers of Islamic bioethics literature in the United States: national Muslim organizations and Islamic jurists. My focus is on health insurance, a somewhat neglected topic in the academic literature on Islamic bioethics, despite its obvious importance.[11] I will compare the discursive frames used by several national American Muslim organizations to craft an "Islamic" argument for healthcare reform in the United States—reform termed "Obamacare" in the popular press but formally known as the Patient Protection and Affordable Care Act (PPACA)—with the Islamic legal opinions (*fatāwā*) of Islamic jurists regarding the permissibility of purchasing health insurance in the United States. Press releases and reports in support of healthcare reform and *fatāwā* providing religious guidance about health insurance may appear to be sufficiently dissimilar as discursive genres to render a comparative examination of their Islamic nature and bioethical framing methodologically contestable. However, I will argue that they in fact display conceptual connections directly relevant to the question of the nature of a putative Islamic bioethics.

In addition to examining the discursive framing present in these textual sources, I will also call attention to the discursive "gaps" between them: that is, considerations that appear in the Muslim organizations' material but not in the jurists' *fatāwā*, and vice versa. This is to highlight the compartmentalized nature of Islamic bioethics discourse, in which different producers of Islamic bioethics material fail to address key considerations that emerge when the problem is analyzed using a different analytic vantage point. Further, by doing so, I hope to stimulate a (re)construction of the field of Islamic bioethics: Once the gaps and discontinuities in the extant discourse have been underscored, scholars should be motivated to undertake multidisciplinary efforts that can accomplish a more wide-reaching theorization of the nature and scope of Islamic bioethics, craft outputs that clarify the Islamic aspects of their bioethics writings, and be attentive to the needs of the multiple different stakeholders that seek out guidance on Islamic bioethics.

THE SOURCES

The sources for this study include press releases and other communiqués concerning American healthcare reform produced, or contributed to, by American Muslim Health Professionals and the Islamic Society of North America.[12] I also analyze online *fatāwā* proffered by scholars at the Fatwa Center of America and the Assembly of Muslim Jurists of America (AJMA), along with Dr. Monzer Kahf, a widely cited scholar of Islamic economics residing in California.[13] These materials are supplemented by selected e-*fatāwā* from outside the United States, but only when these juridical opinions are given in response to a questioner from America. Although the sampling frame is somewhat artificially bounded, since internet *fatāwā* are available globally and some research suggests that juridical decrees from one part of the world influence *fatāwā* and Muslim behavior in other, more distant, parts, restricting the sampling frame to American *fatāwā* in the first instance seems sensible, if only because research has not yet been carried out on which juridical bodies or jurists are most often sought out by American Muslims for bioethical guidance.[14] Furthermore, my recent national survey of American Muslim physicians found that international juridical bodies are looked to for ethical guidance by only a small minority. I present findings from this empirical study in more detail in the next chapter.

Again, with Muslim organizations authoring press releases and reports in support of healthcare reform, on the one hand, and jurists providing religious guidance about health insurance, on the other, these writings may appear to be of different genres, each addressing different situations and divergent audiences. Yet the materials are conceptually linked in at least four ways that are directly relevant to the present study.

For one, both types of producers make "Islamic" moral assessments of the prevailing American healthcare system. Accordingly, the particular religious values that are highlighted in these public communiqués provide insight into what each of these actors considers to be sources of Islamic ethics and their Islamic moral reasoning processes. In other words, the choice of religious values from which to construct the arguments and the language used to communicate these values evidence a particular reading of the Islamic tradition. These readings, in turn, represent different ways of making meaning from sacred source texts and different views on the nature of what constitutes an "Islamic" ethical value. As such, they are a vantage point from which to describe and to critique what an "Islamic" bioethics represents to each of these producers.

Second, both types of producers seek to motivate Muslim behavior. The fashioning of an "Islamic" argument by Muslim organizations results from the aim of spurring American Muslims to support healthcare reform. Likewise, the jurist's reasoning is written into the *fatwā*, at least in part, to persuade the Muslim questioner to act in accordance with the jurist's "Islamic" opinion. We can therefore examine what each group considers aspects of Islam that hold motive force and persuasive power to compel Muslim action.

Third, both sets of Islamic bioethics producers engage a public audience with their materials. While the writings of the national Muslim organizations and those of the jurists address multiple audiences, some of which do not overlap (the policy-makers addressed by the national Muslim organizations, for example, and the specific individuals who asked for the *fatāwā* on the part of the jurists), the publishing of each of these producers' texts on the internet suggests that they also intended to speak to a public audience (Muslim and non-Muslim). Therefore, one can compare the ways in which the outputs describe Islamic ethics to a common nonspecialist audience, and such a comparison may provide insight into the social considerations that influence their discursive framing.

Finally, the writings of these diverse producers are linked by the fact that they are all responding to the problematic American healthcare context. In calling Muslims to support healthcare reform, the national Muslim organizations believed that aspects of the American healthcare system require remedy, and, as I will describe, the jurists also took into consideration the nonideal nature of the American healthcare system while undertaking their ethico-legal deliberations.

AMERICAN MUSLIM ORGANIZATIONS AND U.S. HEALTHCARE REFORM

A brief description of the American healthcare context is warranted before proceeding to a discussion of the discursive frames used by national American Muslim organizations to craft an "Islamic" argument for supporting its reform. The United States remains one of the few developed nations without access to universal healthcare for all its citizens. Instead, most Americans receive health insurance through their employers. Typically, full-time workers receive health insurance packages that provide access to healthcare for themselves and their nuclear families. The elderly and the extremely poor obtain access to healthcare (insurance) subsidized, and in some cases provided free of charge, by the government. Finally, military service personnel and veterans, and some of their family members, are provided low-cost healthcare through a federally administered system of hospitals and clinics known as the Veterans Administration.

Those who do not belong to one of those aforementioned categories must purchase health insurance through the marketplace. It is important to note that American healthcare is extremely expensive, and healthcare costs are one of the leading causes of personal bankruptcy.[15] According to recent estimates, nearly 79 million Americans, almost 30 percent of the American population, are either underinsured or uninsured, which has led to reduced access to routine medical care and delayed healthcare-seeking behaviors.[16]

The historical and cultural reasons behind these peculiarities of American healthcare are numerous and include the provision of healthcare insurance as part of employment benefits during World War II wage increase freezes, the creation of government-run subsidized healthcare programs in 1965 for the elderly and indigent that consume an ever-increasing portion of America's gross domestic product, and a dominant libertarian undercurrent in American society that resists governmental control of essential services, instead promoting the idea that individuals should have control over their own healthcare choices.[17] While there have been multiple attempts to overhaul the U.S. healthcare system and move toward a single-payer universal-coverage healthcare system, and indeed the respondents to most popular surveys favor such a system, healthcare reform in the United States has been piecemeal.[18]

Prior to the 2008 presidential election, momentum had been building toward another round of healthcare reform. The escalating costs of healthcare (accounting for nearly 18 percent of the gross domestic product in 2012), the increasing numbers of Americans without access to routine healthcare (over 47 million persons, or 15 percent of the population), and the relatively poor healthcare outcomes of Americans (ranked thirty-seventh in the world in the World Health Organization's world health report 2000) evidenced the need for drastic change.[19]

Barack Obama's election to the office of president was in part fueled by his promises to enact comprehensive healthcare reform. In March 2010, after much debate, a landmark bill, officially named the Patient Protection and Affordable Care Act (PPACA) but nicknamed "Obamacare," was passed into law and extended financial incentives to purchase health insurance packages in semiregulated private healthcare insurance marketplaces. The law also enacted several mandates on employers of a certain size to provide healthcare insurance to employees, set minimums on the types of care that all health insurance policies must cover, and incentivized states to expand government-covered healthcare insurance for the indigent.[20] The major provisions of this law came into effect in 2014.

Leading up to the passage of the PPACA, several national American Muslim organizations, including American Muslim Health Professionals (AMHP), the Islamic Medical Association of North America (IMANA), and the Islamic Society of North America (ISNA), were all engrossed in the public policy conversations and promoted healthcare reform.[21] Of these groups, AMHP was the most visible in the legislative arena and mobilized allied healthcare professionals, while ISNA tended to work at the community level with mosque leaders. Each group fashioned "Islamic" arguments for healthcare reform by drawing attention to the harms associated with the lack of healthcare insurance and by calling for social justice in healthcare access.

AMHP's Healthcare Reform Messaging

AMHP is a professional community of healthcare workers committed to improving "the health of Americans" by "improving public health through efforts inspired by Islamic tradition," and it has long been involved in promoting healthcare reform.[22] From 2008 through 2009, AMHP created a Task Force on Health Affordability and drafted a health policy brief comparing the various healthcare platforms of the presidential candidates; it met with congressional staffers and partner organizations in Washington, DC, to advocate for reform; it penned a congressional brief; and it also conducted health reform seminars across the country. In its policy brief titled "Principles of Health Care Reform," AMHP notes that Islam motivates its belief in "comprehensive health care reform that will increase access to high-quality, affordable care for all Americans."[23]

While highlighting the social problem represented by the "120 million [Americans] being either uninsured or underinsured," the press release marking AMHP's lobbying visit to Congress simultaneously delineates the Islamic ethos of its efforts. The release highlights both Muslim religious identity and practice in quoting the meeting's lead coordinator's statement that "it was a tremendous opportunity to represent the Muslim voice on this very challenging issue of health reform, [and] we pray that much good" comes from the visit. The AMHP president further affirmed that from "an Islamic and American background it is our duty to support these grassroots efforts."[24] One notes the simultaneous appeal to religious and patriotic values. Following the meeting in Washington, AMHP sent a letter to Muslim staff in Congress noting that supporting healthcare reform was part of an Islamic mandate to serve "the poor and destitute of our society."[25] Soon after the passage of the PPACA, AMHP crafted a press release that again highlighted its Islamic motivations in supporting Obamacare. The release states that "the Islamic faith encourages Muslims to strive towards equity in all things" and cites a Qur'anic verse (3:92) to support this claim.[26] In addition to these outputs, AMHP put its signature on materials of a more interfaith nature crafted by Faithful Reform in Health Care.

Faithful Reform in Healthcare

Faithful Reform in Health Care (FRH) is a national interfaith coalition of more than fifty organizations that aims to use faith-based messaging to advance healthcare reform.[27] The group's initiatives have included mass-media campaigns, prayer vigils, town hall meetings, and conference calls with legislators, including President Obama.[28] The organization's core ideals are captured by its publication "A Faith-Inspired Vision of Health Care," which was developed by constituent members and signed by over four hundred organizations, including AMHP and ISNA.

"A Faith-Inspired Vision of Health Care" uses religious values as well as human rights discourse to frame its support for healthcare reform. Consequently, the document draws attention to humankind's equality in order to advance a human rights conceptualization of healthcare. It notes: "In the bonds of our human family we are created to be equal. . . . Affirming our commitment to the common good, we acknowledge our enduring responsibility to care for one another . . . [and] we are led to discern the human right to health care." This vision statement also says that "as spiritual and sacred vessels we are responsible for . . . the care of one another." The group considers a universal notion of social justice to provide the basis for a (religious) calling "to ensure that all of us have access to health care." Together, these notions contribute to FRH's advocacy for universal healthcare access. FRH states that working to "overcome barriers to and disparities in health care" demonstrates the carrying out of a broader religious obligation to be "partners in health."[29]

With respect to Islamic participation, in addition to the support of the Muslim organizations above, FRH's website also quotes Imām Sa'dullah Khan of the Islamic Center of Southern California. This quotation coheres with the social justice and human rights framing of its advocacy of healthcare reform. Imām Sa'dullah remarks: "The right of every individual to adequate health care flows from the sanctity of human life and that dignity belongs to all human beings. . . . We believe that health is a fundamental human right which has as its prerequisites social justice and equality and that it should be equally available and accessible to all."[30] After the passage of the PPACA, FRH issued a press release lauding the U.S. Supreme Court's upholding of the law. In it the group affirms a "moral imperative to collectively care for one another" and states that "the scriptures of the Abrahamic traditions of Christians, Jews, and Muslims, in addition to the sacred teachings of other faiths, understand that addressing the welfare of the nation includes" meeting the needs of the sick.[31] Both AMHP and ISNA co-signed this press release.

The Islamic Society of North America

ISNA is the largest and most prominent Muslim organization in North America. It presents a Muslim voice to national policy stakeholders and leads civic engagement programs across the nation. In addition to partnering with FRH, ISNA worked with Cover the Uninsured to advance healthcare reform. Cover the Uninsured was a program funded by the Robert Wood Johnson Foundation from 2003 through 2011 that helped to enroll Americans into healthcare insurance programs and raised awareness about the plight of uninsured Americans in support of the goal of generating grassroots support for healthcare reform.[32] Accordingly, the group organized tailored sermons and study circles at mosques, churches, and synagogues. ISNA's director of interfaith and community alliances, Sayyid Syeed, was a member of the National Interfaith Advisory Board for Cover the Uninsured and involved in the Muslim portion of its programming. Cover the Uninsured, presumably in collaboration with ISNA, produced a packet of materials including fliers, a sermon guide, and discussion resources that included narratives of Muslims without health insurance for Muslim consumption. A respected *imām* and Muslim chaplain, Ahmed Kobeisy, was charged with preparing these materials. A quote from Sayyid Syeed incorporated into these materials sets out an Islamic motivation for healthcare reform: "Islam calls on its followers to practice compassion and justice, to act out of concern for the needy. The needs of the 46 million Americans without health care coverage are surely a cause to which we who are Muslim must respond. I encourage every Muslim and masjid to focus attention on the needs of people without health care coverage and to urge solutions to the problem."[33]

The key document in the packet that outlines an Islamic ethos for healthcare reform is titled "An Islamic Perspective on the Plight of Americans without Health Care Coverage" (henceforth referred to as "The Perspective"). The Perspective highlights the "non-Islamic" status quo, where individuals without healthcare coverage suffer, and argues that supporting healthcare reform is part of an Islamic obligation to promote justice. Illustratively, one passage reads:

> Justice means that . . . the value of a human being's health and life is not determined by the level of their wealth or status. . . . It is an Islamic duty, as a step in the pursuit of justice, to raise the awareness of the growing problem of the uninsured and seek to bring about a change in our health care system and public

> policy so that Americans are provided with the health care coverage needed.[34]

The Perspective also proposes that the remedy to the problem of the uninsured is to live out the Prophetic mission of mercy by "providing health care" to them. Near the end of The Perspective, the concepts of justice, mercy, and healthcare coverage are tied together as the basis for an Islamic obligation to promote healthcare reform. "It is hard to imagine a person who claims to be just, merciful and kind who . . . does not work to change" the plight of the uninsured, claims The Perspective, and it says that "health care and treatment must be afforded to every citizen." The Perspective closes by offering a selection of three Qur'anic verses (5:8, 60:8, 16:90) that preachers may draw from to exhort the Muslim community toward healthcare reform. The Perspective directs preachers to use these verses, which assert "the essential nature of justice and standing for justice [and] the obligation to cooperate with everyone—Muslim or non-Muslim—on issues of justice." For example, verse 5:8 urges Muslims to be "witnesses to justice" (*qisṭ*) and not let hatred make them "depart from justice" (*'adl*).[35]

From the above description of AMHP's and ISNA's involvement in healthcare reform we see that they were motivated by Islamic sensibilities and ethics. Indeed, they fashioned "Islamic" arguments by using Qur'anic verses and nominally universal virtues, and they used mosque settings and pulpits to deliver that message to the American Muslim community at large. Therefore, their public communications can be considered examples of Islamic bioethics discourse inasmuch as they directly call on the Islamic tradition to advance ethical arguments related to biomedicine.

Before delving into a deeper analysis of the ethical arguments and language used to signify the Islamic content of AMHP and ISNA's messages, I will briefly describe the contrasting approach of another category of producers of Islamic bioethics material, namely Islamic jurists. Unfortunately, there are no documented opinions from Islamic jurists debating healthcare reform directly. My discussion of the juridical commentary on the American healthcare system is therefore confined to its contextual role in the background of electronic *fatāwā* on the permissibility of purchasing health insurance.

FATĀWĀ ON HEALTH INSURANCE IN THE AMERICAN CONTEXT

In stark contrast to the positive messages of the Islamic organizations considered above, all of the *fatāwā* reviewed consider commercial insurance to be ethico-legally impermissible, or haram. For example, Muftī Ikram ul Haq from the Fatwa Center of America (FCA) states that "according to the research of *'ulamā'* all forms of conventional insurance is [*sic*] *ḥarām*." Corroborating this assertion, Muftī ibn Adam al-Kawthari, the director of the Institute of Islamic Jurisprudence in the United Kingdom, states that the Islamic *Fiqh* Academy of Jeddah, comprised of the "top recognized scholars from around the globe," with "no less than 150 such scholars from 45 Islamic countries," unanimously judged "all types of prevalent insurances to be [Islamically] unlawful."[36] Dr. al-Qudah, from the Assembly of Muslim Jurists of America (AJMA), also cites this opinion.[37]

The jurists explain that this assessment is based on the elements of usury (*ribā*), chancing (*qimār*), and uncertainty (*gharar*) present in conventional insurance contracts. Each of these features is, they agree, expressly forbidden by the Qur'an and *Sunnah*. While the *fatāwā*, generally speaking, do not exhaustively detail the verses and traditions that undergird their prohibitions, the following two verses condemning usury and chancing are cited as sources here:

> Those who swallow usury cannot rise up save as he ariseth whom the devil hath prostrated by (his) touch. That is because they say: Trade is just like usury; whereas Allah permitteth trading and forbiddeth usury. . . . As for him who returneth (to usury)—such are rightful owners of the Fire. They will abide therein. (2:275)
>
> They question thee about strong drink and chancing. Say: In both is great sin, and (some) utility for men; but the sin of them is greater than their usefulness. . . . Thus Allah maketh plain to you (His) revelations, that haply ye may reflect. (2:219)[38]

A core precept in Islamic contractual law, derived from numerous Prophetic traditions, is that the amount paid must be fixed and the product to be transacted clear so as to avoid deception. *Gharar* is the legal term for ambiguity or uncertainty on either point, and Muslims are enjoined to avoid it. As Dr. al-Qudah explains, conventional insurance schema are prohibited "because of the ambiguity and uncertainty built into the contract for neither of the two parties knows whether or not he will pay, how much he will pay and for how long."[39]

While acknowledging the categorical prohibition of commercial insurance, the American *fatāwā* (from Muftī Ikram ul Haq at FCA, Dr. Main al-Qudah and Dr. Salah al-Sawy at the Assembly of Muslim Jurists of America [AMJA], and Dr. Monzer Kahf at islam-online.net) all view health insurance as an exception. For Muftī Ikram and the scholars at AMJA, the exemption stems from the legal maxim "extreme necessity renders the impermissible to be permissible" (*al-ḍarūrāt tubīḥ al-maḥẓūrāt*).[40] These scholars consider the excessive costs of healthcare in the United States to satisfy the threshold for invoking dire necessity (*ḍarūra*). Muftī Ikram notes that "health insurance in America is allowed under the principal [*sic*] of necessity" due to "skyrocketing prices of medicine and medical procedures."[41] Similarly, Dr. al-Qudah states that Muslims in North America have a special dispensation "from the basic rule of prohibition of all kinds of commercial insurance . . . due to the very high and unaffordable healthcare expense."[42] Dr. al-Sawy bolsters the *ḍarūra* rationale with another argument to allow for the exception. He suggests that health insurance is linked to one of the higher objectives of Islamic law, the preservation of life (*ḥifdh al-ḥayāt*), and therefore, given "the lack of Islamic alternatives and also considering the elevated cost of treatment without insurance coverage there would be no blame in getting medical insurance."[43] Finally, Muftī Ikram offers another circumstance that serves to invoke necessity: when health insurance is required by the law of the land, an individual is not considered blameworthy when purchasing it.[44]

While acknowledging that the majority of Islamic scholars deem commercial insurance *ḥarām*, Dr. Kahf's *fatāwā* deem health insurance to be permissible without needing to invoke *ḍarūra*. He notes that, unlike in the case of life insurance, there is no usurious component in health insurance as there is no guaranteed payout. Thus the contract does not contain *ribā* (usury), so the main issue to resolve is that of *gharar*. Following Shaykh Mustafa al-Zarka's opinion (according to Dr. Kahf, a view shared by a minority of jurists),[45] Dr. Kahf suggests that the ambiguity within the contract is remedied by actuarial studies "and the application of the theory of probability." Hence, there is "no *gharar* on the part of the insurer," and purchasing health insurance is ethico-legally permissible (*mubāḥ*).[46]

Although these jurists find the purchasing of healthcare insurance Islamically permitted, it is worth noting that other Islamic jurists do not believe that the high costs of healthcare in America or the argument concerning the preservation of life merit the allowance of exceptions from the normative prohibition of the purchase of commercial insurance. The Permanent Committee for Scholarly Research and Ifta in Saudi Arabia addressed a student's question concerning the permissibility of purchasing health insurance in the United States given that "treatment costs are exorbitant" with the reply that "health insurance falls under commercial insurance which is prohibited."[47] The jurists reject the exceptional nature of the American context, stating elsewhere that there is no contextual difference in ethico-legal rulings here as all commercial insurance involves *gharar*.[48]

While each of the American *fatwā* authors finds an Islamic legal (*shar'ī*) basis for allowing Muslims to purchase health insurance in the United States, all of them consider the Islamic ideal to be a restructuring of conventional health insurance systems. For example, Muftī Ikram remarks that "Muslims should make effort to replace the conventional insurance with the Islamic alternative that is called *takāful*."[49] Dr. Kahf also expresses this view, explaining that *takāful* avoids *ribā* and reduces *gharar*. He states:

> The solution is to create a [*sic*] insurance Islamic cooperative (mutual).... In a cooperative you pay a premium as a contribution to the insurance pool of funds and if anything is left it will be distributed back to the members (contributors) and if the pool wasn't sufficient they [the insurance managers] go back to the members for the deficit.... [T]he condition of avoidance of *gharar* is relaxed in cooperative/contributory entities that are based on some kind of membership relationship.[50]

Dr. al-Sawy, on the other hand, suggests that the Islamically permissible alternative to current health insurance systems would be a government-run single-payer system that "aims to look after the citizens and not to gain profit" by giving them access to a greater quantity of healthcare services than what their fiscal contributions might warrant so that the schema includes an element of gifting beyond simply getting only that amount of healthcare one has "paid" for.[51]

From the above we see that, while insurance schema are normatively prohibited according to Islamic law, in light of the excessive costs associated with American healthcare, the America-based jurists deemed the purchase of healthcare insurance in the United States contingently permissible. They constructed Islamic ethico-legal arguments by drawing on the maxim of dire necessity, calling upon the higher objective of Islamic law to protect life, and in one case considered *gharar* to be offset by actuarial science. These electronic *fatāwā* represent a distinct genre of Islamic bioethics—one often taken as its quintessential form[52]—where the machinery of Islamic law is used to advance ethical arguments concerning biomedicine.

CONNECTIONS AND DISCONNECTIONS

AMHP's and ISNA's textual outputs incorporate two types of discourses, healthcare equity discourse and human rights discourse, not present in the *fatāwā*.[53] The AMHP press releases, the FRH pamphlets, and the ISNA-sponsored Muslim study packet produced for Cover the Uninsured call attention to the numbers of people who are uninsured or underinsured, propose a causal link between lack of insurance and poor health and/or having insurance and maintaining healthy behaviors, and suggest that healthcare be accessible to all. AMHP states that their work toward reform is motivated by the "120 million people" who "are uninsured or underinsured" and that "the status quo is untenable and [we are] prepared to work with all stakeholders to ensure that all Americans have access to high-quality and affordable health care." AMHP also lauds the passage of the PPACA by noting that "the [health] benefits of the Law [PPACA]" will extend to millions of Americans and will include "free preventive checkups for women."[54] The Muslim study packet is also replete with messaging about the health detriments resulting from lack of insurance: "Too many Americans are living without coverage—forced to gamble every day that they won't get sick or injured. Going without insurance means that minor illnesses can become major ones if health care is delayed."[55] The FRH materials co-signed by AMHP and ISNA similarly invoke healthcare equity messages by stating that "all persons should have access to health services" and "that society is whole only when we care for the most vulnerable among us" by "sharing our abundant health care resources with everyone."[56]

FRH materials also incorporate notions of human rights, that is, that human beings have rights that accrue to them simply because they are human and that these rights belong to all humans in equal measure, to support their cause.[57] They note that they "discern the human right to health care" and that the right to healthcare is "grounded in our common humanity."[58] Imām Sa'dullah adopts this lexicon in his words for FRH, calling access to healthcare "a fundamental human right."[59]

Although the *fatāwā*, on the other hand, respond to questioners by acknowledging the high costs of healthcare in the United States, there is no trace of healthcare equity discourse in them. They do not comment on the relationships between not having healthcare insurance and poor health and/or disadvantaged healthcare-seeking behaviors, nor do they suggest that healthcare should be accessible to all. The only oblique references to an "Islamic" responsibility to provide healthcare are those of Dr. al-Sawy when he says that the higher objective of Islamic law is to preserve life and that a single-payer governmental health coverage schema that "aims to look after the citizens" is permitted.[60] These limited statements evidence very little interdiscursivity with the language of health equity. Furthermore, human rights discourse is not invoked by the jurists in their *fatāwā*.

One is thus faced with the question as to why the jurists refer neither to healthcare equity discourse nor to notions of human rights, while both are present in the Muslim organizational material. The lack of language on healthcare equity may be explained by the fact that Islamic jurists in the United States, in general, are not involved in national policy-level dialogue and thus are less likely to be familiar with or adopt the vocabulary of health equity. Illustratively, no Muslims (jurists or otherwise) have been appointed to the Presidential Commission for the Study of Bioethical Issues, although the current commission includes a prominent Franciscan friar and Catholic theologian who can present normative "Christian" perspectives, and several current and former members of the commission, including the current chair, are Jewish.[61] To be fair, the commission has sought out Muslim academics for comment from time to time, but Islamic jurists, to my knowledge, have not been involved in this dialogue, and with no Muslim members on the commission, there is little opportunity for a Muslim representative to voice the need to bring jurists to the table or for that representative to learn (and share this learning with *muftīs*) the health equity lexicon that is relevant to American discussions of bioethics policy.

Muslim-led engagement with health policy issues through ISNA and AMHP also lacks Islamic juridical voices. AMHP has no bioethics committee or *fatwā*-giving body. Most conspicuously, however, the *Fiqh* Council of North America, ISNA's own jurisconsults, does not appear to have engaged with debates on healthcare reform, as none of ISNA's communiqués concerning healthcare reform cite these jurist members. Accordingly, the absence of healthcare equity vocabulary in the *fatāwā* may be attributed to the dislocation between Islamic jurists and the circles of dialogue concerning healthcare equity and policy.

To take a different tack, another underlying reason for the lack of healthcare equity discourse within the *fatāwā* may be intrinsic to the genre. *Fatāwā*, as a discursive medium of Islamic law, are part of a dialogue between a questioner (*mustaftī*), and a jurist (*muftī*). The questioner usually is concerned about whether a certain course of action he or she is considering is Islamically permissible or whether Islamic law requires a specific action of him or her in a given set of circumstances. This particular and local concern occupies the jurist's thinking; larger-scale theorizing may, therefore, not be present within *fatāwā* (although it could be; see below). In other words, a jurist's *fatāwā* generally speak to individual levels of concern, so societal considerations about healthcare equity from a perspective of Islamic bioethics may not be accessible from research limited to *fatāwā* alone.

Admittedly, while the distinctive form of *fatwā*-giving remains one of question and response, *fatāwā* can serve different sorts of purposes and may speak to multiple different audiences beyond the individual questioner.[62] Given their wider electronic dissemination, the *fatāwā* studied in the present chapter could be classified within Skovgaard-Petersen's schema as "public *fatāwā*" that transcend the nexus between the *muftī* and *mustaftī* such that the broader public is addressed and may construe the *fatāwā* to be actionable for them. While Skovgaard-Petersen suggests that in such public *fatāwā muftīs* will "avoid taking individual circumstances of the question into account and seek to issue a generally valid *fatwā*,"[63] the extent to which *muftīs* act in this manner is no doubt variable. In the *fatāwā* I present here, it would seem that the jurists took care to address the individual questioners' circumstances while at the same time presenting accepted ethico-legal doctrine. Society-level considerations—which one might imagine more likely to appear in "public *fatāwā*"—appear to have been absent or, at best, secondary concerns for these jurists.

Regarding the absence of human rights discourse in the *fatāwā*, one might point to a significant tension between the theoretical underpinnings of human rights doctrine and Islamic moral theology, which complicates the adoption of the discourse of human rights by Islamic jurists. The points of contention revolve around the capacities of human reason to discern moral norms and around the notion that rights inhere within the human. In short, orthodox Sunni Islamic theology does not recognize the ontological authority of human reason.[64] Rather, it sees human reason as a fault-prone tool for moral assessment that can, in general, only confirm or corroborate normative values established by revelation (as in the Qur'an and *Sunnah*), and "rights" are conferred by God through revelation. The tension between some versions of human rights and Islam is attested to by the fact that Muslim nations and Islamic authorities crafted their own versions of the Universal Declaration on Human Rights (UDHR), the Cairo Declaration on Human Rights in Islam, and the Universal Islamic Declaration of Human Rights by replacing references to rights inhering within humans with references to the Shariah as the divine source of moral norms and evaluation.[65] Talk of human rights talk has a controversial status within Islamic discourse.

I will now turn, by contrast, to what discourse could be seen as missing from the outputs of the American Muslim organizations. While the dominant concern of the jurists was the prohibited (*ḥarām*) status of commercial health insurance schema, the AMHP and ISNA texts appear to be oblivious to this core Islamic ethico-legal concern. More broadly, instead of using the jurists' ethico-legal vocabulary of permissibility, recommendation, and impermissibility to describe Islamic moral obligations, these communiqués use a vaguer ethical lexicon, employing phrases such as "the Islamic faith encourages . . ." and "Islam calls on its followers to. . . ."[66] This language does not clarify in the same way the precise moral duty one has, in this case, to promote healthcare reform. One must reckon, then, with different sorts of motive forces in play in the effort to change Muslim attitudes and behavior.

In an allied point, one also notes another dominant theme in the practices of interfaith discourse in which Muslim organizations are involved. While FRH aimed to use messaging "embedded in faith values and scriptural narratives" to advance healthcare reform, it by and large incorporated Christian phraseology such as "calling," "sacred vessels," and "spiritual love" rather than much of the conventional Islamic ethico-legal lexicon.[67] Notably, Imām Sa'adullah's statement for FRH is also devoid of conventional Islamic ethico-legal vocabulary and instead uses human rights phraseology. The Christian overtones present in the "interfaith" FRH materials evidence a greater cultural challenge for American Muslims and Islam. Islam and Muslims evoke an emotional response across the sociopolitical spectrum in the post-9/11 era.[68] In particular, references to the Islamic ethico-legal code (Shariah) are met with fears of the Islamization of society. As the principal target audience for FRH was non-Muslim policy-makers, perhaps it appeared prudent for Islamic overtones to remain muted. On the other hand, references to Christian concepts are omnipresent in American sociopolitical discourse, and FRH appears to have remained content to tug subtly at these religious motivations alone. The social conditions contributing to the need for Muslims to discard overt references to their faith, in particular to Islamic law, when engaging in the American civic arena have compounded the marginalization of Islamic jurists and contributed to confusion about what policies, ethical values, and the like qualify as suitably "Islamic." The space vacated by Islamic jurists and their legal discourse has instead been filled by other Muslim figures and other types of values that contribute to what I perceive as a discontinuity between the notion of being Muslim, as a social identity within a plural society, and that of living out Islam—that is, acting in accord with ethico-legal values derived from the scriptural tradition.

CALLING (AND NOT CALLING) ON THE QUR'AN AND *SUNNAH*

The Qur'an and *Sunnah* are the sacred source-texts of Islam. Both represent divine communications (*waḥy*) and thereby represent a link to the

Divine. Thus they are the textual sources of Islamic law and are foundational to all Islamic teachings.[69] Consequently, examining the ways in which the Qur'an and *Sunnah* are called on by our texts should provide some insight into their various orientations toward the tradition. To start with those of the Muslim organizations, the only AMHP writing to call on the Qur'an and/or *Sunnah* is the press release that was written following the Supreme Court's upholding of the PPACA. That document cites the Qur'anic verse "never shall you attain to true piety unless you spend on others out of what you cherish yourselves; and whatever you spend—verily, God has full knowledge thereof" (3:92) to support the claim that Islam enjoins "equity in all things."[70] Leaving aside the exegetical and hermeneutical contestations over this verse, it is notable that the Qur'an and *Sunnah* were not cited in AMHP material advocating for healthcare reform prior to the passage of the final bill. While one can only speculate as to why, this may be further evidence of a cautious approach to invoking Islamic sacred texts in public policy–level dialogue. Once the bill became law, of course, there remained no need for AMHP to suppress such explicit mention of Islamic sources. Indeed, in post-PPACA communiqués AMHP has engaged in further direct quotations of the Qur'an.[71] The interfaith FRH material, signed onto by AMHP and ISNA, also does not cite Islamic scriptures, whether consciously—in light of the political climate—or otherwise. It is, I should say, unclear how much influence AMHP, ISNA, and IMANA had on the FRH publications.

The Cover the Uninsured materials produced in collaboration with ISNA, on the other hand, are replete with Qur'anic references. Since the materials' sole target audience is the Muslim laity, the authors appeal to scripture, presumably in an effort to influence Muslim attitudes and motivate their behavior. An intriguing aspect of these appeals to the Qur'an is that The Perspective uses verses to support "universal" values (justice and mercy) rather than to derive a distinctively "Islamic" position by locating a particular virtue or ethical notion in a verse and then using other verses and *Sunnah* traditions to clarify an Islamic conception of that value before encouraging Muslims to uphold this version of it. An example will make this clearer, in this case with regard to the virtue of justice.

The Perspective notes that the concept of justice is critical to understanding "the Islamic perspective on the issue of the uninsured," for "justice ... requires that health care and services necessary for one's well-being and survival are not offered on the basis of how much the person has or what the person can afford." Linking justice and the Islamic tradition, The Perspective states that justice is central to all of God's revelations and quotes verse 25 of Surat al-Hadid (57). The following translation of the initial part of the verse is offered: "We sent aforetime our apostles with clear signs and sent down with them the Book and the Balance (of Right and Wrong), that they may stand forth in justice," here translating the Arabic *qisṭ* as "justice." The Perspective next defines justice as "equity" and links this notion to the provision of healthcare to all. The final rhetorical move advances the pursuit of healthcare reform as an Islamic obligation by linking it again to justice: "It is an Islamic duty, as a step in the pursuit of justice, to . . . seek to bring about a change in our health care system and public policy so that Americans are provided with the health care coverage needed," as healthcare reform is needed for "justice to be achieved."[72]

The Perspective thus uses the aforementioned verse to support its claim that justice (as a value) is "a core value not only for Islam but also for all previous messages of God" and offers a translation whereby the role of revelation (the Book) is to assist prophets (and, by extension, faith communities) in standing for justice. With respect to our discussion of the content of "Islamic" ethics, The Perspective's discursive framing and interpretative strategy appears to incline toward an ethical framework that is universalist or based on common morality, whereas the Qur'an affirms moral values that are shared by humankind. The same method is used to confirm the value of the concept of mercy but not to define it. The Perspective quotes a verse (21:107) that proclaims that the Prophet was sent as a "mercy for all creatures" and asserts that "providing health care is one of the most important" ways to live out this Prophetic mission of distributing mercy to humankind. The *Sunnah* is called on only once by The Perspective, but for an analogous use.[73]

However, the verse 57:25 can be translated, or interpreted, differently, such that revelation ("the Book") is given primacy in defining moral values and provides the ethico-legal code through which justice is established. For example, Muhammad Asad's translation suggests that it is revelation that is the source of the moral code: "We bestowed revelation from on high, and (thus gave you) a balance (wherewith to weigh right and wrong), so that men might behave with equity."[74] Here he renders the word *qisṭ* as "equity" rather than justice.[75] Several classical Qur'anic commentators further elaborate on the primacy of revelation for establishing justice by considering the word *al-mīzān* ("the Balance") used in verse 57:25 to refer to the divine laws derived from revelation.[76] This gives revelation and the distinctive Islamic ethico-legal tradition primacy, in contrast to The Perspective's usage and translation of Qur'anic verses to affirm conceptions of justice that can be seen as shared within a universalist framework based on common morality.

The manner in which the Qur'an is mobilized by The Perspective to discuss justice (and other concepts such as mercy) is relevant to our discussion regarding the nature of "Islamic" bioethical values. The Perspective would seem to view justice (or mercy) as a universal concept and value, its meaning self-evident.[77] The way in which the Qur'an is translated coheres with this strategy. Yet The Perspective argues for an Islamic moral obligation to support healthcare reform and encourages *imāms* to deliver sermons that follow the reasoning laid out by The Perspective to convey this obligation. Both the message (an "Islamic" obligation) and the medium for delivering the message (the Friday sermon) would appear to be targeted at "practicing" Muslims; it is Muslims who choose to be motivated by Islamic teachings and attend Friday prayer services that The Perspective seeks to persuade to support health reform. While arguments based on common morality may be effective in motivating such support, it is equally possible that many such Muslims would be more motivated by a line of reasoning that argues from the Qur'an outward, as it were, and sets up the moral imperative to support healthcare reform through the vernacular of Islamic law. While Muslim study materials and Friday sermon guides produced for the Muslim laity in collaboration with ISNA do not seek to serve as *fatāwā*, involving jurists in their production might have given a very different flavor to The Perspective's advocacy of an Islamic obligation to support healthcare reform.

THE ISLAMIC JURISTS' *FATĀWĀ*

Given that the Qur'an and *Sunnah* are the primary sources of Islamic law, one might expect an ample number of references to them in the *fatāwā*. Yet, curiously perhaps, none of the *fatāwā* from the Fatwa Center of

America or the Assembly of Muslim Jurists of America cite Qur'anic verses or Prophetic traditions. And while Dr. Monzer Kahf does use the Qur'an and *Sunnah*, he does so in a limited fashion. He paraphrases the verse 2:279 to support the Islamic prohibition of *ribā*, noting of the "*riba* that is mentioned in the Qur'an, it is strongly prohibited with a declaration of war by the Almighty Allah and His messenger." With respect to *Sunnah* traditions, Dr. Kahf notes only that *gharar* is prohibited by several Prophetic statements.[78]

The paucity of references to Qur'anic verses and *Sunnah* traditions in the juridical writings may arise from the conventions of *fatwā*-giving. As mentioned earlier, a questioner usually asks for an Islamic ethico-legal opinion from someone he deems an Islamic ethico-legal authority. Therefore, some Islamic jurists may think that the questioner does not require detailed evidence from the Qur'an and *Sunnah* to substantiate a ruling, because the very act of seeking their opinion signifies the questioner's deference to their expertise. This type of understanding is captured by the saying, oft-repeated in circles of Islamic learning in my experience: "The *fatwā* of a *muftī* constitutes [actionable and sufficient] evidence for the layperson" (*qawl muftī dalīl 'ām; fatāwā al-muftī dalīl mustaftī*). Indeed, the seeker's obligation is only to find a suitably qualified expert to consult; it is not his burden to "know the proof behind a particular ruling."[79] Consequently, *fatāwā* tend to have minimal direct scriptural references, with those who issue them content to deliver the rulings rather than the entire proofs.

If the measure of the "Islamicness" of Islamic bioethics were to be taken as the extent of quotation from the Qur'an and *Sunnah*, one would have to consider the *fatāwā* less "Islamic" than the materials produced by the AMHP and ISNA. But as regards the task of influencing Muslim behavior, it appears that these jurists felt that their statements in themselves carried sufficient motive force and did not require much in the way of Qur'anic verses or *Sunnah* traditions to bolster them. Even if juridical voices had been convened to help craft the AMHP, FRH, and ISNA healthcare reform–related materials, it is not that their quotient of Islamicness as measured by the quotation of scripture would have risen. Rather, it would have entailed the introduction of a set of very different ideas about the Islamic ethical obligation or otherwise of supporting healthcare reform. Islamicness is not something that can be measured on a continuous unitary scale.

THE SOCIAL PRACTICES OF ISLAMIC BIOETHICS DISCOURSE: REPRESENTING THE "ISLAMIC"

Thus far I have demonstrated that two types of producers of what could be characterized as Islamic bioethics discourse, American Muslim organizations and Islamic jurists, have been similarly concerned about the burdensome costs of healthcare in the United States. While both types of producers developed "Islamic" ethical arguments for healthcare reform, the different ways in which they use (and neglect) Qur'anic verses and *Sunnah* traditions, the language and moral reasoning they employ, and the other types of discourses they incorporate into (or leave out of) their communications evince different formulations as to what constitutes Islamic ethics. In this section I want to more closely tie together the social practices and ideological stances that potentially influence their respective representations of the "Islamic" as a means for discussing the challenges in producing an authentic and robust theoretical framework and discourse for Islamic bioethics.

While AMHP describes its work as inspired by an Islamic vision and framed its support of healthcare reform as part of an Islamic duty, the grounding of their Islamic ethical imperative remains unclear in their materials. Unlike in the ISNA materials, however, Qur'an and *Sunnah* supports are not called on by AMHP in order to highlight an ethical framework based on common morality, nor, on the other hand, are the methods and vocabulary of Islamic law deployed to make an ethical argument for supporting healthcare reform.

Again, perhaps the lack of scriptural references was intended as part of a socially conditioned muting of Islamic sources in policy discussions in order to avoid hostile reactions to Islam and Muslims. However, since a major portion of AMHP's target audience was Muslim, avoiding scriptural referencing may have detracted from their ability to affect Muslim attitudes and behavior. Further, if AMHP's ethical framework does require scriptural justification, a strategic or socially conditioned concealment of the scriptural references and the lexicon of Islamic law may have obscured an understanding of what precisely the sources of Islamic ethical imperatives are and rendered problematic the project of developing a distinctive "Islamic bioethics," in the American context at least.

The materials produced under the aegis of ISNA, on the other hand, appear to frame the push for reform as part of living out universal and self-evident virtues such as justice and mercy. As discussed above, this manner of ethical argumentation arguably differs from the inherited orthodox Sunni modes. Sunni *uṣūl al-fiqh* holds that "Islamic" ethical values must be sourced within scripture, and when scripture is silent, there can be no ultimate normative assessment: Actions can be recommended but not obligated.[80]

It is hard to believe that ISNA (and their representative Imām Kobeisy), being closely linked to the *Fiqh* Council of North America, which promotes "classical Islamic jurisprudence" and deliberates according to "accepted norms of Islamic jurisprudence," would be oblivious to the epistemological and theological implications of their messaging.[81] We could lean again on the notion of a perceived need to show similarities between Islam and other moral frameworks in the post-9/11 policy arena. Nonetheless, the discursive framing used by ISNA also renders fuzzy notions of what might be distinctively "Islamic" about Islamic bioethics.

Further muddying the waters is the adoption by AMHP and ISNA of FRH's use of a human rights vocabulary. As noted above, the metaphysical underpinnings of human rights doctrine are arguably in tension with Islamic moral theology. Perhaps these organizations consider there to be no theological divide between human rights doctrine and their Islamic ethico-legal frameworks (one notes again the lack of involvement of jurists in their conversations). Or this may have been another strategic choice made in the hope of achieving a positive policy outcome. Once again, either scenario challenges the development of the field of Islamic bioethics by offering a contested account of, or simply obscuring, the distinctive nature of Islamic content.

With respect to the juridical materials, on the other hand, the lack of explicit arguments from scripture, combined with the conventions of the *fatwā* discourse, suggests that in the jurist's view the text of a *fatwā* contains in itself the legitimating power to label actions as "Islamic." Such an articulation of the Islamic fuels concerns about the scope of Islamic bioethics discourse. Recall that there was little mention of healthcare equity in the *fatāwā*. If one was to take the *fatāwā* as standing for Islamic bioethics on their own, one could justifiably come to the conclusion that Islamic jurists, as a class of Islamic ethical experts, have little concern for social justice and the right ordering of society but are instead concerned only with finding a loophole in the Islamic ethico-legal tradition through which Muslim actions can be deemed permissible (*ḥalāl*). To be sure, the *fatāwā* do note the problem of the escalating costs of American healthcare, and some *muftīs* did mention alternative Islamic insurance schema, but they did not deploy in their *fatāwā* Islamic constructs that take into account harms and benefits at the societal level, such as *maṣlaḥa* (public/universal human interest) and *'umūm al-balwā* (widespread difficulty), for instance, nor did they speak about Islamic ethical obligations to redress the problematic American healthcare situation. Perhaps the *muftīs* felt their duty was only to answer the individuals' (*mustaftis*') questions and that it was inappropriate to use the medium to provide social commentary and construct obligations for American Muslims at large.

Hence, for the developing field of Islamic bioethics it would be a mistake to consider *fatāwā* as complete portrayals of the relevant Islamic values as they pertain to a bioethical issue, as representing the totality of ethico-legal discussions on an Islamic bioethical topic, or even as the final word on Islamic bioethical norms. For one thing, many, perhaps most, *fatāwā* are ephemeral personal interventions rather than published texts. Researchers need to be aware of the bias inherent in taking the latter as standing for the totality of the phenomenon. The contingent nature of *fatāwā* and the pragmatic approach generally taken to giving them should thus give researchers pause when developing comprehensive Islamic bioethics theories from these sources. Perhaps counterintuitively, then, given their totemic status, extant *fatāwā* and their writers also contribute to confusion over the scope of Islamic bioethics and the nature of the "Islamic."

IMPLICATIONS

An order of discourse is a particular social ordering of relationships among different ways of making meaning (i.e., different discourses and genres and styles).[82] Competing perspectives on what is and is not "Islamic" take us to the heart of the question as to the appropriate order of discourse for an emergent Islamic bioethics. These contestations are both epistemological and methodological, because Islam is both a lived tradition recognizable in the social practices of Muslim individuals and communities and a scriptural tradition that holds the Qur'an and *Sunnah* to be transcendental sources of moral guidance. One aspect of a social ordering of discourse is dominance: Some ways of making meaning become mainstream in a particular order of discourse, while others come to be marginalized.[83] As Islamic bioethics coalesces into a field of intellectual inquiry and disciplinary practice, internal social pressure from stakeholders of the field as well as external sociocultural and political forces will affect which mode of meaning-making (the method of moral reasoning) will come to occupy the dominant position in Islamic bioethics discourse. Our snapshot of two orders of Islamic bioethical writing reveals a disconnected Islamic bioethics discourse: The jurists' Islamic concerns about the permissibility of healthcare insurance find no mention in the output of Muslim organizations, while the Muslim organizations' Islamic concerns regarding healthcare equity are absent from the jurists' ethico-legal assessments. Because each party maintains its own perspective on how to construct and label an Islamic bioethical obligation, a lack of clarity regarding the nature of the distinctively Islamic aspect of Islamic bioethics discourse ensues.

The disconnected nature of the production of Islamic bioethical material appears to have further practical effects at the ground level. Although national Muslim organizations sought to mobilize Muslims toward supporting healthcare reform, religious affiliation reportedly had little to do with subsequent attitudes.[84] Perhaps the discursive framing they adopted—one that lacked references to the Qur'an and *Sunnah*, that seemed to employ little of the standard Islamic legal lexicon, and that adopted human rights discourse—failed to have an impact on Muslim attitudes. In other words, the attempt to present Islamic values in the public policy arena according to secular conventions may have removed the potential power of more explicitly Islamic motivators over the Muslim laity. Or, conversely, perhaps religious arguments have little influence over Muslim attitudes in the United States and the impact of religion on health policy attitudes is more limited than is generally believed.

Alternatively, perhaps it was not the messaging but rather its dissemination that contributed to the less-than-ideal impact of these programmatic efforts; perhaps they did not reach enough members of the target Muslim audience. While the PPACA did become law, there is no data as to the impact of Muslim voices on its passage, rendering it almost impossible to evaluate the effect of Muslim engagement in the healthcare reform debate.

We can, however, point to a different possible effect of the absence of jurists collaborating with these Muslim organizations. The *fatāwā* suggested that an ideal Islamic schema of healthcare coverage would involve either a single-payer governmental system or a cooperative insurance scheme (*takāful*). Unfortunately, these types of transformative ideas never made it to the proverbial policy market. No national Muslim organization brought forth such notions, which would arguably have been more potent in bringing about healthcare equity than was the expanded commercial healthcare insurance set out by the PPACA. Since some religious groups, such as the Amish, with a mutual aid system of paying for healthcare, were granted exemptions from the PPACA insurance mandate, it seems that there would have been precedent (and potential partners) for Muslim voices to promote a *takāful* system for national healthcare reform, or at the least for Muslims to seek an exemption of their own based on religious grounds.[85]

Islamic bioethics producers, whether they are jurists or Muslim organizations, tend to give inadequate attention to the implications of the language they use as they make their determinations of the Islamic. The myriad notions they put forth create problems for the field. If one were to examine the output of Muslim organizations, one would wonder what is distinctive about the Islamic bioethics they call for. On the other hand, when one looks to juridical writings that seem devoid of sufficient theorization and consideration of social reality, one might view the vision of these scholars as missing the forest for the trees. Neither the national Muslim organizations nor the jurists have the upper hand in instituting the social order of Islamic bioethics discourse, and neither group presents a comprehensive and cohesive Islamic bioethics theory or meets the needs of the myriad Islamic bioethics stakeholders.

Multi- and interdisciplinary methods are necessary to understand the present state of Islamic bioethics discourse. The different categories of Islamic bioethics producers also need to come together so that they can effect a more holistic discourse through a mutual understanding of their respective disciplinary tools and areas of concern and by generating a common conceptual Islamic bioethics vocabulary. In this chapter, with its reliance on a range of methods and source texts, I have sought to provide fodder for such much-needed conversation.

NOTES

This chapter is a slightly modified version of my article "Muslim Perspectives on the American Healthcare System: The Discursive Framing of 'Islamic' Bioethical Discourse," *Die Welt des Islams* 55, nos. 3–4 (2015). Permission to reproduce was obtained from the publisher.

1. I adopt Professor Mohamed Fadel's usage of the English term "moral theology" to refer to the Islamic science of *uṣūl al-fiqh*: M. Fadel, "The True, the Good, and the Reasonable: The Theological and Ethical Roots of Public Reason in Islamic Law," *Canadian Journal of Law and Jurisprudence* 21, no. 1 (2008). I use the terms "Islamic ethico-legal tradition" and "Islamic law" to refer to the notions of *fiqh* and *aḥkām taklīfiyya* interchangeably.

2. For example, A. I. Padela et al., "The Perceived Role of Islam in Immigrant Muslim Medical Practice within the USA: An Exploratory Qualitative Study," *Journal of Medical Ethics* 34, no. 5 (October 8, 2008): 365–69; M. C. Inhorn, "Globalization and Gametes: Reproductive 'Tourism,' Islamic Bioethics, and Middle Eastern Modernity," *Anthropology of Medicine* 18, no. 1 (April 2011): 87–103; Kiarash Aramesh, "The Influences of Bioethics and Islamic Jurisprudence on Policy-Making in Iran," *American Journal of Bioethics* 7, no. 10 (2007): 42–44; M. ur Rahman, S. Abuhasna, and F. M. Abu-Zidan, "Care of Terminally Ill Patients: An Opinion Survey among Critical Care Healthcare Providers in the Middle East," *African Health Sciences* 13, no. 4 (2013): 893–98; A. I. Padela et al., "Religious Values and Healthcare Accommodations: Voices from the American Muslim Community," *Journal of General Internal Medicine* 27, no. 6 (2012): 708–15; A. I. Padela and F. A. Curlin, "Religion and Disparities: Considering the Influences of Islam on the Health of American Muslims," *Journal of Religion and Health* 52, no. 4 (2013): 1333–45; Aasim I. Padela, "Islamic Bioethics: Between Sacred Law, Lived Experiences, and State Authority," *Theoretical Medicine and Bioethics* 34, no. 2 (April 1, 2013): 65–80; A. I. Padela, "Islamic Verdicts in Health Policy Discourse: Porcine-Based Vaccines as a Case Study," *Zygon* 48, no. 3 (September 2013): 655–70; Janneke T. Gitsels-van der Wal et al., "The Role of Religion in Decision-Making on Antenatal Screening of Congenital Anomalies: A Qualitative Study amongst Muslim Turkish Origin Immigrants," *Midwifery* 30, no. 3 (March 1, 2014): 297–303.

3. See A. I. Padela, A. Arozullah, and E. Moosa, "Brain Death in Islamic Ethico-Legal Deliberation: Challenges for Applied Islamic Bioethics," *Bioethics* 27, no. 3 (March 2013): 132–39; Aasim I. Padela, Hasan Shanawani, and Ahsan Arozullah, "Medical Experts and Islamic Scholars Deliberating over Brain Death: Gaps in the Applied Islamic Bioethics Discourse," *Muslim World* 101, no. 1 (2011): 53–72; A. I. Padela, "Public Health Measures and Individualized Decision-Making: The Confluence of the H1N1 Vaccine and Islamic Bioethics," *Human Vaccines* 6, no. 9 (2010); Hasan Shanawani and Mohammad Hassan Khalil, "Reporting on 'Islamic Bioethics' in the Medical Literature: Where Are

the Experts?," in *Muslim Medical Ethics: From Theory to Practice*, ed. Jonathan E. Brockopp and Thomas Eich (Columbia: University of South Carolina Press, 2008), 213–28.

4. Avraham Steinberg, *Encyclopedia of Jewish Medical Ethics: A Compilation of Jewish Medical Law on All Topics of Medical Interest*, 3 vols. (Jerusalem and New York: Feldheim, 2003).

5. When I first penned the article at the core of this chapter, such an encyclopedia was not at hand. However, since then, with funding from the Qatar National Resource Fund and under the chief editorship of Ayman Shabana, an encyclopedia of Islamic bioethics of such scope is being produced. I am one of the senior editors of this encyclopedia, which is available at http://www.oxfordislamicstudies.com/ReferenceWorks/guide_21.html.

6. Padela, Shanawani, and Arozullah, "Medical Experts."

7. A. R. Jonsen, "A History of Religion and Bioethics," in *Handbook of Bioethics and Religion*, ed. David E. Guinn (Oxford: Oxford University Press, 2006), 22–36; H. Brody and A. Macdonald, "Religion and Bioethics: Toward an Expanded Understanding," *Theoretical Medical Bioethics* 34, no. 2 (2013): 133–45.

8. Brody and Macdonald, "Religion and Bioethics," 133–45.

9. Abdulaziz Abdulhussein Sachedina, *Islamic Biomedical Ethics: Principles and Application* (Oxford and New York: Oxford University Press, 2009); E. Moosa, "Translating Neuroethics: Reflections from Muslim Ethics; Commentary on 'Ethical Concepts and Future Challenges of Neuroimaging: An Islamic Perspective,'" *Science and Engineering Ethics* 18, no. 3 (2012): 519–28; "Muslim Ethics and Biotechnology," in *The Routledge Companion to Religion and Science*, ed. Gregory R. Peterson, James W. Haag, and Michael L. Spezio, 455–65 (New York: Routledge Taylor and Francis Group, 2012); Tariq Ramadan, *Radical Reform: Islamic Ethics and Liberation* (Oxford: New York: Oxford University Press, 2008).

10. Ruth Wodack and Michael Meyer, "Critical Discourse Analysis: History, Agenda, Theory and Methodology," in *Methods of Critical Discourse Analysis*, ed. Ruth Wodack and Michael Meyer, Introducing Qualitative Methods (London: Sage, 2009); Norman Fairclough, "A Dialectical-Relational Approach to Critical Discourse Analysis in Social Research," in ibid.

11. Much of the contemporary Islamic bioethics discussions focus on issues that are perceived as controversial or "hot" in the public domain, e.g. abortion ethics, or arise from biotechnological advancements, e.g. CRISPR-Cas 9. Topics that are more germane to medical practice, e.g. the patient-doctor relationship, or involve the social structure of healthcare, e.g. insurance-based schemas granting people access to medical treatment, are often overlooked yet arguably have greater impact upon the lives of patients and clinicians.

12. While ISNA is not a health-related organization per se, I include its statements in this study both because ISNA is the premier unifying civic organization for Muslims in North America and because the Islamic Medical Association of North

America (IMANA), which is a medical organization, is a founding partner of ISNA and some of its members play key roles in it.

13. askamufti.com, "Fatwa Center of America," http://askamufti.com; Assembly of Muslim Jurists of America, "Assembly of Muslim Jurists of America," http://amjaonline.com.

14. Padela, "Islamic Verdicts in Health Policy Discourse"; Padela, "Public Health Measures and Individualized Decision-Making: The Confluence of the H1N1 Vaccine and Islamic Bioethics"; Mohammed Ghaly, "Organ Donation and Muslims in the Netherlands: A Transnational Fatwa in Focus," *Recht Van De Islam* 26 (2012): 39–52; "Religio-Ethical Discussions on Organ Donation among Muslims in Europe: An Example of Transnational Islamic Bioethics," *Medicine, Health Care, and Philosophy* 15 (2012): 207–20; "Milk Banks through the Lens of Muslim Scholars: One Text in Two Contexts," *Bioethics* 26, no. 3 (2012): 117–27.

15. cnbc.com, "Medical Bills Are the Biggest Cause of US Bankruptcies: Study," http://www.cnbc.com/id/100840148.

16. C. Schoen et al., "America's Underinsured: A State-by-State Look at Health Insurance Affordability Prior to the New Coverage Expansions" (New York: Commonwealth Fund), http://www.commonwealthfund.org/Publications/Fund-Reports/2014/Mar/Americas-Underinsured.aspx.

17. P. Starr, *The Social Transformation of American Medicine: The Rise of a Sovereign Profession and the Making of a Vast Industry* (New York: Basic Books, 1982).

18. Western PA Coalition for Single-Payer Healthcare, "Why Is the Public Option in Danger of Stalling?," http://www.wpasinglepayer.org/PollResults.html.

19. World Bank, "Health Expenditure, Total (% of Gdp)," http://data.worldbank.org/indicator/SH.XPD.TOTL.ZS; C. J. Murray and J. Frenk, "Ranking 37th—Measuring the Performance of the U.S. Health Care System," *New England Journal of Medicine* 362, no. 2 (January 14, 2010): 98f.

20. "National Federation of Independent Business v. Sebelius," http://www.supremecourt.gov/opinions/11pdf/11-393c3a2.pdf; "About the Law," http://www.hhs.gov/healthcare/rights/index.html.

21. A. Rosen and S. Clement, "Religious Groups Weigh in on Healthcare Reform" (Washington, DC: Pew Research Center, 2009).

22. American Muslim Health Professionals (AMHP), "About Us," http://amhp.us/aboutus/#OurHistory.

23. *Principles of Health Care Reform*, ed. American Muslim Health Professionals (Palatine, IL: American Muslim Health Professionals, n.d.).

24. AMHP, *Muslim Health Professionals from across the Nation Meet with the Senate and Congress* (Palatine, IL: AMHP, 2009).

25. F. Qazi, "Muslim Free Clinics and Health Reform" (Palatine, IL: American Muslim Health Professionals, 2009).

26. AMHP, "AMHP Lauds Supreme Court Decision," http://amhp.us/american-muslim-health-professionals-lauds-supreme-court/.

27. Faithful Reform in Health Care (FRH), "About Us," http://www.faithfulreform.org/index.php?option=com_content&task=view&id=13&Itemid=77. FRH comprises a loose coalition of national and state-based organizations that signed their core document, "A Faith-Inspired Vision of Health Care." Most of the signing organizations are of Christian affiliation, and the organization's director is an ordained minister in the Christian Church (Disciples of Christ). Nonetheless, FRH's messaging is developed in consultation with multiple faith groups and identifies theological perspectives and scriptural narratives that inform dialogue about healthcare reform that are common to all participating faith communities.

28. Rosen and Clement, "Religious Groups Weigh in on Healthcare Reform."

29. FRH, "A Faith-Inspired Vision of Health Care," faithfulreform.org, Vision Statement.

30. FRH, "Perspectives," http://www.faithfulreform.org/index.php?option=com_content&task=view&id=136&Itemid=162.

31. L. Walling, "Faith Groups Applaud the U.S. Supreme Court for Upholding the Affordable Health Care Act" (Wilson, NC: Faithful Reform in Health Care, Washington Interreligious Staff Community, 2012).

32. The Robert Wood Johnson Foundation is America's largest philanthropy dedicated solely to the health sector. Through grant funding and collaborative projects and programs, the foundation seeks to improve the health and healthcare of all Americans. For more information, see www.rwjf.org.

33. Ahmed Kobeisy, "Materials for Muslim Prayer and Study," http://covertheuninsured.org/materials/files/2007/InterfaithMuslimPrayerStudy.pdf.

34. Ibid.

35. Ibid.

36. Ikram ul Haq, "Life Insurance and Health Insurance: Fatwa No. 1918," Fatwa Center for America, http://www.askamufti.com/Answers/ViewQuestion.aspx?QuestionId=1918; M Al-Kawthari, "Islam's Position on Prevalent Forms of Insurance: Fatwa No. 383," Qibla, http://spa.qibla.com/issue_view.asp?HD=1&ID=383&CATE=43.

37. M. al-Qudah, "Offering Medical-Health Insurance: Fatwa Number 77826," amjaonline.org, http://www.amjaonline.org/fatwa-77826/info. Given the varied nature of America's Muslim communities, some comment on the various backgrounds of the American scholars mentioned might be apposite here. Mufti Ikram ul Haq is the founding president of the Fatwa Center of America. He graduated with the degree of Takhassus Fil-Ifta and certification as a mufti from Jamiah Darul-Uloom in Karachi, Pakistan, and studied there with Shaykhul-Islam Mufti Muhammad Taqi Usmani and Mufti Muhammad Rafi Usmani, the current grand mufti of the Islamic Republic of Pakistan. He holds traditional licenses (*ijazat*) to teach hadith, alongside an Aalim degree (master's equivalent) from Dar-ul-loom Al-Madania in Buffalo, New York (see http://askamufti.com/1/mufti-ikram-ul-haq and http://masjidalislam.wordpress.com/imams-bio/). Dr. Main al-Qudah, on

the other hand, currently an assistant professor of Islamic Studies at the American Open University and member of the *Fatwā* Committee of the Assembly of Muslim Jurists of America, holds a PhD in the science of economics in Islam from the American Open University, a master's degree in Islamic studies from Yarmouk University in Jordan, and a bachelor's degree in economics from Al-Azhar University in Egypt. But he also holds traditional licenses (*ijazat*) to teach the Qur'an (see http://www.amjaonline.org/en/dr-main-al-qudah). Dr. Salah al-Sawy holds a PhD and bachelor's degrees from the Faculty of Islamic Legislation and Law at Al-Azhar University in Egypt. He is a former professor at the same university as well as at Umm Al Qura University in Saudi Arabia. He is a founder, and served as president, of the American Open University and also co-founded the Assembly of Muslim Jurists of America. He currently serves on the *Fatwā* Committee of the Assembly of Muslim Jurists of America (see http://www.amjaonline.org/en/dr-salah-alsawy). Dr. Monzer Kahf holds a PhD in economics from the University of Utah and a bachelor's degree in business from the University of Damascus. He worked as a research economist at the Islamic Research and Training Institute of the Islamic Development Bank in Jeddah, Saudi Arabia (1985–99), and as professor of Islamic economics and banking at the School of Shari'ah of Yarmouk University in Jordan (2004–5). He is a collaborating expert for the Islamic *Fiqh* Academy of the Organisation of the Islamic Conference (see http://monzer.kahf.com/about.html). One notes that even though he does not have a formal Islamic degree, his writings on islamonline.net and elsewhere are labeled as *fatāwā*.

38. al-Kawthari, "Islam's Position on Prevalent Forms of Insurance: Fatwa No. 383." The translation is that used in the source cited.

39. al-Qudah, "Offering Medical-Health Insurance: Fatwa Number 77826."

40. On this, see, e.g., Mohammad Hashim Kamali, *Principles of Islamic Jurisprudence*, 3rd rev. and enl. ed. (Cambridge: Islamic Texts Society, 2003).

41. ul Haq, "Life Insurance and Health Insurance: Fatwa No. 1918"; "Medical Insurance from Employer: Fatwa No. 2516," Fatwa Center of America, http://www.askamufti.com/Answers/ViewQuestion.aspx?QuestionId=2516.

42. M. al-Qudah, "Health Benefits [*sic*] in Canada: *Fatwā* No. 83603," http://www.amjaonline.org/fatwa-83603/info.

43. S. al-Sawy, "Getting Health Insurance for Family Coming to Visit: Fatwa No. 23107," amjaonline.org, http://www.amjaonline.org/fatwa-23107/info.

44. Ikram ul Haq, "Car Insurance, Home Insurance, Health Insurance: Fatwa No. 2921," Fatwa Center of America, http://www.askamufti.com/Answers/ViewQuestion.aspx?QuestionId=2921.

45. The late Shaykh Mustafa al-Zarka was a prominent Ḥanafī jurist of Syrian origin who passed away in 1999. He was a prominent member of the Islamic *Fiqh* Council of Makkah and was awarded the King Faisal International Prize for his work in Islamic *fiqh*. He is credited with being one of the earliest jurists involved in matters of Islamic finance and one of the first to judge certain types of commercial insurance to be permissible. See http://www.arabnews.com/node/212596.

46. M. Kahf, "Fatawa on Insurance" (2002), http://monzer.kahf.com/fatawa/2000-2002/FATAWA_INSURANCE.pdf.

47. "The first question of Fatwa No. 9580: Health Insurance Cards for Students in the USA," Permanent Committee for Scholarly Research and Ifta', http://www.alifta.net/Search/ResultDetails.aspx?languagename=en〈=en&view=result&fatwaNum=true&FatwaNumID=9580&ID=5665&searchScope=7&SearchScopeLevels1=&SearchScopeLevels2=&highLight=1&SearchType=EXACT&SearchMoesar=false&bookID=&LeftVal=0&RightVal=0&simple=&SearchCriteria=AnyWord&PagePath=&siteSection=1&searchkeyword=#firstKeyWordFound.

48. Permanent Committee for Scholarly Research and Ifta', "Fatwa No. 7723," http://www.alifta.net/Search/ResultDetails.aspx?languagename=en〈=en&view=result&fatwaNum=true&FatwaNumID=7723&ID=5664&searchScope=7&SearchScopeLevels1=&SearchScopeLevels2=&highLight=1&SearchType=EXACT&SearchMoesar=false&bookID=&LeftVal=0&RightVal=0&simple=&SearchCriteria=AnyWord&PagePath=&siteSection=1&searchkeyword=#firstKeyWordFound.

49. ul Haq, "Car Insurance, Home Insurance, Health Insurance: Fatwa No. 2921."

50. Kahf, "Fatawa on Insurance."

51. al-Sawy, "Getting Health Insurance for Family Coming to Visit: Fatwa No. 23107."

52. See the introduction to this volume.

53. Here I draw on the critical discourse analysis approach as presented by Wodack and Meyer in "Critical Discourse Analysis: History, Agenda, Theory and Methodology," and by Norman Fairclough in "A Dialectical-Relational Approach to Critical Discourse Analysis in Social Research," in *Methods of Critical Discourse Analysis*. I have structured the following sections according to Fairclough's analytical paradigm by examining social practices, interdiscursivity, and gaps.

54. AMHP, "AMHP Lauds Supreme Court Decision," and "Muslim Health Professionals from across the Nation Meet with the Senate and Congress."

55. Kobeisy, "Materials for Muslim Prayer and Study."

56. FRH, "A Faith-Inspired Vision of Health Care."

57. For this framing of human rights, see Abdulaziz Abdulhussein Sachedina, *Islam and the Challenge of Human Rights* (Oxford and New York: Oxford University Press, 2009).

58. FRH, "A Faith-Inspired Vision of Health Care."

59. FRH, "Perspectives."

60. al Sawy, "Getting Health Insurance for Family Coming to Visit: Fatwa No. 23107."

61. Members of the commision are chosen by the U.S. president. Daniel P. Sulmasy, MD, PhD, http://bioethics.gov/daniel-sulmasy, accessed January 3, 2014; Transcript: Meeting 1, Session 5, 2010, http://bioethics.gov/node/168, accessed January 4, 2014; Transcript: Meeting 9, Session 8, 2012, http://www.bioethics.gov/node/717, accessed January 4, 2014.

62. Jakob Skovgaard-Petersen, "A Typology of Fatwas," *Die Welt des Islams* 55, nos. 3–4 (2015).

63. Ibid.

64. D. Brown, "Islamic Ethics in Comparative Perspective," *Muslim World* 89, no. 2 (1999): 181–92; E. Moosa, "The Dilemma of Islamic Rights Schemes," *Worlds and Knowledges Otherwise*, Fall 2004; A. M. Emon, "On Islam and Islamic Natural Law: A Response to the International Theological Commisson's 'Look at Natural Law,'" in *Searching for a Universal Ethic*, ed. John Berkman and William C. Mattison (Grand Rapids, MI: Eerdmans, 2011).

65. Dariusch Atighetchi, *Islamic Bioethics: Problems and Perspectives*, International Library of Ethics, Law, and the New Medicine, vol. 31 (New York: Springer, 2007).

66. AMHP, "AMHP Lauds Supreme Court Decision"; Kobeisy, "Materials for Muslim Prayer and Study."

67. AMHP, "About Us"; FRH, "A Faith-Inspired Vision of Health Care"; Walling, "Faith Groups Applaud the U.S. Supreme Court for Upholding the Affordable Health Care Act"; L. Walling, "A Moral Vision for Our Healthcare Future," ed. Faithful Reform in Health Care (Cleveland, OH: FRH, 2010); and "An Open Letter to President Barack Obama and to Members of the United States Senate and House of Representatives" (Cleveland, OH: Faithful Reform in Healthcare, 2010).

68. L. Cainkar, "The Impact of 9/11 on Muslims and Arabs in the United States," in *The Maze of Fear: Security and Migration after September 11*, ed. J. Tirman (New York: New Press, 2004); M. Potok, "FBI Reports Dramatic Spike in Anti-Muslim Hate Violence," *Huffington Post*, November 11, 2011; Council on American-Islamic Relations, "The Status of Muslim Civil Rights in the United States 2005: Unequal Protection," *Jurist*, May 11, 2005.

69. There are many different hermeneutical approaches to these scriptural source-texts, and such differences undergird the development of different schools of Islamic theology and law. Islamic law is thus inherently plural, and there can be multiple different authentically scripturally derived rulings that are deemed correct and actionable.

70. AMHP, "AMHP Lauds Supreme Court Decision."

71. AMHP, "Get Covered Outreach Materials," http://amhp.us/get-covered-outreach-materials.

72. Kobeisy, "Materials for Muslim Prayer and Study."

73. Ibid.

74. "Verse 57:25," http://corpus.quran.com/translation.jsp?chapter=57&verse=25, in Asad, *The Message of the Qur'an*.

75. Ibid. The Perspective translates the Qur'anic terms *'adl* and *qisṭ* equally as "justice." While the two are, to a certain extent, interchangeable, and while for The Perspective's purposes any difference between them is perhaps irrelevant, the two words are used differently in the Qur'an. *Qisṭ* refers to the notion of equity and balance and is metaphorically used to indicate justice, while *'adl* has a much broader

meaning, including judging with equity, and is used to refer to both God's actions and those of humankind in different verses. See "The Qur'an: An Encyclopedia," in *The Qur'an: An Encyclopedia*, ed. O. Leaman (New York: Routledge, 2006), and J. E. Brockopp, "Justice and Injustice 3:69–74," in *The Encyclopedia of the Qur'ān*, ed. J. McAuliffe (Washington, DC: Brill Online, 2015).

76. Maulana Mufti Muhammad Shafi, *Maariful Quran* (Karachi, Pakistan, 2004).

77. In a certain way, The Perspective's locating ethical values as part of a vision of a shared common human morality could be argued to resemble Mu'tazilite moral reasoning, and this approach may be influenced by similar social motivations. According to Reinhart, the sociopolitical circumstances in the Islamic world under a stable Abbasid caliphate in the late seventh centry and early eighth century CE contributed to the development of religious doctrines whose developers sought to find commonalities across the ethnic and cultural diversity of Muslims and between Muslims and non-Muslims. As the caliphate came to govern peoples from vastly different cultural backgrounds and sought to bring more peoples into the Islamic faith, and as Islamic scholars came into contact with Greek thought, some Islamic scholars began to mine the Islamic scriptures to build an argument for humankind's sharing a moral common sense and for human reason's being sufficient to distinguish moral acts from immoral ones. See A. K. Reinhart, *Before Revelation: The Boundaries of Muslim Moral Thought*, SUNY Series in Middle Eastern Studies (Albany: State University of New York Press, 1995). While American Muslims are not a dominant cultural and political force (as Muslims in the Abbasid caliphate were), their status as a minority group within the secular liberal democracy of America motivates them to ally with other groups and find common moral frameworks. In modern times, some Islamic scholars have advocated for the incorporation of Mu'tazilite moral sensibilities into contemporary Muslim civic and ethico-legal discourses. See Khaled Abou El Fadl, "The Human Rights Commitment in Modern Islam," in *Human Rights and Responsibilities in the World Religions*, ed. J. Runzo, Nancy M. Martin, and A. Sharma (Oxford: Oneworld Publications, 2002), 301–65.

78. Kahf, "Fatawa on Insurance."

79. Hamza Karamali, "Questions about Taqlid and Ijtihad," Qibla, http://spa.qibla.com/issue_view.asp?HD=3&ID=1568&CATE=389.

80. Emon, "On Islam and Islamic Natural Law: A Response to the International Theological Commisson's 'Look at Natural Law'"; Reinhart, *Before Revelation*; A. M. Emon, *Islamic Natural Law Theories* (New York: Oxford University Press, 2010). An Islamic obligation refers to refraining from actions and nonactions that carry sin and therefore have the potential for punishment in the afterlife.

81. *Fiqh* Council of North America, "The Fiqh Council of North America," fiqhcouncil.org.

82. Fairclough, "A Dialectical-Relational Approach to Critical Discourse Analysis in Social Research."

83. Fairclough, *Discourse and Social Change* (Cambridge, UK, and Cambridge, MA: Polity Press, 1992).

84. Rosen and Clement, "Religious Groups Weigh in on Healthcare Reform."

85. "National Federation of Independent Business v. Sebelius"; K. O'Brien, "Obamacare Religious Exemption Hard to Get," http://www.religionnews.com/2014/04/28/obamacare-religious-exemption-hard-get/.

REFERENCES

Abou El Fadl, Khaled. "The Human Rights Commitment in Modern Islam." In *Human Rights and Responsibilities in the World Religions*, ed. J. Runzo, Nancy M. Martin, and A. Sharma, 301–65. Oxford: Oneworld Publications, 2002.

al-Kawthari, M. "Islam's Position on Prevalent Forms of Insurance: Fatwa No. 383." Qibla. http://spa.qibla.com/issue_view.asp?HD=1&ID=383&CATE=43.

al-Qudah, M. "Offering Medical-Health Insurance: Fatwa Number 77826." amjaonline.org, http://www.amjaonline.org/fatwa-77826/info.

———. "Health Benefits [*sic*] in Canada: *Fatwā* No. 83603." http://www.amjaonline.org/fatwa-83603/info.

al-Sawy, S. "Getting Health Insurance for Family Coming to Visit: Fatwa No. 23107." amjaonline.org, http://www.amjaonline.org/fatwa-23107/info.

American Muslim Health Professionals (AMHP). "About Us." http://amhp.us/aboutus/#OurHistory.

———. "AMHP Lauds Supreme Court Decision." http://amhp.us/american-muslim-health-professionals-lauds-supreme-court/.

———. *Muslim Health Professionals from across the Nation Meet with the Senate and Congress*. Palantine, IL: AMHP, 2009.

———. *Principles of Health Care Reform*, ed. American Muslim Health Professionals. Palantine, IL: AMHP.

Aramesh, Kiarash. "The Influences of Bioethics and Islamic Jurisprudence on Policy-Making in Iran." *American Journal of Bioethics* 7, no. 10 (October 8, 2007): 42–44.

Asad, Muhammad. *The Message of the Qur'an*. Mecca and Zurich: Muslim World League, European Representative, Islamic Foundation, 1964.

askamufti.com. "Fatwa Center of America." http://askamufti.com.

Assembly of Muslim Jurists of America (AMJH). "Assembly of Muslim Jurists of America." http://amjaonline.com.

Atighetchi, Dariusch. *Islamic Bioethics: Problems and Perspectives*. International Library of Ethics, Law, and the New Medicine, vol. 31. New York: Springer, 2007.

Brockopp, J. E. "Justice and Injustice 3:69–74." In *The Encyclopedia of the Qur'ān*, ed. J. McAuliffe, 69–74. Washington, DC: Brill Online, 2015.

Brody, H., and A. Macdonald. "Religion and Bioethics: Toward an Expanded Understanding." *Theoretical Medical Bioethics* 34, no. 2 (April 2013).

Brown, D. "Islamic Ethics in Comparative Perspective." *Muslim World* 89, no. 2 (1999).

Cainkar, L. "The Impact of 9/11 on Muslims and Arabs in the United States." In *The Maze of Fear: Security and Migration after September 11*, ed. J. Tirman, 215–39. New York: New Press, 2004.

cnbc.com. "Medical Bills Are the Biggest Cause of US Bankruptcies: Study." http://www.cnbc.com/id/100840148.

Council on American-Islamic Relations. "The Status of Muslim Civil Rights in the United States 2005: Unequal Protection." *Jurist* (May 11, 2005), x.

Emon, A. M. *Islamic Natural Law Theories*. New York: Oxford University Press, 2010.

———. "On Islam and Islamic Natural Law: A Response to the International Theological Commisson's 'Look at Natural Law.'" In *Searching for a Universal Ethic*, ed. John Berkman and William C Mattison. Grand Rapids, MI: Eerdmans, 2011.

Fadel, M. "The True, the Good, and the Reasonable: The Theological and Ethical Roots of Public Reason in Islamic Law." *Canadian Journal of Law and Jurisprudence* 21, no. 1 (2008): 5–69.

Fairclough, Norman. "A Dialectical-Relational Approach to Critical Discourse Analysis in Social Research." In *Methods of Critical Discourse Analysis*, ed. Ruth Wodack and Michael Meyer. Introducting Qualitative Methods. London: Sage Publications, 2009.

———. *Discourse and Social Change*. Cambridge, UK, and Cambridge, MA: Polity Press, 1992.

———. "A Faith-Inspired Vision of Health Care." Vision Statement. faithfulreform.org.

———. Faithful Reform in Health Care. "About Us." http://www.faithfulreform.org/index.php?option=com_content&task=view&id=13&Itemid=77.

———. "A Moral Vision for Our Healthcare Future." Ed. Faithful Reform in Health Care. Cleveland, OH: Faithful Reform in Healthcare, 2010.

———. "Perspectives." http://www.faithfulreform.org/index.php?option=com_content&task=view&id=136&Itemid=162.

Fiqh Council of North America (FCNA). "Fiqh Council of North America." fiqhcouncil.org.

Ghaly, Mohammed. "Milk Banks through the Lens of Muslim Scholars: One Text in Two Contexts." *Bioethics* 26, no. 3 (2012): 117–27.

———. "Organ Donation and Muslims in the Netherlands: A Transnational Fatwa in Focus." *Recht Van De Islam* 26 (2012): 39–52.

———. "Religio-Ethical Discussions on Organ Donation among Muslims in Europe: An Example of Transnational Islamic Bioethics." *Medicine, Health Care, and Philosophy* 15 (2012): 207–20.

Gitsels-van der Wal, Janneke T., Judith Manniën, Mohammed M. Ghaly, Pieternel S. Verhoeven, Eileen K. Hutton, and Hans S. Reinders. "The Role of Religion in Decision-Making on Antenatal Screening of Congenital Anomalies: A Qualitative Study amongst Muslim Turkish Origin Immigrants." *Midwifery* 30, no. 3 (March 1, 2014): 297–302.

Inhorn, M. C. "Globalization and Gametes: Reproductive 'Tourism,' Islamic Bioethics and Middle Eastern Modernity." *Anthropology of Medicine* 18, no. 1 (April 2011): 87–103.

Jonsen, A. R. "A History of Religion and Bioethics." In *Handbook of Bioethics and Religion*, ed. David E. Guinn, 23–36. Oxford: Oxford University Press, 2006.

Kahf, M. "Fatawa on Insurance." 2002. http://monzer.kahf.com/fatawa/2000–2002/FATAWA_INSURANCE.pdf.

Kaiser Commision on Medicaid and the Uninsured. "Key Facts about the Uninsured Population." Henry J. Kaiser Family Foundation. http://kff.org/uninsured/fact-sheet/key-facts-about-the-uninsured-population/.

Kamali, Mohammad Hashim. *Principles of Islamic Jurisprudence*. 3rd rev. and enl. ed. Cambridge: Islamic Texts Society, 2003.

Karamali, Hamza. "Questions about Taqlid and Ijtihad." Qibla. http://spa.qibla.com/issue_view.asp?HD=3&ID=1568&CATE=389.

Kobeisy, Ahmed. "Materials for Muslim Prayer and Study." http://covertheuninsured.org/materials/files/2007/InterfaithMuslimPrayerStudy.pdf.

Moosa, E. "The Dilemma of Islamic Rights Schemes." *Worlds and Knowledges Otherwise*, Fall 2004, 1–25.

———. "Muslim Ethics and Biotechnology." In *The Routledge Companion to Religion and Science*, ed. Gregory R. Peterson, James W. Haag, and Michael L. Spezio, 455–65. New York: Routledge Taylor and Francis Group, 2012.

———. "Translating Neuroethics: Reflections from Muslim Ethics; Commentary on 'Ethical Concepts and Future Challenges of Neuroimaging: An Islamic Perspective.'" *Science and Engineering Ethics* 18, no. 3 (September 2012): 519–28.

Murray, C. J., and J. Frenk. "Ranking 37th—Measuring the Performance of the U.S. Health Care System." *New England Journal of Medicine* 362, no. 2 (January 14, 2010): 98–99.

"National Federation of Independent Business v. Sebelius." http://www.supremecourt.gov/opinions/11pdf/11-393c3a2.pdf.

O'Brien, K. "Obamacare Religious Exemption Hard to Get." http://www.religionnews.com/2014/04/28/obamacare-religious-exemption-hard-get/.

Padela, Aasim I. "Islamic Bioethics: Between Sacred Law, Lived Experiences, and State Authority." *Theoretical Medicine and Bioethics* 34, no. 2 (April 1, 2013): 65–80.

———. "Islamic Verdicts in Health Policy Discourse: Porcine-Based Vaccines as a Case Study." *Zygon* 48, no. 3 (September 2013): 655–70.

———. "Public Health Measures and Individualized Decision-Making: The Confluence of the H1n1 Vaccine and Islamic Bioethics." *Human Vaccines* 6, no. 9 (September 12, 2010).

Padela, Aasim I., and F. A. Curlin. "Religion and Disparities: Considering the Influences of Islam on the Health of American Muslims." *Journal of Religion and Health* 52, no. 4 (December 2013): 1333–45.

Padela, Aasim I., H. Shanawani, J. Greenlaw, H. Hamid, M. Aktas, and N. Chin. "The Perceived Role of Islam in Immigrant Muslim Medical Practice within the USA: An Exploratory Qualitative Study." *Journal of Medical Ethics* 34, no. 5 (October 8, 2008): 365–69.

Padela, Aasim I., Hasan Shanawani, and Ahsan Arozullah. "Medical Experts and Islamic Scholars Deliberating over Brain Death: Gaps in the Applied Islamic Bioethics Discourse." *Muslim World* 101, no. 1 (2011): 53–72.

Padela, Aasim I., K. Gunter, A. Killawi, and M. Heisler. "Religious Values and Healthcare Accommodations: Voices from the American Muslim Community." *Journal of General Internal Medicine* 27, no. 6 (2012): 708–15.

Permanent Committee for Scholarly Research and Ifta'. "Fatwa No. 7723." http://www.alifta.net/Search/ResultDetails.aspx?languagename=en⟨=en&view=result&fatwaNum=true&FatwaNumID=7723&ID=5664&searchScope=7&SearchScopeLevels1=&SearchScopeLevels2=&highLight=1&SearchType=EXACT&SearchMoesar=false&bookID=&LeftVal=0&RightVal=0&simple=&SearchCriteria=AnyWord&PagePath=&siteSection=1&searchkeyword=#firstKeyWordFound.

———. "The First Question of Fatwa No. 9580: Health Insurance Cards for Students in the USA." http://www.alifta.net/Search/ResultDetails.aspx?languagename=en⟨=en&view=result&fatwaNum=true&FatwaNumID=9580&ID=5665&searchScope=7&SearchScopeLevels1=&SearchScopeLevels2=&highLight=1&SearchType=EXACT&SearchMoesar=false&bookID=&LeftVal=0&RightVal=0&simple=&SearchCriteria=AnyWord&PagePath=&siteSection=1&searchkeyword=#firstKeyWordFound.

Potok, M. "FBI Reports Dramatic Spike in Anti-Muslim Hate Violence." *Huffington Post*, November 11, 2011.

Qazi, F. "Muslim Free Clinics and Health Reform." Palatine, IL: American Muslim Health Professionals, 2009.

"The Qur'an: An Encyclopedia." In *The Qur'an: An Encyclopedia*, ed. O. Leaman, 804. New York: Routledge, 2006.

Ramadan, Tariq. *Radical Reform: Islamic Ethics and Liberation*. Oxford and New York: Oxford University Press, 2008.

Reinhart, A. K. *Before Revelation: The Boundaries of Muslim Moral Thought*. SUNY Series in Middle Eastern Studies. Albany: State University of New York Press, 1995.

Rosen, A., and S. Clement. "Religious Groups Weigh in on Healthcare Reform." Washington, DC: Pew Research Center, 2009.

Sachedina, Abdulaziz Abdulhussein. *Islam and the Challenge of Human Rights.* Oxford and New York: Oxford University Press, 2009.

———. *Islamic Biomedical Ethics: Principles and Application.* Oxford and New York: Oxford University Press, 2009.

Schoen, C., S. L. Hayes, S. R. Collins, J. A. Lippa, and D. C. Radley. "America's Underinsured: A State-by-State Look at Health Insurance Affordability Prior to the New Coverage Expansions." New York: Commonwealth Fund. http://www.commonwealthfund.org/Publications/Fund-Reports/2014/Mar/Americas-Underinsured.aspx.

Shafi, Maulana Mufti Muhammad. *Maariful Quran.* Karachi, Pakistan, 2004.

Shanawani, Hasan, and Mohammad Hassan Khalil. "Reporting on 'Islamic Bioethics' in the Medical Literature: Where Are the Experts?" In *Muslim Medical Ethics: From Theory to Practice*, ed. Jonathan E. Brockopp and Thomas Eich. Columbia: University of South Carolina Press, 2008.

Skovgaard-Petersen, Jakob. "A Typology of Fatwas." *Die Welt des Islams* 55, nos. 3–4 (2015): 278–85.

Starr, P. *The Social Transformation of American Medicine: The Rise of a Sovereign Profession and the Making of a Vast Industry.* New York: Basic Books, 1982.

Steinberg, Avraham. *Encyclopedia of Jewish Medical Ethics: A Compilation of Jewish Medical Law on All Topics of Medical Interest.* 3 vols. Jerusalem and New York: Feldheim, 2003.

ul Haq, Ikram. "Car Insurance, Home Insurance, Health Insurance: Fatwa No. 2921." Fatwa Center of America. http://www.askamufti.com/Answers/ViewQuestion.aspx?QuestionId=2921.

———. "Life Insurance and Health Insurance: Fatwa No. 1918." Fatwa Center for America. http://www.askamufti.com/Answers/ViewQuestion.aspx?QuestionId=1918.

———. "Medical Insurance from Employer: Fatwa No. 2516." Fatwa Center of America. http://www.askamufti.com/Answers/ViewQuestion.aspx?QuestionId=2516.

ur Rahman, M., S. Abuhasna, and F. M. Abu-Zidan. "Care of Terminally Ill Patients: An Opinion Survey among Critical Care Healthcare Providers in the Middle East." *African Health Sciences* 13, no. 4 (2013).

Walling, L. "Faith Groups Applaud the U.S. Supreme Court for Upholding the Affordable Health Care Act." Wilson, NC: FRH, Washington Interreligious Staff Community, 2012.

———. "A Moral Vision for Our Healthcare Future." Ed. Faithful Reform in Health Care. Cleveland, OH: FRH, 2010.

———. "An Open Letter to President Barack Obama and to Members of the United States Senate and House of Representatives." Cleveland, OH: Faithful Reform in Healthcare, 2010.

Western PA Coalition for Single-Payer Healthcare. "Why Is the Public Option in Danger of Stalling?" http://www.wpasinglepayer.org/PollResults.html.

Wodack, Ruth, and Michael Meyer. "Critical Discourse Analysis: History, Agenda, Theory and Methodology." In *Methods of Critical Discourse Analysis*, ed. Ruth Wodack and Michael Meyer. Introducting Qualitative Methods. London: Sage, 2009.

World Bank. "Health Expenditure, Total (% of GDP)." http://data.worldbank.org/indicator/SH.XPD.TOTL.ZS.

SEVEN

Muslim Doctors and Islamic Bioethics

Insights from a National Survey of Muslim Physicians in the United States

AASIM I. PADELA

Muslim clinicians are active participants in Islamic bioethics discourse. On the production side, many draw from the tradition to author pieces outlining Islamic bioethical positions. Some even play key roles in juridical academies. In this latter venue, Muslim clinicians assist jurists in understanding the biomedical science and technology in question and help detail the larger bioethical landscape that contextualizes the specific questions under debate. At the same time, Muslim clinicians also seek Islamic bioethical guidance. They desire to know the Islamically sanctioned boundaries of their profession: what procedures they can and cannot perform, what types of medication are licit to prescribe, and what particular virtues and mannerisms mark the "Islamic" physician.[1] The knowledge and insights gained from these roles is applied both to clinical encounters and to community settings. Most obviously, the medical practices of Muslim clinicians who are strongly informed by an Islamic ethos give life to religious teachings about interactions with patients, both Muslim and non-Muslim.[2] In community settings, Muslim physicians are also trusted resources for addressing biomedical and bioethical issues. For example, a national survey of 431 Muslim American physicians in 2012 found that over half provided health-related expertise to local community organizations outside of work.[3] It was also found that religiously inclined physicians are often sought out by community members for advice on Islamic bioethics. While Muslim clinicians can play many different roles in the Islamic bioethical discourse, there is no research, of which we are aware, that quantifies these tendencies or delineates how Muslim physicians interact with Islamic bioethics actors and literature.

Aside from better characterizing Islamic bioethics discourse by understanding the bioethics-related activities of Muslim clinicians, studying the ways in which Muslim clinicians engage with the Islamic bioethics literature helps to explicate the role of religion in physicians' behaviors. Religiosity, defined as "the extent to which an individual embraces his religion as the 'master motive,'"[4] is measured through a variety of constructs and scales and mediates the impact of a formal religious worldview on professional medical practices. A series of recent surveys have demonstrated the multiple impacts of physician religiosity on clinical practice. For example, a significant proportion of U.S. physicians are motivated to pursue medical careers out of a sense of "calling," and this sense of a religiously inflected purpose is associated with higher levels of career satisfaction and less burnout.[5] Furthermore, American primary care physicians and psychiatrists who believe that religion is an important part of their lives appear to practice in medically underserved areas, or in religiously oriented practices, more so than their colleagues.[6]

In addition to providing a set of normative beliefs about the medical profession and one's role in it, religions also provide ethical frameworks by which physicians evaluate their commitments to patients and the scope of the treatments they provide. For example, among practicing U.S. obstetrician/gynecologists, those with high levels of religiosity when compared to those with medium or low levels, as well as those who were Catholics or Protestants when compared to those with no religious affiliation, were significantly less likely to provide abortion services.[7] Similarly, practicing obstetricians and gynecologists in New York report that one of the most important factors influencing their decision not to perform abortions is their religion.[8] In the same vein, a survey of primary care physicians in the United Kingdom reported a significant difference between Christian physicians and those with no religion in their attitudes toward abortion, with the former group less likely to find abortion justifiable than the latter.[9] Given the condemnation abortion generates in religious circles, these findings illustrate how the religious views of clinicians influence the clinical services they provide. Similar associations between religiosity and a physician's recommendations of medical procedures have been observed in clinical areas such as those providing care for newborns with congenital anomalies,[10] and also end-of-life care.[11] In the first study, physicians who were more religiously active were more likely to recommend surgery for congenital anomalies than their less religiously active colleagues. The latter study found that religious physicians were less likely to recommend or implement more controversial medical procedures such as sedation to death or physician-assisted death than their less religious colleagues. Such research demonstrates that religiously informed bioethical views are important sources of variations in the provision of clinical care and that religion is a source of self-understanding for many practicing physicians.[12]

With respect to Islam and Muslims, few studies delineate the impact of Islam on physicians' bioethical attitudes and professional practices. In my interview-based study of immigrant Muslim physicians working in the United States, Islam was consistently identified as the source of their professional virtues, and Islamic bioethical teachings informed physicians' reluctance to recommend certain procedures, such as abortion. Muslim identity also fueled sociocultural conflicts with the medical community.[13] Another interview-based study of twenty clinicians in the United Kingdom reported that Muslim clinicians experienced significant ethical challenges in medicine, with professional conventions suggesting certain courses of action and religious teachings others. These clinicians often resorted to scriptural interpretation to develop Islamic bioethical guidelines for themselves.[14] Aside from regulating practice boundaries, religious views also impact clinical recommendations and advice. For example, a study of Muslim physicians in Saudi Arabia found that physicians with higher levels of religiosity were more likely to share their own religious ideas and experiences with patients.[15] This finding suggests that patients' decisions about medical procedures might be influenced by their physicians' religious views. In sum, this scant research calls for more detailed studies regarding how Muslim clinicians live out their faith and how they interact with Islamic bioethics literature and other stakeholders. In this chapter I start to fill in these gaps by presenting data from a national survey of American Muslim physicians to better quantify their engagement with other Islamic bioethics stakeholders (both consumers and producers) and resource materials; their perceptions regarding the importance of Islamic bioethics, as well as their familiarity with it; and their conceptions of "brain death" and dire necessity (*ḍarūra*).

METHODS

Participant Recruitment and Data Collection

Since national databases of physicians, such as the American Medical Association Masterfile, do not collect data on religious affiliation and algorithms for selecting subjects by surname or country of origin have poor specificity for identifying Muslims,[16] generating a national sample of Muslim physicians is methodologically challenging. Hence our survey drew on the membership of the largest professional Muslim health organization in the United States, the Islamic Medical Association of North America (IMANA, with 1,968 members in 2013) to generate a national pool of clinicians who self-identify with Islam.[17]

We used Dillman's Total Design Survey methodology to guide survey administration and questionnaire design.[18] A random sample of 746 participants was drawn from the 2013 membership list, and each was mailed a letter introducing the study. For letters returned undeliverable, we sought alternative addresses through postal records and the internet. After excluding members with nonworking addresses (n = 100), those no longer in the United States (n = 1), deceased persons (n = 2), those not practicing medicine (n = 17), and non-Muslims (n = 1), we mailed a questionnaire to a total of 626 potential respondents for self-administration. The first questionnaire mailing included a $2 incentive. We sent a postcard reminder ten days after the first mailing and another copy of the survey five weeks later to nonrespondents. A third survey mailing was sent approximately five weeks after the second and included the promise of a book on Islam and medicine as an additional incentive. Several weeks after the third mailing, we sent to the remaining nonrespondents a final postcard reminder that included a web address linked to an online version of the questionnaire. During the data collection period, intermittent email reminders about the study were sent via an IMANA listserv and, several weeks after the final postcard we sent a final email noting that all respondents would be entered into a raffle for an iPad.

Survey Instrument Development and Key Measures

The survey instrument drew on instruments and items available in the literature and others we created de novo. It was pilot-tested through cognitive interviews with a group of experienced Muslim and non-Muslim physician-researchers. Survey domains relevant to this chapter include (1) participants' perceptions of Islamic bioethics and their relationships with other stakeholders (this domain includes several subdomains noted below), (2) their conception of brain death, (3) their views on *ḍarūra*, (4) their religiosity, and (5) their sociodemographic characteristics.

Perceptions of Islamic bioethics and their relationships with other stakeholders

This domain was comprised of several subdomains. (1) *Participants' familiarity with Islamic bioethics and study methods* was assessed by two questions. The first was "How familiar would you say you are with Islamic bioethics?," with response choices being very, somewhat, or not at all familiar. The second question was about the methods participants used to study Islamic bioethics and was answered with a series of yes/no responses to questions about these methods, including receiving formal training in Islamic law, attending Islamic seminars and workshops either online or in person, or reading books and articles on the topic. (2) *The importance of Islamic bioethics to participants' clinical practice* was assessed with two questions. The first was "To what extent does Islamic bioethics influence your medical practice?," with responses from not at all to a great deal, and the second inquired as to whether "Islamic values influence(d) your choice of specialty," with yes/no response options. (3) *Participants' assistance of* imāms *and patients with Islamic bioethics questions* was assessed using two questions. The first asked how often participants assisted *imāms* with bioethics cases (with six response choices, from never to daily), and the second asked, "How frequently do you advise Muslim patients to seek guidance from an Islamic religious authority?" (with response options never, rarely, sometimes, and often). (4) *Participants' bioethics resource use* was measured by asking, "How often do you seek guidance from the following resources when facing an ethical challenge in medicine?" The specific resources were local *imāms*, Islamic jurists, Islamic bioethics books, Muslim clinicians, IMANA publications, Islamic *fiqh* academy opinions, and hospital ethics committees. The response options were never, rarely, sometimes, and often.

Conceptions of "brain death"

This domain was comprised of three questions recorded on a four-point level-of-agreement scale (strongly disagree to strongly agree). The first proffered that "brain death and cardiac death are the same state (i.e., both signifying a dead individual)" and thus assessed agreement with the dominant medical convention (which is reflected legally in the Uniform Determination of Death Act, which considers both states to be legal death). The second question tested participants' agreement with the statement "Brain death signifies the departure of a person's soul from the body," which incorporates the theological understanding of death as the separation of one's soul from one's body. The third question inquired about the participant's agreement with the idea that death equated to the "irreversible loss of personhood and consciousness."

Views on ḍarūra

This domain had to do with how participants translated the Islamic ethico-legal maxim *al-ḍarūrāt tubīḥ al-maḥẓurāt* (dire necessity overturns prohibitions) into the clinical realm.[19] Accordingly, five case scenarios were constructed that focused on ethically controversial procedures. These cases described Muslim patients faced with the decision of whether to pursue procedures that are normatively proscribed in Islam (tubal ligation, abortion, porcine-based vaccination, receipt of a pelvic exam by a male clinician) or one that is debated by scholars (kidney transplantation).[20]

These procedures may become permissible according to Islamic law under conditions of dire necessity (*ḍarūra*). The clinical context for each of these cases entailed a possible extenuating circumstance that might qualify as a medical necessity and/or represent a life threat. The participants were asked whether the scenario qualified as a medical necessity or represented a life threat in order to assess which they thought demonstrated *ḍarūra*. A "do not know" option was included along with yes and no responses. Importantly, the definition of "ethico-legal maxim" was provided prior to each scenario. The case histories follow.

- Tubal Ligation Scenario: HA is a 36-year-old Muslim female patient who was diagnosed with dilated cardiomyopathy associated with severe heart failure. The patient's OB/GYN physician advised her to undergo surgical sterilization (bilateral tubal ligation) to prevent conception in the future.
- Abortion Scenario: SM is a 30-year-old Muslim female who has been diagnosed with leukemia and is on intensive chemotherapy. The patient is found to be pregnant at a stage where according to Islamic tradition fetal ensoulment has already occurred. The hematology/oncology and obstetrics/gynecology physicians recommend an abortion.
- Kidney Transplant Scenario: BA is a 46-year-old Muslim male patient with chronic renal failure on hemodialysis for the last 10 years. The patient's condition is deteriorating because of frequent catheter infections. The patient's physician recommends a kidney transplant.
- Porcine-Based Vaccine Scenario: There is an influenza outbreak. Although no deaths have been reported, the Centers for Disease Control is recommending that all individuals without contraindications be vaccinated. The only vaccination available contains porcine components.
- Pelvic Exam Scenario: LS is a 30-year-old Muslim female who comes to the emergency department with a fever and vaginal discharge. There are no female physicians available to care for this patient.

Participants' religiosity

Survey items assessed *religious importance* and *religious practice*. *Religious importance* was assessed by the question "How important would you say your religion is in your life?"[21] This question has been used in multiple physician surveys assessing religion-associated variations in physicians' clinical practices.[22] Five items inquired about *religious practice*. The first three assessed the frequency with which participants (1) attended congregational worship, (2) performed Islamic ritual prayers, and (3) read the Qur'an. Each of these was a slightly modified version of items that have been used widely to assess Islamic religiosity. The fourth assessed the extent to which the participant keeps the Ramadan fasts (strictly to not at all). Additionally, we constructed a fifth item to assess participants' adherence to guidelines around meat consumption (participants reported whether they would eat meat slaughtered according to Islamic law [*dhabīha*], kosher meat, any meat save for pork, or did not eat meat).

Sociodemographic characteristics

The questionnaire captured standard physician sociodemographic descriptors such as gender, age, ethnicity/race, state of residence, location of medical school, and immigration status, as well as practice-level data that included years in medical practice and medical specialty. Religious affiliation was also recorded.

Data Analysis

Descriptive analyses are reported below using means for continuous data and frequencies and percentages for categorical data. Responses to the vignette questions are reported as frequencies and percentages. Response categorizes were dichotomized or collapsed for ease of interpretation when appropriate.

RESULTS

Participants' Sociodemographic Characteristics

Two hundred fifty-five physicians completed the survey (a 41 percent response rate). The mean age of respondents was 52 years. Most respondents were male (70 percent), South Asian (70 percent), and adult migrants to the United States (64 percent). Muslim patients' panels comprised a very small proportion (less than 14 percent) of the overwhelming majority's (87 percent) patient panels. (See table 7.1.)

TABLE 7.1 Physicians' Characteristics (N = 255)

Characteristic[a]	N	%
Age in years (Mean ± SD) (n = 238)	52.0 ± 15.8	
24–39	66	(27.7)
40–55	58	(24.4)
56–69	76	(31.9)
70–84	38	(16.0)
Gender (n = 246)		
Male	172	(69.9)
Race/ethnicity (n = 247)		
Arab	54	(21.9)
South Asian	172	(69.6)
Residency status (n = 247)		
Immigrated as a child/born in U.S.A.	86	(34.8)
Immigrated as an adult	158	(64.0)
Completed medical school in the U.S. (n = 243)	77	(31.7)
Primary medical specialty (n = 241)		
Primary care specialty	72	(29.9)
Internal medicine subspecialty	43	(17.8)
Surgical subspecialty	30	(12.4)
Obstetrics/gynecology	13	(5.4)
Psychiatry	13	(5.4)
Percentage of patients who are Muslim		
0–5	5	(2.1)
1–14	206	(85.1)
15–28	15	(6.2)
29–98	16	(6.6)

Source: Author's compilation.

[a] The sum of the subcategories does not equal n because the "other" categories were dropped.

Participants' Religiosity Profiles

The overwhelming majority of participants identified as Sunni Muslims (91 percent) (table 7.2). Most felt religion was the most important or a very important part of their lives (89 percent) and strictly performed Ramadan fasting (85 percent). The majority also reported praying five times daily (63 percent). There was considerable variability in participants'

TABLE 7.2 Religiosity Profiles of Participants ($N = 255$)

Characteristic[a]	*No.*	*(%)*
Religious affiliation within Islam ($n = 244$)		
Sunni	222	(91.0)
Shia	11	(4.50)
Importance of religion in respondent's life ($n = 254$)		
The most important part	136	(53.5)
Very important	90	(35.4)
Fairly important	25	(9.80)
Not at all important	3	(1.20)
Frequency of attendance at congregational worship service ($n = 251$)		
More than once a year but less often than once a month	59	(23.5)
More than once a month but less often than several times a week	128	(51.0)
Several times a week or daily	64	(25.5)
Frequency of performing ritual prayers ($n = 251$)		
Never/at least once a week but less often than once a day	28	(11.2)
At least once a day but less often than five times a day	65	(25.9)
Five times a day	158	(62.9)
Observance of Ramadan fast ($n = 253$)		
Not at all	7	(2.80)
Somewhat	31	(12.3)
Strictly	215	(85.0)
Frequency of reading the Qur'an outside of prayer ($n = 251$)		
Never/on special occasions	90	(35.9)
Weekly or less often	82	(32.7)
Daily	79	(31.5)
Dietary practices ($n = 248$)		
Not religious	14	(5.70)
Fairly religious	96	(38.7)
Very religious	74	(29.8)
Most religious	64	(25.8)

Source: Author's compilation.

[a]The sum of the subcategories does not equal n where another category was dropped.

frequency of attending congregational prayers, habits of reading the Qur'an, and dietary practices.

Participants' Perceptions of Islamic Bioethics and Their Relationships with Other Stakeholders

With respect to *familiarity with Islamic bioethics and study methods*, most respondents felt somewhat familiar with Islamic bioethics (63 percent) (table 7.3a). The preferred method of studying Islamic bioethics was reading books and articles (61 percent) rather than attending seminars and workshops (45 percent), and almost none of the participants sought formal Islamic law degrees (fewer than 1 percent). In terms of the *importance of Islamic bioethics in clinical practice*, a third (33 percent) felt Islamic bioethics greatly impacted their medical practices, with over a quarter responding somewhat (26 percent). Similarly, over a quarter reported choosing their clinical specialty in light of Islamic values (29%). With respect to *assisting* imāms *and patients with Islamic bioethics questions*, over three-quarters (77%) never assisted *imāms* and most never or rarely advised patients to seek Islamic authorities on the matter (60%). Finally, in terms of *bioethics resource use*, the majority of respondents (59 percent) sometimes or often sought the advice of fellow Muslim clinicians, and nearly half (45 percent) sought

TABLE 7.3a Participants' Perceptions of Islamic Bioethics and Relationships with Other Stakeholders ($N = 255$)

Characteristic	*No.*	*(%)*
Islamic Bioethics Familiarity and Study Methods		
Familiarity with Islamic bioethics ($n = 253$)		
Not at all familiar	37	(14.7)
Somewhat familiar	159	(62.7)
Very familiar	57	(22.6)
Study of Islamic bioethics by		
Seeking a formal degree in Islamic law ($n = 254$)	2	(0.80)
Attending Islamic bioethics seminars and workshops ($n = 254$)	113	(44.5)
Reading books and articles on Islamic bioethics ($n = 254$)	154	(60.5)

(*continues*)

TABLE 7.3a *Continued*

Importance of Islamic Bioethics to Clinical Practice		
None at all	44	(17.5)
A little	59	(23.5)
Somewhat	67	(26.3)
A great deal	82	(32.7)
Islamic values influenced specialty choice (*n* = 249)	71	(28.5)
Assisting Imāms *and Patients with Islamic Bioethics Questions*		
Frequency of assisting *Imāms* with bioethics cases (*n* = 252)		
Never	192	(76.6)
A few times a year or less often	46	(18.3)
Monthly or more often	13	(5.17)
Frequency of advising patients to seek guidance from an Islamic jurist (*n* = 251)		
Never	68	(27.2)
Rarely	83	(33.2)
Sometimes	64	(25.6)
Often	36	(14.0)

Source: Author's compilation.

TABLE 7.3b Use of Bioethics Resources (*N* = 255)

Characteristic	*No.*	*(%)*
Frequency of seeking guidance from		
Imāms at local mosques when facing a bioethics challenge (*n* = 249)		
Never	113	(45.4)
Rarely	65	(26.1)
Sometimes	59	(23.4)
Often	12	(4.83)
Islamic jurists when facing a bioethics challenge (*n* = 250)		
Never	106	(42.4)
Rarely	56	(22.4)
Sometimes	68	(27.2)
Often	20	(8.00)

(continues)

TABLE 7.3b *Continued*

Islamic bioethics books when facing a bioethics challenge (*n* = 244)		
Never	86	(35.2)
Rarely	48	(19.7)
Sometimes	80	(32.8)
Often	30	(12.3)
Other Muslim physicians when facing a bioethics challenge (*n* = 248)		
Never	52	(21.0)
Rarely	49	(19.8)
Sometimes	117	(47.4)
Often	30	(11.7)
Hospital ethics committee(s) when facing a bioethics challenge (*n* = 246)		
Never	64	(26.0)
Rarely	70	(28.5)
Sometimes	77	(31.3)
Often	35	(14.2)
Specialist *fiqh* academies when facing a bioethics challenge (*n* = 247)		
Never	139	(56.3)
Rarely	56	(22.7)
Sometimes	41	(16.6)
Often	11	(4.50)
IMANA publications when facing a bioethics challenge (*n* = 245)		
Never	123	(50.4)
Rarely	50	(24.2)
Sometimes	47	(18.9)
Often	16	(6.6)

Source: Author's compilation.

out hospital ethics committees (table 7.3b). Islamic bioethics-related books were used sometimes or often by nearly half of the group (45 percent). On the other hand, all other resources were infrequently sought for guidance. Islamic jurists were never or rarely sought out by the majority of participants (65 percent), nor were local *imāms* (71 percent). Nearly three quarters

TABLE 7.4a Conceptions of Brain Death

Belief	*No.*	*(%)*
Brain death and cardiac death are the same state (n = 246)		
Strongly disagree	27	(11.0)
Disagree	87	(35.4)
Agree	86	(35.0)
Strongly agree	46	(18.7)
Brain death signifies the departure of a person's soul (n = 243)		
Strongly disagree	26	(10.7)
Disagree	96	(39.5)
Agree	87	(35.8)
Strongly agree	34	(14.0)
Death is the irreversible loss of personhood and consciousness (n = 245)		
Strongly disagree	31	(12.7)
Disagree	110	(44.9)
Agree	75	(30.6)
Strongly agree	29	(11.8)

Source: Author's compilation.

never or rarely looked to IMANA publications (74 percent), and the overwhelming majority never or rarely referred to the bioethical opinions of specialized *fiqh* academies (79 percent).

Conceptions of "Brain Death"

Over half of the respondents agreed that brain death and cardiac death are the same state (54 percent); yet almost half disagreed (46 percent) (table 7.4a). Similarly, half saw brain death as signifying the departure of the soul (50 percent), but half did not (50 percent). More than half (58 percent) viewed death as the irreversible loss of personhood and consciousness.

Views on *Ḍarūra* (Dire Necessity)

In response to the tubal ligation scenario, over half of respondents saw the procedure as a medical necessity (57 percent), while the overwhelming majority viewed continued pregnancy in the face of cardiomyopathy as a life

TABLE 7.4b Views on *Ḍarūra* (Dire Necessity and Life Threat) (N = 255)

	Tubal Ligation Scenario N (%)	*Abortion Scenario N (%)*	*Kidney Transplant Scenario N (%)*	*Vaccination Scenario N (%)*	*Pelvic Exam Scenario N (%)*
Medical Necessity					
Yes	145 (57.1)	113 (44.8)	226 (89.0)	155 (61.2)	223 (88.1)
No	78 (30.7)	68 (27.0)	20 (7.90)	82 (32.4)	19 (7.5)
Do not know	31 (12.2)	71 (28.1)	8 (3.16)	16 (6.30)	11 (4.4)
Life Threat					
Yes	206 (81.1)	123 (49.2)	140 (55.8)	154 (61.1)	63 (25.1)
No	14 (5.50)	52 (20.8)	79 (31.1)	74 (29.3)	152 (60.2)
Do not know	34 (13.4)	75 (30.0)	33 (13.1)	24 (9.50)	37 (14.7)

Source: Author's compilation.

threat (81 percent) (table 7.4b). Responding to the scenario involving a physician's recommendation of abortion in order for the patient to obtain intensive chemotherapy, almost half of respondents viewed the situation as involving a life threat (49 percent) for the patient and as making abortion a medical necessity (45 percent). In the scenario involving a kidney transplant for kidney failure, nearly all viewed organ transplantation as a medical necessity (89 percent), but just slightly over half saw continued hemodialysis as a life threat (56 percent). For the scenario involving seeking porcine-based vaccines for the flu, the majority saw the scenario involving a medical necessity (61 percent) and as a life threat (61 percent). In the scenario entailing a pelvic examination of a Muslim female by a male clinician, nearly all respondents viewed examination as a medical necessity (89 percent), yet only a quarter saw vaginal discharge as a life threat (25 percent).

DISCUSSION

This first-of-its-kind national survey of Muslim physicians' engagement with Islamic bioethics provides key insights into demographic characteristics and habits of this group. In what follows I would like to comment on several of the more salient findings.

American Muslim Physicians Have High Levels of Religiosity

By and large, the respondent pool deemed religion an important part of their lives. The majority were also regular in their worship practices, strictly adhered to the obligatory fasts of Ramadan, and performed the ritual prayer five times daily. While there was greater variance among the group in performing nonobligatory forms of worship such as reading the Qur'an outside of prayer or attending congregational services, over a quarter were regular in such practices as well. This sample's high level of religiosity might be attributable to selection bias; sampling physicians from the Islamic Medical Association of North America may have skewed our participant pool's religiosity profile, and this is a limitation of our study. Since this organization likely draws its membership from more religiously inclined clinicians, our data may not accurately reflect the general population of Muslim American physicians and should be interpreted with caution. However, our respondent pool was similar in religiosity to that of another national study of American Muslim physicians in which physicians were not sampled from religious organizations.[23] Considering this important similarity, these data suggest that Muslim physicians in the United States are highly religious.

Moreover, it appears that Muslim physicians might be more religious than the general American Muslim population. Illustratively, a 2011 population-based survey of American Muslims revealed that 81 percent attended a mosque more often than once a month (47 percent at least weekly and 34 percent once or twice a month or a few times a year),[24] and a 2008 poll found that 41 percent attended a mosque at least weekly.[25] In comparison, 76 percent of our sample attended a mosque monthly or more often. The same surveys find that 69 to 80 percent of American Muslims rate Islam as "important" in their lives,[26] yet 89 percent of the physicians in our study indicated that Islam is a "very important" or "the most important" part of their lives.

Perhaps more significant is that American Muslim physicians appear to have higher levels of participatory religiosity than their non-Muslim counterparts. A nationally representative survey of physicians in the United States conducted in the early 2000s found that 54 percent attended religious services *less* often than once a month, compared to only 24 percent of our sample.[27] Interestingly, however, physicians (both

Muslim and non-Muslim) appear to attend worship services more often than the general population.

American Muslim Physicians Engage with Islamic Bioethics Literature and Producers Only to a Slight Degree

Given the high levels of religiosity of respondents, we anticipated that participants would be very familiar with Islamic bioethics, find it important to their practice, and have high levels of engagement with other Islamic bioethics stakeholders. The data, however, suggests several different, and potentially conflicting, stories. For one thing, most respondents reported being somewhat familiar with Islamic bioethics (63 percent), and nearly another quarter (23 percent) reported being very familiar with Islamic bioethics. This familiarity with the field appears to come from their reading of books and articles on the subject, since the majority of respondents use this method for study of religious bioethics (61 percent). Yet, while more than half read books and are familiar with the subject, only a third believe that Islamic bioethics greatly impacts their clinical practices (33 percent). And only about a quarter indicated that Islamic values influenced their choice of a clinical specialty (29 percent).

There may be several explanations for these findings. It could be that "Islamic" considerations come into play at the margins of practice and surround controversial treatments and thus the influence of Islamic bioethics on clinical medicine is modest. This line of reasoning is supported by the fact that much of the extant literature on Islamic bioethics, particularly articles on Medline, which are the most readily available to clinicians, present Islamic ethico-legal perspectives on topics such as abortion, organ transplant, and end-of-life care. While these areas generate ethical controversy, the daily clinical practice of most clinicians does not involve these procedures. Indeed, a minority of our sample, and doctors in general, were obstetrician/gynecologists, surgeons, or critical-care physicians who would deal with these ethically charged procedures routinely. Further supporting this view is the finding that a minority saw Islamic values as informing their choice of specialty. A related explanation is that Muslim clinicians do not see the importance of "Islamic" bioethics to their practice because they associate Islamic bioethics with legal injunctions (as this is the dominant genre of the field) and not with virtue cultivation or other ethical dimensions of medical practice. Another interpretation can be advanced as a critique of the extant Islamic bioethics literature. Chapters in this volume have outlined shortcomings and gaps in Islamic bioethics writings, so the fact that Muslim clinicians report being familiar with and reading the literature yet do not find that it influences their practice may be because the writings are not sufficiently practical and thus do not impact clinical care delivery. Or the literature may be unconvincing in other ways so that Muslim clinicians do not find it impactful in their practices.

When American Muslim clinicians face bioethical dilemmas, the minority seek out Islamic experts or Islamic bioethics resources. This finding was unexpected, as we had assumed that our religiously inclined sample would consult such individuals and materials more often. The finding may result from Muslim clinicians' feeling secure in their own Islamic bioethics knowledge, as most perceived themselves to be somewhat or very familiar with the subject. Indeed, further analyses of our data demonstrate statistically significant differences in resource use between those who feel somewhat or very familiar with Islamic bioethics and those who report not being familiar with the field. Physicians who perceive themselves to be somewhat or very familiar with Islamic bioethics are less likely to seek the assistance of *imāms*, jurists, or *fiqh* academy rulings when faced with bioethics challenges than those who consider themselves unfamiliar with Islamic bioethics. Indeed, it appears that Muslim clinicians trust in the Islamic bioethics knowledge of their professional guild, as other Muslim clinicians were the most common resources sought for bioethical advice. This interpretation aligns with our unexpected finding that Islamic jurists, local *imāms*, and the bioethics-related verdicts of Islamic *fiqh* academies were consulted "often" by fewer than 10 percent of respondents. These data points underscore the discursive "silo" in which Muslim clinicians remain.

Only two respondents had engaged in formal study of Islamic law, and the fact that only a small minority interacted with experts in Islamic law and juridical rulings when facing bioethical challenges suggests that Muslim doctors may not find value in these "legal" perspectives of Islamic bioethics. This finding somewhat coheres with an in-depth analysis of the writings on Islamic bioethics undertaken by Hasan Shanawani and Mohammad Khalil. In it they reviewed 112 papers that represented more than fifty years of Islamic bioethics papers in Medline (overwhelmingly authored by Muslim clinicians) and found that the Qur'an was most often cited ($n = 55$) as the basis for the Islamic bioethical perspectives offered. On the other hand, Islamic legal devices and constructs (e.g., *qiyās*) were referenced by a very small minority ($n = 18$).[28] Thus it appears that Muslim clinicians may confidently draw on the Qur'an for ethical values but are less familiar with, or attach less importance to, the constructs and devices of Islamic law. Similarly, in "all of the articles there were fewer than thirty references to statements made by a Muslim professional society, Shariah council, or other organization with a professed interest in or focus on either medicine or Islamic law."[29] This finding aligns with ours in that Muslim physicians appear to "go it alone" and do not read or engage with the writings of juridical academies or even the ethics publications of their own medical organization (IMANA). On these bases, Shanawani and Khalil conclude that "few professionals [Muslim clinicians] with an interest in Islamic bioethics are turning to organized forums of discourse" for guidance and knowledge.[30] Our data lends support to their finding, as the majority of our sample does not engage with such resources when confronting ethical challenges in medicine. Given the above, it is not surprising that our respondents rarely assist *imāms* with bioethics cases and rarely refer Muslim patients to Islamic jurists for Islamic bioethical advice.

In my view, these findings are profoundly troubling. As I have argued elsewhere, a multidisciplinary approach is needed to derive Islamic bioethical opinions. Islamic ethico-legal pronouncements regarding the permissibility of a certain technology or procedure requires an in-depth understanding of the biomedical science involved, as well as the social implications of the procedure or technology in question. When jurists issue verdicts without the input of relevant biomedical and social scientists, their judgements are often imprecise and unable to be acted upon in clinical practice.[31] At the same time, when physicians do not have knowledge of Islamic theology and law and/or do not consult Islamic scholars for such input, they neglect critically important ethical considerations and may misrepresent Islamic ethics and law.[32] Consequently, if jurists, physicians, and other experts were to come together to assess the "Islamic" position on a biomedical issue, the group together would better understand the problem at hand and offer a more holistic bioethical perspective.

By neglecting *fiqh* academies and other bodies that involve multidisciplinary Islamic bioethical deliberation, Muslim physicians ignore potentially beneficial sources of ethical guidance. And by not helping *imāms* with bioethics cases or advising patients to seek out other Islamic ethics experts, they might perpetuate incomplete understandings and render ineffectual guidance.

Muslim Physicians Are "Polarized" on Brain Death

According to the Uniform Determination of Death Act, brain death and cardiac death are considered equivalent in the United States. In other words, this equivalence is sanctioned both by medical convention and by law. Despite this, nearly half of Muslim clinicians disagreed with this view (46 percent). In turn, half of the respondents (50 percent) held that brain death did not correspond to a religious understanding of death whereby the soul detaches from the body.[33] On the other hand, nearly half held the opposite view, that brain death signified the soul's departure from the body and was equivalent to cardiac death. Furthermore, those who disagreed that brain death was equivalent to cardiac death were more likely to view brain death as not signifying departure of the soul, and vice versa (data analyses not shown). Among respondents, slightly less than half (42 percent) held that death is the irreversible loss of personhood and consciousness, perhaps being more comfortable with death's being tied to personhood through the notion of brain death than it being tied to a metaphysical event.

These data suggest that there are two camps in the American Muslim clinician community, one ascribing to the medical convention about brain death and the other abjectly disagreeing. Now, one may assert that this ambivalence toward brain death reflects the juridical ambivalence toward brain death. Some Islamic jurists and academies consider brain death to be legal death in Islam, others hold it to represent a dying but not dead state, and still others consider a patient in this state to be fully living.[34] However, we know that our sample rarely looks to the outputs of Islamic juridical academies, and thus the source of polar opinions among clinicians is not *fiqh*. Future studies should examine how Muslim clinicians reason that brain death does or does not indicate the departure of the soul and why it is or is not equivalent to cardiac death. Such data would shine light on the interplay between biomedical and theological understandings in the minds of practicing doctors.

It is more important, perhaps, to examine how these views implicate medical practice and bioethical advice. In other words, do Muslim clinicians who disagree that brain death indicates the departure of the soul claim they are acting according to conscience when they refuse to withdraw life support from a patient who meets the criteria for neurological death? Or do they withdraw life support anyway? Alternatively, do these clinicians advise families to continue "futile" care or to hope for miracles? Furthermore, what advice do these clinicians offer community members about beating-heart organ donation, that is, organ donation when a patient is in a brain-dead state? Do clinicians who agree that brain death indicates the departure of the soul support organ donation, and those who do not, disagree? These and other questions merit further investigation.

This data is also relevant to collective Islamic bioethical deliberation among jurists and clinicians. It is curious that all the physicians who provided testimony on brain death at the meetings of the Islamic Organization for Medical Science as well as the Organisation of Islamic Cooperation's *Fiqh* Academy agreed that brain death was death proper. They voiced one position even though the medical academy at the time was debating, and continues to debate, the significance and accuracy of brain-death diagnoses.[35] Moreover, it was this consensus that influenced some jurists to consider that brain death meets the threshold for legal death in Islam. One wonders whether the ambivalence over brain death today would be reason for Islamic jurists to reconsider their views on brain death. Furthermore, this story underscores the fact that jurists rely on clinicians to accurately portray the biomedical science and clinical context of brain death. Given the importance of such "testimony," having multiple different viewpoints represented at the dialogue table is critical for those present to have accurate conceptualizations of the state of the science and clinical practice.

Another chapter in this volume comments on brain death and plays on the clinical uncertainty about brain death. Dr. Stodolsky and Shaykh Kholwadia argue that Muslim clinicians overstepped their bounds in the aforementioned Islamic *fiqh* academies and that Islamic jurists incorrectly deferred the matter of deciding when death occurs to clinicians. Specifically, they say, "Even though the only type of *ijtihād* (Islamic ethico-legal reasoning) that physicians are capable of doing is *taḥqīq al-manāṭ* (certification that the criteria for a ruling are present), the proponents entrust them with *takhrīj al-manāṭ*, or, in other words, determining the criterion based not on the *Sunna* of the Prophet and the Companions, but on medical practice." They argue that Islamic bioethics cannot admit a biomedical understanding of death even though they concede that there is no definitive scriptural text that indicates signs of death. Instead, they suggest that the views of classical Islamic jurists must be taken into account. They argue that "all four extant Sunni legal schools agreed upon certainty as the criterion for the determination of death when there is doubt" and that, since brain death is an uncertain state—that is, its diagnosis and the resulting prognosis are not 100 percent certain—Muslim clinicians are morally obligated *not* to declare brain-dead patients dead. One could complicate this view by marshalling evidence that Islamic law, for the most part, considers dominant probability and not certainty sufficient grounds for rulings.[36] Thus, if the epidemiological data and diagnostic certainty of brain death accord with dominant probability, these could serve as admissible criteria for death, particularly when no scriptural indicants conclusively determine the matter. Indeed, such an argument was advanced by jurists at the Islamic *fiqh* academies. My point is not to respond to these authors' arguments, but rather to underscore that Islamic bioethical perspectives on brain death still remain to be worked out.

Indeed, Professor Moosa takes a different approach to the conundrum by leaving the legal register and instead focusing on the question of personhood on several Islamic ontological, epistemological, metaphysical registers. He concludes his analyses by arguing that the spirit-soul complex serves a body that has full integrity and that when the body is irreversibly damaged it is no longer tenable to conclude that the soul subsists. Thus, death can faithfully be ascertained by indicators of the brain's function and that a brain-dead organism is identical to a corpse, except for the fact that techno-science allows us to simulate life in it. Moosa's idea of tying death to loss of personhood bears resemblance to arguments Professor Sachedina makes on the same topic,[37] and also secular advocates for definitions of death based on loss of higher brain functions.

Our data seems to suggest that a lesser proportion of Muslim physicians may agree with the idea that death equates to the irreversible loss of personhood and consciousness than do to the idea that brain death equates to the departure of the soul. But neurological criteria for death ("brain death") represents the irreversible loss of consciousness according to the limits of present-day biomedical technology and understanding. Hence, our data is unclear as to what exactly Muslim clinicians understand the physiological state of brain death to represent and what their views are on the relationships between the metaphysical soul and the physical brain in such a state.

Consequently, this area remains one that requires bringing together multidisciplinary perspectives. When trying to understand and evaluate the moral significance of the brain-dead individual, Islamic jurists and biomedical scientists must engage each other with epistemic humility given that there are ambiguities on the matter within their own respective disciplines. Perhaps, as a report from the Prophet states, the plurality of views reflects God's mercy upon mankind,[38] and Muslim clinicians, patients, and families can treat the multiple different ethico-legal rulings as actionable.

Muslim Physicians May Not See Medical Necessity and Life Threat as Equivalent

Clinical medicine involves plenty of morally charged scenarios and ethically controversial procedures. When a patient's life is at stake, there is a heightened impetus to intervene, but what if the necessary intervention contravenes the religious values of the patient or the clinician? Our survey contained such scenarios, and through it we sought to understand how Muslim clinicians might invoke the Islamic ethico-legal maxim of *al-ḍarūrāt tubīḥ al-maḥẓurāt* ("circumstances of necessity make the unlawful lawful"). We asked, in particular, how participants related the concept of medical necessity to the notion of life threat. As Islamic juridical explanations of *ḍarūra* invoke concepts of threat to life and significant harms, we were interested in whether Muslim clinicians mapped their notions of medical necessity onto the concept of *ḍarūra*. Interestingly our data reveals no consistent correlation between the two concepts in the minds of Muslim clinicians. More specifically, in the abortion and porcine-based vaccination scenarios nearly the same percentage of respondents viewed the scenarios as representing a life threat as well as a medical necessity. Yet, in the cases involving kidney transplantation and pelvic examination, the overwhelming majority (>88 percent) held that a medical necessity existed, and over half (56 percent) viewed lack of transplant as a life threat, yet only a quarter felt that vaginal discharge threatened the patient's life. The opposite trend was noted in the case involving tubal ligation, in which more clinicians saw future pregnancy as posing a life threat but did not view performing sterilization as a medical necessity. This latter case might be explained by the fact that there are other forms of preventing pregnancy, albeit not as effective. But how might one interpret the data about the other cases?

For one thing, it is reasonable to advance that the two concepts are not always equivalent in clinical practice. Some situations may represent medical necessity, others life threat, and some both. Another way to explain the variance in responses among the cases would be that when it comes to the scenarios that involve procedures that are nearly categorically forbidden, or widely assumed to be (abortion and treatment with porcine products), physicians resort to seeing life threat and medical necessity as aligned. However, when there is some ambiguity among the juridical views, as is the case when some jurists permit organ transplant and others do not or when the patient's medical condition is not severe (for example, vaginal discharge), less equivalence is perceived. Regardless of these speculations, it is important to note that there is variance among clinicians as to when a life threat exists and when a medical necessity is present. It was only in the kidney transplantation and pelvic exam scenarios that views on medical necessity where nearly uniform. Wide variance was present in all other cases.

Based on this data, some important implications for applied Islamic bioethics arise. As Dr. Stodolsky and Shaykh Kholwadia suggest, Islamic jurists defer to Muslim clinicians as to whether a particular ruling applies to a certain patient case. The passing of authority is even more pronounced when overturning normative prohibitions because of the great moral significance of the matter. In this area of ethical controversy, our data suggests that there would not be a clinical consensus on when a medical necessity or life threats exists. Such uncertainty presents a significant challenge for rendering Islamic bioethical guidance because the jurists would not have the requisite knowledge to assess the biomedical data on necessity and risk to life, and the clinicians might be uncertain or disagree about the data as well. Islamic bioethical paralysis would ensue, leaving all parties—patients, families, jurists, and clinicians—unsure about the most appropriate and Islamically sanctioned course of action.

The chapter in this volume co-authored by Professor Mohsen Ebrahim and me arguably increases the clinical boundaries of *ḍarūra*. Professor Ebrahim suggests that *ḍarūra* can be invoked to make vaccination with porcine products licit because of the known benefits vaccination has had upon global rates of mortality. He also suggests that the same argument allows for the abortion of a fetus that has contracted congenital rubella, because the medical data notes that disabilities may arise in the future child. Professor Ebrahim uses medical data about harms and benefits as the basis for invoking *ḍarūra*. While it is beyond the scope of this chapter to review the data on the harms and benefits of various vaccines and the prognoses of children born with rubella, our data suggests that clinicians could look at the same case and come to different conclusions as to whether a patient's life is under threat or medical necessity is involved.

Consequently, insofar as we would like to support the invocation of dire necessity based on a uniform interpretation of biomedical data and consensus among physicians, such consensus may be out of reach based on this survey. Aside from this concern, one could also argue that all vaccinations are not "life-saving" and a blanket ruling based on *ḍarūra* is specious. Some vaccinations reduce the duration of disease if contracted, some lessen the severity of disease, and others reduce the incidence of disease through herd immunity. Similarly, one could argue that congenital rubella is not a life threat to the mother or the fetus and that fear of disability does not serve as grounds for invoking *ḍarūra*. Regardless of these shortcomings, *ḍarūra* arguments reflect the mapping of an ethico-legal construct onto a biomedical context. For this construct to be properly applied in practice requires an understanding of the scriptural evidence for *ḍarūra*, the ethico-legal understandings of the construct, and the biomedical aspects of the clinical case. The interplay among these fields of knowledge allows for the provision of precise Islamic bioethical guidance. As I have argued elsewhere, we need to bring these types of knowledges together; epidemiological and statistical data can increase precision by giving jurists a more accurate understanding of biomedical evidence, tying notions of life threat to statistical probabilities, and clarifying when *ḍarūra* can serve as the grounds for an Islamic bioethical argument.[39]

In conclusion this first-of-its-kind national survey of Muslim physicians details their self-perceptions of Islamic bioethics knowledge, their interactions with other producers and consumers of the discourse, and their uncertainties about certain ethically controversial clinical issues. It also illustrates how these critical stakeholders of Islamic bioethics remain disconnected from other experts in the developing academic field, as well as the need for multidisciplinary engagement to provide credible "Islamic" answers to bioethical controversies.

NOTES

The survey data presented here was collected as part of a project funded by the John Templeton Foundation through the University of Chicago's Program on Medicine and Religion Faculty Scholars Program. I thank the Islamic Medical Association of North America (IMANA) for collaborating on the survey by providing access to the membership roster. Notably, I acknowledge the efforts of Rasheed Ahmed, Akrama Hashmi, and Dr. Ayaz Samadani through IMANA. I also acknowledge the following individuals for their valuable assistance: Zahra Hosseinain and Maha Ahmad for survey administration; Dr. Farr Curlin for assistance with study conceptualization, grant writing, instrument development, and survey design; Julie Johnson for data entry; Heba Abdel-Latief for literature review and survey instrument development; and Stephen Hall for survey analysis.

1. A. I. Padela et al., "The Perceived Role of Islam in Immigrant Muslim Medical Practice within the USA: An Exploratory Qualitative Study," *Journal of Medical Ethics* 34, no. 5 (2008); Thalia A. Arawi, "The Muslim Physician and the Ethics of Medicine," *Journal of the Islamic Medical Asscociation of North America* 42, no. 3 (October 26, 2010).

2. Padela et al., "The Perceived Role of Islam in Immigrant Muslim Medical Practice within the USA."

3. W. Abu-Ras, L. D. Laird, and F. Sensai, "A Window into American Muslim Physicians: Civic Engagement and Community Participation, Their Diversity, Contributions and Challenges" (Washington, DC: Institute for Social Policy and Understanding, 2012).

4. G. W. Allport and J. M. Ross, "Personal Religious Orientation and Prejudice," *Journal of Personality and Social Psychology* 5, no. 4 (1967).

5. J. D. Yoon, B. M. Daley, and F. A. Curlin, "The Association between a Sense of Calling and Physician Well-Being: A National Study of Primary Care Physicians and Psychiatrists," *Academic Psychiatry* 41, no. 2 (April 2017); A. J. Jager, M. A. Tutty, and A. C. Kao, "Association between Physician Burnout and Identification with Medicine as a Calling," *Mayo Clinical Proceedings* 92, no. 3 (March 2017).

6. J. Lio et al., "Religious Characteristics of Physicians Who Care for Underserved Populations or Work in Religiously Oriented Practices." *Southern Medical Journal* 111, no. 9 (September 2018).

7. D. B. Stulberg et al., "Abortion Provision among Practicing Obstetrician-Gynecologists," *Obstetrics and Gynecology* 118, no. 3 (September 2011).

8. A. N. Aiyer et al., "Influence of Physician Attitudes on Willingness to Perform Abortion," *Obstetrics and Gynecology* 93, no. 4 (April 1999).

9. E. Abdel-Aziz, B. N. Arch, and H. Al-Taher, "The Influence of Religious Beliefs on General Practitioners' Attitudes towards Termination of Pregnancy—a Pilot Study," *Journal of Obstetrics and Gynaecology* 24, no. 5 (August 2004).

10. I. D. Todres et al., "Pediatricians' Attitudes Affecting Decision-Making in Defective Newborns," *Pediatrics* 60, no. 2 (August 1977).

11. C. Seale, "The Role of Doctors' Religious Faith and Ethnicity in Taking Ethically Controversial Decisions during End-of-Life Care," *Journal of Medical Ethics* 36, no. 11 (November 2010); K. M. Wolenberg et al., "Religion and United States Physicians' Opinions and Self-Predicted Practices Concerning Artificial Nutrition and Hydration," *Journal of Religion and Health* 52, no. 4 (December 2013); J. Cohen et al., "Influence of Physicians' Life Stances on Attitudes to End-of-Life Decisions and Actual End-of-Life Decision-Making in Six Countries," *Journal of Medical Ethics* 34, no. 4 (April 2008).

12. F. A. Curlin et al., "Physicians' Observations and Interpretations of the Influence of Religion and Spirituality on Health," *Archives Journal of Internal Medicine* 167, no. 7 (2007); "Religion, Conscience, and Controversial Clinical Practices," *New England Journal of Medicine* 356, no. 6 (February 8, 2007); "The Association of Physicians' Religious Characteristics with Their Attitudes and Self-Reported Behaviors Regarding Religion and Spirituality in the Clinical Encounter," *Medical Care* 44, no. 5 (2006): 446–53.

13. Padela et al., "The Perceived Role of Islam in Immigrant Muslim Medical Practice within the USA."

14. Aminah Molloy, "Attitudes to Medical Ethics among British Muslim Medical Practitioners," *Journal of Medical Ethics* 6 (1980): 139–44.

15. N. A. Al-Yousefi, "Observations of Muslim Physicians Regarding the Influence of Religion on Health and Their Clinical Approach," *Journal of Religion and Health* 51, no. 2 (June 2012).

16. F. Curlin, "Ob-Gyns Approaches to Sexual and Reproductive Health Care: A National Survey, Survey Methodology Report" (Chicago: University of Chicago Program on Medicine and Religion, 2010); K. A. Rasinski, "Religion and Care of Patients with Advanced Illness at the End of Life: A National Physician Study, Survey Methodology Report" (Chicago: University of Chicago Program on Medicine and Religion, 2010).

17. IMANA is the largest professional Muslim health organization in the United States. Founded in 1968, IMANA aims to provide a networking forum and Islamic medical ethics resources on Islamic medicine for Muslim health

professionals. It maintains an active ethics committee and a publication arm that produces resources for these professionals.

18. D. A. Dillman, *Mail and Internet Surveys: The Tailored Design Method*, 2nd ed. (New York: John Wiley and Sons, 2000).

19. Sobhi Mahmassani, *Falsafat Al-Tashri' Fi Al-Islām: The Philosophy of Jurisprudence in Islam*, trans. Farhat Ziadeh (Leiden: E. J. Brill, 1961).

20. On tubal ligation, see Dariusch Atighetchi, *Islamic Bioethics: Problems and Perspectives*, International Library of Ethics, Law, and the New Medicine, vol. 31 (New York: Springer, 2007). On abortion, see Oren Asman, "Abortion in Islamic Countries—Legal and Religious Aspects," *Medicine and Law* 23, no. 1 (2004); A. Sachedina, "Islamic Bioethics," in *Religious Perspectives in Bioethics*, ed. J. F. Peppin et al. (London: Taylor and Francis, 2004): 153–71. On porcine-based vaccination, see A. I. Padela and H. Zaganjor, "Relationships between Islamic Religiosity and Attitude toward Deceased Organ Donation among American Muslims: A Pilot Study," *Transplantation*, March 18, 2014; N. M. Isa, "Darurah (Necessity) and Its Application in Islamic Ethical Assessment of Medical Applications: A Review on Malaysian Fatwa," *Science and Engineering Ethics* 22, no. 5 (2015): 1319–32. On receipt of a pelvic exam by a male clinician, see Vardit Rispler-Chaim, *Islamic Medical Ethics in the Twentieth Century* (Leiden: Brill, 1993); A. I. Padela et al., "Patient Choice of Provider Type in the Emergency Department: Perceptions and Factors Relating to Accommodation of Requests for Care Providers," *Emergency Medicine Journal* 27, no. 6 (June 2010). On kidney donation, see M. Y. Rady, J. L. Verheijde, and M. S. Ali, "Islam and End-of-Life Practices in Organ Donation for Transplantation: New Questions and Serious Sociocultural Consequences," *HEC Forum* 21, no. 2 (June 2009); Y. I. el-Shahat, "Islamic Viewpoint of Organ Transplantation," *Transplant Proceedings* 31, no. 8 (1999); Mohammed Ghaly, "Organ Donation and Muslims in the Netherlands: A Transnational Fatwa in Focus," *Recht Van De Islam* 26 (2012); O. Ghannam, "Organ Donation and Islam," ed. Saad Ismail (Bangor, Wales: Muslim Healthcare Student Network, 2012).

21. Curlin et al., "The Association of Physicians' Religious Characteristics with Their Attitudes and Self-Reported Behaviors Regarding Religion and Spirituality in the Clinical Encounter."

22. G. S. Chung et al., "Obstetrician-Gynecologists' Beliefs about When Pregnancy Begins," *American Journal of Obstetrics and Gynecology* 206, no. 2 (2012); J. D. Yoon et al., "Religion, Sense of Calling, and the Practice of Medicine: Findings from a National Survey of Primary Care Physicians and Psychiatrists," *Southern Medical Journal* 108, no. 3 (March 2015).

23. Abu-Ras, Laird, and Sensai, "A Window into American Muslim Physicians: Civic Engagement and Community Participation, Their Diversity, Contributions and Challenges."

24. Pew Research Center, "Muslim Americans: No Signs of Growth in Alienation or Support for Extremism" (Washington, DC, 2011).

25. "Muslim Americans: A National Portrait—an in-Depth Analysis of America's Most Diverse Religious Community" (Gallup, NM: Gallup Center for Muslim Studies, Muslim West Facts Project, 2009).

26. Pew Research Center, "Muslim Americans: No Signs of Growth in Alienation or Support for Extremism."

27. F. A. Curlin et al., "Religious Characteristics of U.S. Physicians: A National Survey," *Journal of General Internal Medicine* 20, no. 7 (July 2005): 629–34.

28. Hasan Shanawani and Mohammad Hassan Khalil, "Reporting on 'Islamic Bioethics' in the Medical Literature: Where Are the Experts?," in *Muslim Medical Ethics: From Theory to Practice*, ed. Jonathan E. Brockopp and Thomas Eich (Columbia: University of South Carolina Press, 2008).

29. Ibid., 221.

30. Ibid.

31. A. I. Padela, H. Shanawani, and A. Arozullah, "Medical Experts and Islamic Scholars Deliberating over Brain Death: Gaps in the Applied Islamic Bioethics Discourse," *Muslim World Journal* 101, no. 1 (2011): 53–72; A. I. Padela, A. Arozullah, and E. Moosa, "Brain Death in Islamic Ethico-Legal Deliberation: Challenges for Applied Islamic Bioethics," *Bioethics* 27, no. 3 (2013).

32. A. I. Padela, "Muslim Perspectives on the American Healthcare System: The Discursive Framing of 'Islamic' Bioethical Discourse," *Die Welt des Islams* 55, nos. 3–4 (November 2015).

33. Jane I. Smith and Yvonne Yazbeck Haddad, *The Islamic Understanding of Death and Resurrection* (Albany: State University of New York Press, 1981).

34. A. I. Padela and T. A. Basser, "Brain Death: The Challenges of Translating Medical Science into Islamic Bioethical Discourse," *Medicine and Law* 31, no. 3 (September 2012); Padela, Shanawani, and Arozullah, "Medical Experts and Islamic Scholars Deliberating over Brain Death: Gaps in the Applied Islamic Bioethics Discourse"; A. I. Padela, "The Perspectives of Islamic Jurists on the Brain Death as Legal Death in Islam," *Journal of Religion and Health* 55, no. 4 (2016); E. Moosa, "Brain Death and Organ Transplantation—an Islamic Opinion," *South African Medical Journal* 83 (1993): 385–86; Sachedina, "Islamic Bioethics"; Padela, Arozullah, and Moosa, "Brain Death in Islamic Ethico-Legal Deliberation: Challenges for Applied Islamic Bioethics."

35. Ebrahim Moosa, "Languages of Change in Islamic Law: Redefining Death in Modernity," *Islamic Studies* 38, no. 3 (October 1, 1999).

36. Franz Rosenthal, *Knowledge Triumphant: The Concept of Knowledge in Medieval Islam*, vol. 2 (Leiden: Brill, 1970).

37. See chapter 6, "Death and Dying," in A. Sachedina, *Islamic Biomedical Ethics: Principles and Application* (Oxford and New York: Oxford University Press, 2009).

38. There is debate among *ḥadīth* scholars about the veracity of statements attributed to the Prophet Muhammad that convey meanings such as "Difference of opinion among my Companions is a mercy for you." My intent is not to weigh in on

these debates but to reference a feature of Islamic discourse whereby scholars have suggested that differences in opinion can be beneficial.

39. Padela and Zaganjor, "Relationships between Islamic Religiosity and Attitude toward Deceased Organ Donation among American Muslims"; O. Qureshi and A. I. Padela, "When Must a Patient Seek Healthcare? Bringing the Perspectives of Islamic Jurists and Clinicians into Dialogue," *Zygon* 51, no. 3 (2016): 592–625.

REFERENCES

Abdel-Aziz, E., B. N. Arch, and H. Al-Taher. "The Influence of Religious Beliefs on General Practitioners' Attitudes towards Termination of Pregnancy—a Pilot Study." *Journal of Obstetrics and Gynaecology* 24, no. 5 (August 2004): 557–61.

Abu-Ras, W., L. D. Laird, and F. Sensai. "A Window into American Muslim Physicians: Civic Engagement and Community Participation, Their Diversity, Contributions and Challenges." Washington, DC: Institute for Social Policy and Understanding, 2012.

Aiyer, A. N., G. Ruiz, A. Steinman, and G. Y. Ho. "Influence of Physician Attitudes on Willingness to Perform Abortion." *Journal of Obstetrics and Gynecololgy* 93, no. 4 (April 1999): 576–80.

Allport, G. W., and J. M. Ross. "Personal Religious Orientation and Prejudice." *Journal of Personality and Social Psychology* 5, no. 4 (1967): 432–43.

al-Yousefi, N. A. "Observations of Muslim Physicians Regarding the Influence of Religion on Health and Their Clinical Approach." *Journal of Religion and Health* 51, no. 2 (June 2012): 269–80.

Arawi, Thalia A. "The Muslim Physician and the Ethics of Medicine." *Journal of the Islamic Medical Association of North America* 42, no. 3 (2010): 111–16.

Asman, Oren. "Abortion in Islamic Countries—Legal and Religious Aspects." *Medicine and Law* 23, no. 1 (2004): 73–89.

Atighetchi, Dariusch. *Islamic Bioethics: Problems and Perspectives.* International Library of Ethics, Law, and the New Medicine, vol. 31. New York: Springer, 2007.

Chung, G. S., R. E. Lawrence, K. A. Rasinski, J. D. Yoon, and F. A. Curlin. "Obstetrician-Gynecologists' Beliefs about When Pregnancy Begins." *American Journal of Obstetrics and Gynecology* 206, no. 2 (February 2012): 132e1–7.

Cohen, J., J. van Delden, F. Mortier, R. Lofmark, M. Norup, C. Cartwright, K. Faisst, et al. "Influence of Physicians' Life Stances on Attitudes to End-of-Life Decisions and Actual End-of-Life Decision-Making in Six Countries." *Journal of Medical Ethics* 34, no. 4 (April 2008): 247–53.

Curlin, F. "Ob-Gyns Approaches to Sexual and Reproductive Health Care: A National Survey, Survey Methodology Report." Chicago: University of Chicago Program on Medicine and Religion, 2010.

Curlin, F. A., M. H. Chin, S. A. Sellergren, C. J. Roach, and J. D. Lantos. "The Association of Physicians' Religious Characteristics with Their Attitudes and Self-Reported Behaviors Regarding Religion and Spirituality in the Clinical Encounter." *Medical Care* 44, no. 5 (May 2006): 446–53.

Curlin, F. A., J. D. Lantos, C. J. Roach, S. A. Sellergren, and M. H. Chin. "Religious Characteristics of U.S. Physicians: A National Survey." *Journal of General Internal Medicine* 20, no. 7 (July 2005): 629–34.

Curlin, F. A., R. E. Lawrence, M. H. Chin, and J. D. Lantos. "Religion, Conscience, and Controversial Clinical Practices." *New England Journal of Medicine* 356, no. 6 (February 8, 2007): 593–600.

Curlin, F. A., S. A. Sellergren, J. D. Lantos, and M. H. Chin. "Physicians' Observations and Interpretations of the Influence of Religion and Spirituality on Health." *Archives of Internal Medicine* 167, no. 7 (April 9, 2007): 649–54.

Dillman, D. A. *Mail and Internet Surveys: The Tailored Design Method.* 2nd ed. New York: John Wiley and Sons, 2000.

el-Shahat, Y. I. "Islamic Viewpoint of Organ Transplantation." *Transplant Proceedings* 31, no. 8 (December 1999): 3271–74.

Ghaly, Mohammed. "Organ Donation and Muslims in the Netherlands: A Transnational Fatwa in Focus." *Recht Van De Islam* 26 (2012): 39–52.

Ghannam, O. "Organ Donation and Islam." Ed. Saad Ismail. Bangor, Wales: Muslim Healthcare Student Network.

Isa, N. M. "Darurah (Necessity) and Its Application in Islamic Ethical Assessment of Medical Applications: A Review on Malaysian Fatwa." *Science and Engineering Ethics* 22, no. 5 (2015): 1319–32.

Jager, A. J., M. A. Tutty, and A. C. Kao. "Association between Physician Burnout and Identification with Medicine as a Calling." *Mayo Clinical Proceedings* 92, no. 3 (March 2017): 415–22.

Lio, J., H. J. Tak, Y. Duan, F. Dadani, B. Ali, and J. D. Yoon. "Religious Characteristics of Physicians Who Care for Underserved Populations or Work in Religiously Oriented Practices." *Southern Medical Journal* 111, no. 9 (September 2018): 511–15.

Mahmassani, Sobhi. *Falsafat Al-Tashri' Fi Al-Islām: The Philosophy of Jurisprudence in Islam.* Trans. Farhat Ziadeh Leiden: E. J. Brill, 1961.

Molloy, Aminah. "Attitudes to Medical Ethics among British Muslim Medical Practitioners." *Journal of Medical Ethics* 6 (1980): 139–44.

Moosa, E. "Brain Death and Organ Transplantation—an Islamic Opinion." *South African Medical Journal* 83 (1993): 385–86.

Moosa, Ebrahim. "Languages of Change in Islamic Law: Redefining Death in Modernity." *Islamic Studies* 38, no. 3 (October 1, 1999): 305–42.

"Muslim Americans: A National Portrait—an In-Depth Analysis of America's Most Diverse Religious Community." Gallup, NM: Gallup Center for Muslim Studies, Muslim West Facts Project, 2009.

Padela, A. I. "Muslim Perspectives on the American Healthcare System: The Discursive Framing of 'Islamic' Bioethical Discourse." *Die Welt des Islams* 55, nos. 3–4 (November 2015).

Padela, A. I., Ahsan Arozullah, and Ebrahim Moosa. "Brain Death in Islamic Ethico-Legal Deliberation: Challenges for Applied Islamic Bioethics." *Bioethics* 27, no. 3 (2013).

Padela, A. I., and H. Zaganjor. "Relationships between Islamic Religiosity and Attitude toward Deceased Organ Donation among American Muslims: A Pilot Study." *Transplantation*, March 18, 2014.

Padela, A. I., and T. A. Basser. "Brain Death: The Challenges of Translating Medical Science into Islamic Bioethical Discourse." *Medicine and Law* 31, no. 3 (September 2012): 433–50.

Padela, A. I., H. Shanawani, and A. Arozullah. "Medical Experts and Islamic Scholars Deliberating over Brain Death: Gaps in the Applied Islamic Bioethics Discourse." *Muslim World Journal* 101, no. 1 (2011): 53–72.

Padela, A. I., H. Shanawani, J. Greenlaw, H. Hamid, M. Aktas, and N. Chin. "The Perceived Role of Islam in Immigrant Muslim Medical Practice within the USA: An Exploratory Qualitative Study." *Journal of Medical Ethics* 34, no. 5 (2008): 365–69.

Padela, A. I., S. M. Schneider, H. He, Z. Ali, and T. M. Richardson. "Patient Choice of Provider Type in the Emergency Department: Perceptions and Factors Relating to Accommodation of Requests for Care Providers." *Emergency Medicine Journal* 27, no. 6 (June 2010): 465–69.

Pew Research Center. "Muslim Americans: No Signs of Growth in Alienation or Support for Extremism," 1–127. Washington, DC, 2011.

Qureshi, O., and A. I. Padela. "When Must a Patient Seek Healthcare? Bringing the Perspectives of Islamic Jurists and Clinicians into Dialogue." *Zygon* 51, no. 3 (September 2016): 592–625.

Rady, M. Y., J. L. Verheijde, and M. S. Ali. "Islam and End-of-Life Practices in Organ Donation for Transplantation: New Questions and Serious Sociocultural Consequences." *HEC Forum* 21, no. 2 (June 2009): 175–205.

Rasinski, K. A. "Religion and Care of Patients with Advanced Illness at the End of Life: A National Physician Study, Survey Methodology Report." Chicago: University of Chicago Program on Medicine and Religion, 2010.

Rispler-Chaim, Vardit. *Islamic Medical Ethics in the Twentieth Century*. Leiden: Brill, 1993.

Rosenthal, Franz. *Knowledge Triumphant: The Concept of Knowledge in Medieval Islam*. Vol. 2. Leiden: Brill, 1970.

Sachedina, A. "Islamic Bioethics." In *Religious Perspectives in Bioethics*, ed. J. F. Peppin et al., 153–71. London: Taylor and Francis, 2004.

———. *Islamic Biomedical Ethics: Principles and Application*. Oxford and New York: Oxford University Press, 2009.

Seale, C. "The Role of Doctors' Religious Faith and Ethnicity in Taking Ethically Controversial Decisions during End-of-Life Care." *Journal of Medical Ethics* 36, no. 11 (November 2010): 677–82.

Shanawani, Hasan, and Mohammad Hassan Khalil. "Reporting on 'Islamic Bioethics' in the Medical Literature: Where Are the Experts?" In *Muslim Medical Ethics: From Theory to Practice*, ed. Jonathan E. Brockopp and Thomas Eich. Columbia: University of South Carolina Press, 2008.

Smith, Jane I., and Yvonne Yazbeck Haddad. *The Islamic Understanding of Death and Resurrection*. Albany: State University of New York Press, 1981.

Stulberg, D. B., A. M. Dude, I. Dahlquist, and F. A. Curlin. "Abortion Provision among Practicing Obstetrician-Gynecologists." *Obstetrics and Gynecology* 118, no. 3 (September 2011): 609–14.

Todres, I. D., D. Krane, M. C. Howell, and D. C. Shannon. "Pediatricians' Attitudes Affecting Decision-Making in Defective Newborns." *Pediatrics* 60, no. 2 (August 1977): 197–201.

Wolenberg, K. M., J. D. Yoon, K. A. Rasinski, and F. A. Curlin. "Religion and United States Physicians' Opinions and Self-Predicted Practices Concerning Artificial Nutrition and Hydration." *Journal of Religion and Health* 52, no. 4 (December 2013): 1051–65.

Yoon, J. D., B. M. Daley, and F. A. Curlin. "The Association between a Sense of Calling and Physician Well-Being: A National Study of Primary Care Physicians and Psychiatrists." *Academic Psychiatry* 41, no. 2 (April 2017): 167–73.

Yoon, J. D., J. H. Shin, A. L. Nian, and F. A. Curlin. "Religion, Sense of Calling, and the Practice of Medicine: Findings from a National Survey of Primary Care Physicians and Psychiatrists." *Southern Medical Journal* 108, no. 3 (March 2015): 189–95.

EIGHT

Jurists, Physicians, and Other Experts in Dialogue

A Multidisciplinary Vision for Islamic Bioethical Deliberation

AASIM I. PADELA

As I described in the previous chapter, data from my national survey of Muslim physicians in the United States supports the characterization of Islamic bioethics discourse as one in which various experts remain in their disciplinary circles and rarely interact with one another. As a result, those involved often "do not know what they do not know." Notably, the American Muslim physicians we surveyed perceived themselves to be familiar with Islamic bioethics, but only slightly more than half read books on the subject and fewer than half attend workshops and courses on the topic. Tellingly, even when facing a bioethical challenge, Muslim clinicians do not avail themselves of the Islamic ethics expertise of jurists and *imāms* or of the bioethics-related analyses of *fiqh* academies. Thus one wonders what the sources of their "Islamic" bioethical knowledge are.

As illustrated by the discussions about *ḍarūra* and brain death in this volume, when morally assessing biomedicine, Islamic jurists depend on others to describe the scientific data and the clinical practice context that shapes an ethical quandary. Thus, in several *fiqh* academies, physicians decode and interpret the medical data for jurists and also explain the technology or procedure in question. Controversially, some physician partners in these deliberations also advance their own Islamic ethico-legal arguments. Given these features of the dialogue, one could argue that physicians have the upper hand in Islamic bioethical deliberation. They pose and frame the Islamic bioethics questions, interpret and describe the biomedical contexts for jurists, and even fashion Islamic arguments.[1] Jurists could thus be marginalized—or, worse, instrumentalized—leading to rulings based on incomplete understandings or selectively chosen biomedical data. This risk is not unknown to jurists and might be the reason that juridical academies are particular about the Muslim clinicians they invite into their midst. Aside from these academies, however, my research finds that, at least in the American context, physicians and Islamic scholars rarely get together to discuss matters of Islamic bioethics.

Against this backdrop, it is the consumers of the discourse who suffer. Muslim patients and families do not know whom to trust and may be left with nonactionable guidance. Policy-makers are bewildered by the diverse and at times conflicting Islamic bioethics position statements offered by physicians and jurists, and researchers find the literature of poor quality and hard to navigate.

As a remedy to this disconnected discourse, I would like to offer a conceptual model to improve Islamic bioethics deliberation (figure 8.1). This multidisciplinary model would better account for the various disciplines required to derive "Islamic" ethical views and understand the "biomedical" contexts. While I admit that the model is provisional and not comprehensive, it offers a starting point for enhancing the discourse beyond doctors and jurists.[2]

Beginning with the right side of the figure, I see the foundations for Islamic bioethics to draw from at least three distinct genres of the Islamic intellectual tradition: (1) law, (2) theology, and (3) the sciences of virtue and practical ethics. Islamic law principally focuses on assessing the morality of an act but also provides an axiology via frameworks of the higher

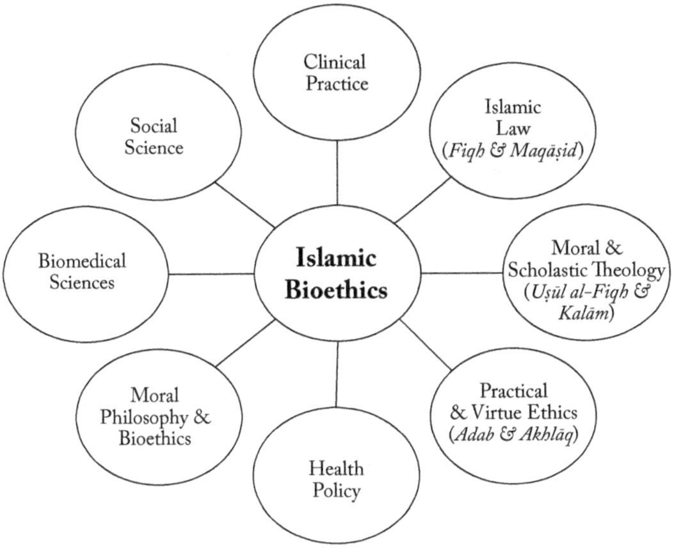

FIGURE 8.1 A Multidisciplinary Vision for Islamic Bioethics Deliberation

intents of Islamic law, *maqāṣid al-Sharī'ah*. Islamic law thus carries forward the act-based moral vision for Islamic bioethics.

Islamic moral theology, *uṣūl al-fiqh*, provides a hermeneutical science for deriving law from scripture, and this is related to act-based morality, stated as above, but also furnishes tools for explicating theological understandings of illness, cures, health, and other critical concepts related to biomedicine. This latter aspect is complementary to the science of *kalām*, scholastic theology, where metaphysical and ontological frameworks are aids to explicating such concepts. The *maqāṣid*, together with *uṣūl* and *kalām*, attend to outcome-based morality and help build out a holistic Islamic bioethical vision.

The various Islamic sciences of moral formation and literary genres cultivating virtue and practical ethics, including *'ilm al-ahklāq* and *adab*,[3] attend to the reformation of one's inner being, molding one to incline toward righteous action. These sciences therefore facilitate holism within Islamic bioethics by outlining agent-based morality. *Adab* manuals specific to various professions go further in connecting the inner and the outer by motivating one to live out virtues in one's vocational practice. While *adab* can be wedded to scriptural understanding of the virtues, the genre also incorporates practice-based virtues that are not wholly scripturally based. These are gleaned from exemplars within the profession, since the internal goods of the profession are best known to, and demonstrated by, those in the practice.[4]

Together, then, broadly speaking, law, theology, and the sciences of virtue and practical ethics offer a more complete assessment of the moral dimensions of biomedicine, as they attend to the morality of the act, the goals to be achieved and actualized, and the agent. Indeed, the agent, act, and outcome are inter-related in complex ways so as to collectively contribute to morality: A comprehensive ethics framework must be constructed to assess and evaluate this confluence. Truisms such as "one can do the right thing for the wrong reason" and "the path to hell is paved with good intentions" illustrate the pitfalls of focusing on only one part of the whole—the act to the exclusion of the agent's inner motivation in the former and the inner motivation to the exclusion of ultimate outcomes/consequences of the act in the latter. Indeed, anything other than a purely consequentialist moral theory demands that righteous outcomes be produced through righteous actions that are, in turn, informed by right intentions. In my view, a bioethics rooted in Islam must also evidence such holism.

Building on this view, the moral machinery of Islam would be represented by experts in Islamic law, theology, and moral formation deliberating at the proverbial table of Islamic bioethics. The convener may bring to the table a scholar who has mastery in many or all of these areas or might seek out multiple scholars who can provide perspectives from these fields. In any case, these different vantage points are needed to ground Islamic bioethical perspectives within the moral frameworks of the Islamic tradition.

At the six and twelve o'clock positions of the figure are the two areas from which ethical questions often emerge. In other words, a particular clinical practice or a health policy concern becomes the subject of ethical debate and leads individuals and institutions to seek out Islamic bioethics resources and rulings. For example, a Muslim patient might wonder whether xenotransplantation is permitted by Islam as she considers treatment options for liver failure; a Muslim surgeon may desire to know whether sex-change operations are Islamically sanctioned as he sets up his clinical practice; or a health insurer may want to know whether male circumcision is a religious obligation for Muslims as they delineate coverage policies for patients. To fully understand the clinical and policy contexts informing such questions, experts from these domains need to be at the dialogue table. They can provide insight into the reasons that various clinical and policy questions are being debated, the data supporting various solutions, and the social, legal, and practice conventions that frame the debate. Given the conventions of *fatwā* giving, Islamic scholars are used to a single individual or institution presenting an ethical query and providing data on the clinical or policy context. But in light of the complexity of biomedicine today and the different ways in which clinicians can interpret the same data, I suggest that multiple clinical and policy experts offer interpretations of such data so that the various dimensions of the ethical problem-space are fully understood. Indeed, it may be that historians, social scientists, and ethicists can provide insight into contexts that lead to the particular clinical or policy question at hand. And they can describe how contemporary world-views prefigure ethical questions and answers. Importantly, clinical and policy experts can "check" one another by helping individuals understand the interplay between their fields, how policies shape clinical practices, and how certain clinical practices demand policy action.

Moving to the left side of the figure, the social and biomedical sciences offer scientific data that further frames the biomedical contexts and Islamic perspectives. For example, the health benefits of new biomedical technologies or the science behind a particular research breakthrough is better assessed when presented by the theoreticians, investigators, and technical experts involved in the research and development of such technologies and advancements. While applied scientists, such as clinicians, can detail the practice implications, the potentialities are better described by those at the forefront of the science and research. At the same time, social scientists can present a clearer picture of the meanings attached to technologies, therapeutics, and policies and how they are understood by various stakeholders. They can help explicate the interplay among medicine, technology, law, policy, and the broader society and can also provide a historical perspective on these issues. Such data is critically important for Islamic scholars making moral assessments because Islamic notions of harm (*ḍarar*) and benefit (*maṣlaḥa*) hinge on an accurate accounting of individual and societal harms and benefits. Truly, demarcating an Islamic perspective that adheres to the overarching maxim of Islamic ethics and law, *dar al-mafāsid 'awla min jalb al-maṣāliḥ* (the removing of harms/

wrongs is prioritized over bringing about benefits), requires an in-depth sociological understanding of the biomedical contexts at play. Accordingly, biomedical and social scientists must be present at the dialogue table alongside jurists and doctors.

Finally, I see contemporary moral philosophy and bioethics as discursive partners in an Islamic bioethics deliberation forum. In terms of philosophers, I mean both political and moral philosophers, and when I refer to bioethicists I refer to all types of bioethicists, be they clinicians, lawyers, theologians, or other disciplinary experts. Interacting with secular voices and religious ethicists can sharpen ethical analyses and also clarify points of convergence and divergence between these perspectives and Islamically grounded ones. Given that bioethics is a pluralistic and a global discourse, such experts may also aid those in the dialogue in finding policy solutions that meet the needs of both Muslims and non-Muslims. Moreover, the emergence of the need for an "Islamic bioethics" is tied to a particular arrangement between the modern state and civil society, and the extent to which Islamic bioethics is given space in the clinical and policy domain rests on specific political allowances given to religion in the public square. Islamic scholars and Muslim physicians are likely less versed in these matters and would thus benefit from the input of moral philosophers and professional bioethicists.

I began this volume by defining Islamic bioethics as a discourse that uses the Islamic tradition to address moral questions and ethical issues arising out of the biomedical sciences and allied health practice. This discourse has largely been shaped by the writings of Muslim physicians and Islamic jurists. At times, these two types of disciplinary experts derive their views of the "Islamic" and the "bioethical" by working in concert, but more often they do it alone. To develop the field, we must extend beyond these domain experts to incorporate a more holistic perspective of the "Islamic" and to furnish more comprehensive understandings of the biomedical/bioethical contexts. Consequently, in the model outlined in figure 8.1 I attempt to enhance the discourse and incorporate multiple perspectives into Islamic bioethical deliberation. Living out the maxim of Islamic law, *al-ḥukm 'ala shay far' 'an taṣawwurihi* (the ethico-legal assessment of a matter comes from its conceptualization), demands, at a minimum, that these different disciplines be brought together to achieve an accurate conceptualization of the problem-space and potential solutions.

While I have noted the various disciplinary experts needed for multidisciplinary deliberation, I recognize that a deliberative method that brings these groups into a fruitful and humble dialogue is also required. Some scholars may suggest that the collective *ijtihād* methods of *fiqh* academies could be used to bring about equitable dialogue, while others may assert that the classical method of *ijtihād* should be deployed so that jurists have the final say in order to prevent mistaken views of the "Islamic."[5] As one who avidly reads and seeks to inform his own clinical practices based on the Islamic bioethics-related rulings of *fiqh* academies and traditional jurists, I dare say that there are gaps in both *fiqh* academy verdicts and traditional *fatāwā*. These knowledge gaps render some of these outputs inapplicable to clinical practice and ineffective for policy generation. As an academic, I also desire discursive outputs that are more convincing in argument and comprehensive in scope. Perhaps as Islamic bioethics becomes more multidisciplinary, innovative approaches to ethico-legal deliberation and the penning of ethico-legal verdicts will be needed. I look forward to working with others to study and develop such process models.

NOTES

1. Anecdotally, my own experiences and research have disclosed that they may even pen the *fatāwā* jurists sign.

2. As I mention in the opening chapter of this book, some *fiqh* academies have begun to broaden the expertise brought to the deliberative table by including experts outside of the fields of medicine and Islamic law. However, in my view, most *fiqh* academies have yet to adopt a truly multidisciplinary perspective, and none bring together all of the experts I note in the figure. Illustratively, I discuss how the presence of health policy stakeholders impacted the uptake of *fiqh* council rulings on porcine vaccines in my "Islamic Verdicts in Health Policy Discourse: Porcine-Based Vaccines as a Case Study," *Zygon* 48, no. 3 (September 2013): 655–70. In that paper I also suggest that jurists might have been more careful in their rulings had they fully appreciated the health policy implications of their judgements. Similarly, I point out missing biomedical and bioethical perspectives that problematize the ruling of the Organisation of the Islamic Conference's Islamic *Fiqh* Academy on brain death in A. I. Padela, H. Shanawani, and A. Arozullah, "Medical Experts and Islamic Scholars Deliberating over Brain Death: Gaps in the Applied Islamic Bioethics Discourse," *Muslim World Journal* 101, no. 1 (2011). I believe my model offers a sort of

checklist that *fiqh* academy conveners can use to ensure that the relevant experts are given a voice as ethico-legal assessments are proffered.

3. The sciences of *taṣawwuf* and some Sufi practices aim at similar goals and can also be included in this group. I recognize that such a proposal may be controversial in light of the excesses of some purportedly Sufi circles, public misconceptions of traditional *taṣawwuf* because of misguided polemic debates, and the like. My conceptualization here refers only to those practices that remain within the bounds of Islamic law.

4. Such virtues are complementary to, and must not conflict with, scriptural teachings.

5. Collective *ijtihād*, *ijtihād jamāʿī*, brings together groups of scholars to issue *fiqh* rulings via joint deliberation. Such joint fora are increasingly being used in the Muslim world because of growing scientific and social complexities that are critical to the rendering of juridical verdicts. The methodology for such deliberation remains unsettled. For an overview of the history and methodology of collective *ijtihād*, see Aznan Hasan's "An Introduction to Collective Ijtihad (Ijtihad Jamai): Concept and Applications," *American Journal of Islamic Social Sciences* 20, no. 2 (2003): 26–49.

REFERENCES

Hasan, Aznan. "An Introduction to Collective Ijtihad (Ijtihad Jamai): Concept and Applications." *American Journal of Islamic Social Sciences* 20, no. 2 (2003): 26–49.

Padela, A. I. "Islamic Verdicts in Health Policy Discourse: Porcine-Based Vaccines as a Case Study." *Zygon* 48, no. 3 (September 2013): 655–70.

Padela, A. I., H. Shanawani, and A. Arozullah. "Medical Experts and Islamic Scholars Deliberating over Brain Death: Gaps in the Applied Islamic Bioethics Discourse." *Muslim World* 101, no. 1 (2011): 53–72.

CONTRIBUTORS

Bilal Ali is an academic advisor and liaison in the Department of Hadith at Darul Qasim Islamic Institute in Glendale, Illinois, and a religious consultant, researcher, and board member at the Khalil Center, a psychological and spiritual wellness center in Chicago. Mawlana Bilal received his undergraduate education at the University of Illinois in Urbana in computer engineering and received his bachelor's diploma from National-Louis University in Lisle, Illinois, in the field of applied behavioral sciences. Mawlana Bilal completed his formal *dars niẓāmī* studies (equivalent to a master's degree in Arabic and Islamic studies) at Jāmiʿat Dār al-Ulūm in Karachi and has *ijāzahs* in hadith from the most senior generation of hadith masters in Pakistan. He has since continued his studies in various fields, including discursive theology (*kalām*), Islamic jurisprudence (*uṣūl al-fiqh*), and Islamic philosophy under Shaykh Mohammed Amin Kholwadia at Darul Qasim. His research interests include *ḥadīth*, Ḥanafī law, education and curriculum development, mental health, and Islamic bioethics.

Abul Fadl Mohsin Ebrahim is an emeritus professor in the School of Religion, Philosophy, and Classics at the University of KwaZulu-Natal; a senior professor and researcher at the Regent Business School in Durban, South Africa; a member of the editorial board of the Federation of Islamic Medical Association's Yearbook; and the academic research director at the International Institute of Islamic Thought (IIIT) in Herndon, Virginia. His recent publications include *Muslims in Seychelles: A Historical Appraisal of Their Legacy* (South Africa: iMedia Limited, 2016); "Ethics of Fertility Treatment: A Case Study of Nadya Suleman's Feat," in *In Islam and Knowledge—Al Faruqi's Concept of Religion and Islamic*

Thought (London: I. B. Taurus, 2012); and *Reproductive Health and Islamic Values—Ethical and Legal Insights* (Cape Town: Islamic Medical Association of South Africa, 2011). His research interests include bioethics and Islamic law.

Hooman Keshavarzi is the founding director of the Khalil Center, the first Islamically oriented psychological and spiritual wellness center in the United States, in Chicago; an instructor of psychology for Islamic Online University; and an adjunct professor of psychology at Argosy University Chicago, American Islamic College in Chicago, and Hartford Seminary in Hartford, Connecticut. He is a licensed psychotherapist in Illinois, has completed his PsyD, and holds a master's of clinical psychology and a bachelor's of science, with a specialist psychology track/minor in Islamic studies. In addition to receiving this academic training, he has studied Islamic theology both formally and informally. He has also authored several academic papers that have appeared in recognized peer-reviewed journals on integrating Islamic spirituality into modern psychological practice.

Mohammed Amin Kholwadia is the founder and director of Darul Qasim Islamic Institute in Glendale, Illinois, an institute of higher Islamic learning where both undergraduate and postgraduate studies are conducted under his direction and leadership. Shaykh Amin received training in the Islamic sciences on the Indian subcontinent, culminating at the world-renowned Islamic seminary in Deoband, India. He received further instruction in Islamic law at the Shariah Court of Patna in Bihar, India, and in Islamic theism and theosophy from his mentor, Shaykh Meeran, at Sabil al-Rashad Institute in Bangalore, India. Shaykh Amin has co-authored *Islamic Banking and Finance: What It Is and What It Could Be* (London: First Ethical Charitable Trust, 2010). He has also written a book on Qur'anic exegesis titled *A Spark from the Dynamo of Prophethood.* In the works is a book on Ghazalian eschatology. His intellectual pursuits span both community and academic settings, and his speaking and counseling engagements span the globe.

Ebrahim Moosa is professor of Islamic studies at the University of Notre Dame's Keough School of Global Affairs and in the Department of

History. Professor Moosa's interests span both classical and modern Islamic thought, with a special focus on Islamic law, history, ethics, and theology. He is the author of many books, including *What Is a Madrasa?* (Chapel Hill: University of North Carolina, 2015); *Ghazali and the Poetics of Imagination* (University of North Carolina, 2005), which was awarded the American Academy of Religion's Best First Book in the History of Religions (2006); and edited the last manuscript of the late Professor Fazlur Rahman, *Revival and Reform in Islam: A Study of Islamic Fundamentalism* (London: Oneworld, 1999). Other publications include the co-edited book *The African Renaissance and the Afro-Arab Spring* (Washington, DC: Georgetown University Press, 2015), *Islam in the Modern World* (New York: Routledge, 2014), and *Muslim Family Law in Sub-Saharan Africa: Colonial Legacies and Post-Colonial Challenges* (Amsterdam: Amsterdam University Press, 2010). Born in South Africa, Moosa earned his MA and PhD degrees from the University of Cape Town. He also holds a degree in Islamic and Arabic studies from Darul Uloom Nadwatul Ulama in Lucknow, India; a BA degree from Kanpur University; and a postgraduate diploma in journalism from City University in London.

Aasim I. Padela is a professor of emergency medicine, bioethics, and humanities at the Medical College of Wisconsin in Milwaukee, as well as vice chair of research and scholarship in the Department of Emergency Medicine. He is also chairman and director of the Initiative on Islam and Medicine, an independent nonprofit organization dedicated to Islamic bioethics and Muslim health research and training. Much of this volume was completed during his tenure as associate professor of medicine in the Section of Emergency Medicine and a faculty member at the MacLean Center for Clinical Medical Ethics and Divinity School at the University of Chicago. Dr. Padela holds an MD from Weill Cornell Medical College and received an MSc in healthcare research from the University of Michigan. He completed residency training in emergency medicine at the University of Rochester, New York, and a clinical ethics fellowship at the MacLean Center for Clinical Medical Ethics at the University of Chicago. Prior to that he received bachelor's degrees in biomedical engineering and classical Arabic and literature from the University of Rochester. His Islamic studies expertise comes from part-time seminary studies, tutorials and formal coursework with traditionally trained Islamic scholars, and fellowships at the Oxford Centre for Islamic Studies and the International Institute of Islamic Thought in Herndon, Virginia. Dr. Padela uses diverse methodologies, from health services research and religious studies to comparative ethics, to examine the encounter of Islam with contemporary biomedicine through the lives of Muslim patients and clinicians and in the scholarly writings of Islamic authorities. Through systematic research and strategic interventions, he seeks (1) to improve American Muslim health outcomes and healthcare experiences and (2) to construct a multidisciplinary field of Islamic bioethics. Dr. Padela is associate editor for the *Encyclopedia of Islamic Bioethics* and the "Ethics in Public Health, Medical Law, and Health Policy" section of *BMC Medical Ethics*, as well as section editor for *Global Bioethics*. He also serves on the editorial boards of the *American Journal of Bioethics*, *TAFHIM: IKIM Journal of Islam and the Contemporary World*, the *Journal of Islam and the Contemporary World*, and the *BETIM Journal of Medical Humanities*. He has authored dozens of peer-reviewed articles and book chapters, and his work has been featured in international media outlets including the *New York Times*, *USA Today*, the *Chicago Tribune*, the *Washington Post*, the BBC, CNN, and NPR.

Vardit Rispler-Chaim is an associate professor in the Department of Arabic Language and Literature at the University of Haifa, Israel. She obtained her PhD in Near Eastern studies from the University of California–Berkeley. Her main fields of research and publication are Islamic law, Islamic medical ethics, and human rights in Islam, the Qur'an, and commentaries. She has published several articles on Islamic ethical positions related to abortion, genetic engineering, postmortem examinations, the beginning of life, selecting the sex of an embryo, restoration of virginity, and other topics. She is also the author of several books on Islamic bioethics, including *Islamic Medical Ethics in the Twentieth Century* (Leiden: E. J. Brill, 1993) and *Disability in Islamic Law* (Dordrecht: Springer, 2007).

Muhammed Volkan Yildiran Stodolsky is a liaison in the Department of Theology at Darul Qasim Islamic Institute in Glendale Heights, Illinois. He received his undergraduate education from Bates College in Lewiston, Maine; completed his MPhil degree in classical and medieval Islamic history at Oxford University; and earned his MA and PhD from the University of Chicago's Department of Near Eastern Languages and Civilizations. In 2008, he traveled to Syria as a Fulbright fellow to conduct research concerning the Ḥanafī school of Islamic law. His research interests include Islamic law and legal history, historiography, the instrumental Islamic sciences (syntax, semantics, logic, and rhetoric), *ḥadīth* and its methodology, Islamic theology (especially that of the Māturīdī school), and Sufism.

INDEX

Page numbers in italics refer to figures and tables.

Abbasid caliphate, 185n77
Abdul-Basser, Taha, 76
abortion: on the grounds of *ḍarūra*, 63; judicial reasoning on, 43, 135; as medical necessity, 64; permissibility of, 49, 123, 217; psychological factors of, 135; religious attitudes of physicians and, 194–95
Abū Dharr Jundab b. Junādah al-Ghifārī, 74
Abū Ḥanīfah Nuʿmān ibn Thābit, 73
Abū Zahrah, Muhammad, 59
accident (*ʿaraḍ*), 89, 91, 94
adab literature, 6, 10, 229
al-Azhar University, 47
Ali, Bilal, 27
American healthcare system: "Islamic" moral assessments in, 154; public debates on, 27
American Muslim Health Professionals (AMHP): creation of, 156; documents of, 153, 164; ethical framework of, 173; healthcare reform and, 156–57, 160, 169; human rights vocabulary, 174; scriptural references, 169, 173; target audience of, 173
animal soul, 116n81
Aristotle, 89
artificial insemination, Islamic comments on, 42–43
Assembly of Muslim Jurists of America (AJMA), 153
ʿatah, mental category of, 137, 139
autopsies, 46–47
ʿawra, 47

Bakr, Abū, 72
Baṣāʾir Wa-Al-Dhakhāʾir, Al-, 87
becoming, idea of, 100, 101
being: categories of, 90–91; criteria of existence of, 91; divine origin of, 89; idea of skepticism and, 115n66; knowing and, 111; movement of, 102; question of, 94, 95, 96; studies of, 26; as truth, 102–3
Bihārī, Muḥibbullāh Ibn ʿAbd al-Shakūr al-, x
bioethics, vii, 7, 11, 29n5, 232
biomedicine, 229, 230, 231
bipolar manic disorder, 145
blood donation, 49
body-soul relationship, 110–12
brain death: cardiac death and, 212; as criterion of death, 76–77, 81, 107, 108–9, 213; as departure of the soul, 214–15; Islamic debate on, 46, 53n18, 84n15, 87; juridical

brain death (*continued*)
ambivalence toward, 212, 214; as legal death, 77–78, 81, 213; Muslim physicians' perception of, 198, 212–15; organ transplantation and, 81–82, 213; signs of life after, 80
Broeckaert, Bert, 21

Cairo Declaration on Human Rights in Islam, 167
Callahan, Daniel, 7
canonical discursive approach, 97–98, 99
Charmez, K., 126
Clark, Kelly James, 111
clinical practice, ethical problems of, 230–31
cloning, 45, 53n12
collective *ijtihād*, 8, 13, 24, 31n24, 233, 234n5
congenital rubella syndrome (CRS), 62–63, 64
consciousness, 100
contraceptives, in Islam, use of, 47, 53n11
Corbin, Henri, 102, 103
corporeal monism, 111
Cover the Uninsured, 159, 164, 169

Dardīr, al-, 60
ḍarūra (dire necessity): clinical boundaries of, 217; in the context of vaccination, 61; definition of, 25–26, 28, 58, 59–60; ethico-legal maxim on, 59; foundation for invoking, 66, 67; Islamic bioethics rulings on, 65; juridical explanations of, 215; life threat and, 64–65, 66, 215–16; medical necessity and, 64–65; physicians' views of, 64, 65, 66, 67, 198–99, 217; Qur'anic verses on, 58–59; scenarios of, 199; scholarship on, 60; theological construct of, 58–60, 64
death: in age of techno-science, 100; brain death as criterion of, 76–77, 81, 107, 108–9, 213; certainty of, 79–80; clinical concerns of, 81–82; definitions of, 77, 106; from drowning, 79; legal, 77–78; as loss of personhood, 214–15; metaphysics of, 103–7; methods of determining, 46, 76, 198; in Muslim bioethics, 107–8; organs transplantation and, 81–82; religious criterion of, 78; Shaykh Walīyullāh's description of, 103–4; signs of, 80, 107–8
Deleuze, Gilles, xi, 100
Department of Islamic Development Malaysia (JAKIM), 8, 24
dhū-l-ghafla al-shadīda (person afflicted by severe heedlessness), 138, *140*
dire necessity. See *ḍarūra*
Djaīt, Kameleddine, 46

Ebrahim, Abul Fadl Mohsin, 26
Ebrahim, Mohsen, 217
emotional states, 138, *140*
Encyclopedia of Jewish Medical Ethics, 150
ensoulment, Muslim perspective on, 63
ethico-legal maxims, 58, 59, 60, 198, 199
European Council for Fatwā and Research (ECFR), 24

Faithful Reform in Health Care (FRH): human rights vocabulary, 168, 174; mission of, 157, 181n27; pamphlets of, 164; support of healthcare reform, 157–58, 165, 168; target audience of, 168

Faith-Inspired Vision of Health Care, A, 157–58
Fārābī, Abū Naṣr al-, 89
fatāwā (nonbinding ethico-legal opinions): absence of human rights discourse in, 167; definition of, 29n8, 40, 166; discussions of Islamic bioethics in, 4–5, 12, 21, 174–75; on health insurance, 161–64, 174, 175; of Islamic jurists, 171–72, 174; legal framework for issuing, 132–33; on medical issues, 41, 51; of *muftī*, 172; nonbinding nature of, 8; online sources, 153, 164; public, 166–67; vs. *qarārāt* (collective resolutions), 57; on scientific discoveries, 44; scriptural references, 171–72; types of, 29n8, 40
Fatwa Center of America, 153
Federation of Islamic Medical Associations (FIMA), 23
fiqh (discipline of juristic ethics), x, 13, 30n13, 72
fiqh academies: assessment of brain death, 26; bioethics-related analyses of, 13, 24, 227; establishment of, 7–8; interpretation of medical data, 228; multidisciplinary perspectives of, 233n2
Fiqh Council of North America, 166, 174
Flanagan, Owen, 96
forensic psychiatry/psychology, 123, 144

Ghaly, Mohammed, 24
gharar (legal term for ambiguity), 162, 163, 172
Ghazālī, Abū-Ḥāmid al-: on the beginning of life, 108; on intellect, 92, 93; on metaphysics, 89, 97; on Muslim knowledge framework, 92; on obedience to God, 92; on objectives of the Shariah, 59, 62; on ontological question of God, 90, 91–92; on reality, 93; on sources of knowledge, 92; on spiritual organ, 92
Glaser, B. G., 126
God: creation of humans, 45; intervention in medical treatment, 43–44; knowledge of, 45; obedience to, 92; ontological question of, 90, 91–92
Goodman, Lenn, 91, 103
Greer, David, 81
Guattari, Félix, 100

Ḥajjī, 'Abd al-Raḥmān 'Alī al-, 40
Hamdy, Sherine, 22, 46
Ḥanafī, al-Hamawī al-, 60
Haque, Omar Sultan, 111
Harari, Yuval Noah, 94
harm (*ḍarar*), 123, 231
Hasker, William, 111
Haydar Efendi, Ali, 75
health, Avicenna's idea of, x–xi
healthcare: cost of, 156; moral dimensions of, 14
healthcare equity discourse, 164, 165, 166
healthcare reform: American Muslim organizations and, 152, 155–60; ethical arguments for, 171, 173; history of, 155–56; Islamic bioethics and, 152; Islamic rhetoric on, 154, 158, 169–71; of Obama administration, 156; promotion of, 167–68; sources of, 153–54
health insurance: access to, 155, 159; *fatāwā* on, 161–64; Islamic perspective on, 152, 159–60, 163–64, 177; as part of employment benefits, 155; permissibility of, 162–63, 164, 167, 176

heart, idea of, 103
Heidegger, Martin, 101
hospitals, 17
human being, 82, 101, 108, 111, 116n81
human brain: development of, 44–45; limitations of, 44; in neuroscience, treatment of, 109–10
human personhood, 107–8, 109, 110, 111, 112
human rights discourse, 164, 165, 167
human skeletons, ethical issues of using, 47
hygiene standards, 48, 51
hymenoplasty controversy, 49–50, 54n32

Ibn Hindū, Abū Al-Faraj ʻAlī ibn al-Husayn, 6
Ibn Kaldūn, ʻAbd al-Raḥmān, 93
Ibn Qudāma al-Maqdisī, ʻAbdallāh Ibn-Aḥmad, 80
Ibn Rushd, Abū al-Walīd Muḥammad b. Aḥmad (a.k.a. Averroes), 79
Ibn Sīnā, Abū Alī (a.k.a. Avicenna), x–xi, 89
Iftaa, Darul, 49
Ījī, ʻAḍud al-Dīn al-, x
ijtihād: call for reform in, 13; definition of, 72; jurisprudential framework of, 72–74, 76; types of, 26, 73–74, 76. *See also* collective *ijtihād*
illness, concept of, xi
imāms, 130–31, 144
impure substances, medical use of, 68n9
intellect, 92, 93
in vitro fertilization (IVF) treatments, 45
Islam: formation of religious doctrine of, 185n77; immanent ontology of, 103; progress and, 40; science and, 40–41
Islamic bioethics: applied, 9; assessment of, vii, 8, 151; conferences on, 2; consumers of, 14, *15*, 16, 18, 154, 195; definitions of, 3–5; as discipline, construction of, 149, 151, 228–29, *229*; ethical scope of, 11–12; experts in, 12–14; *fatāwā* as source for, xiv, 4–5, 12, 21, 25, 175; guidance and manuals, 39–40, 150, 216–17; history of, 5–8; idea of encyclopedia of, 179n5; “Islamic” aspects of, 2, 8–11, 172; Islamic jurists and, 20–21, 176; lawmaking and, 17; methodology of, 13, 150, 151–52; moral sciences and, 10–11, 232; vs. Muslim bioethics, 5, 9; Muslim physicians’ engagement with, 21, 28, 193–98, *203–4*, 209, 210, 218, 227–28; neuroscience and, 110; philosophical perspective on, ix; public health ethics and, 11; references to the Qur’an and *Sunnah*, 10, 176; religious leaders and, 15–16; scholarship, xiii–xiv, 1–2, 4, 6, 12, 25–28, 152, 210–11, 232; social practices of, 173–75; sources for, 4–5, 10, 232; as a subfield of bioethics, 11, 151; traditionalist perspectives, viii–ix; training in, 12–13, 23
Islamic bioethics deliberation, 228, *229*, 230, 232, 233
Islamic bioethics producers: academic religious studies experts as, *19*, 22; Islamic jurists as, *19*, 20–21; Islamic/Muslim bioethicists as, *20*, 23, 177; juridical academies as, *20*, 24; Muslim clinicians as, 15–16,

19, 21; Muslim health professional organizations as, *20*, 23–24, 27; social scientists as, *19*, 22; state authorities as, *20*, 24–25; typology of, *19–20*, 173
Islamic contractual law, 161–62
Islamic ethico-legal guidance, 14, 66–67
Islamic ethics, 150, 174, 185n77
Islamic *Fiqh* Academy of India, 24
Islamic judicial process (case study): data analysis, 126–27; data collection, 126; discussion, 142–45; limitations of, 145–46; participants of the study, 123, 124–25, 127–28, *128*; qualitative interview design, 124, 125–26; results, 127–42; sample characteristics, 127–29
Islamic jurisprudence, 60, 124
Islamic jurists: attitudes to medicine, 12, 40; background of, 143; bioethics rulings of, 21; dialogue with *muftī*, 20; *fatwā*-making practices, 142–43, 171–72; healthcare policy dialogue and, 27, 165–66; Islamic bioethics and, *19*, 21, 41; proposal on training in sciences, 141–42; roles and duties of, 130; social status of, 20; view of brain death, 212
Islamic law: accountability in, 136; definition of, 83n2; five objectives of, 59, 62; Islamic values and, 12, 121–22; on killing human beings, 82; maxims of, 232; meaning of justness in, 72–73; medical judgments and, 48–49; mental status in, 136–40; Muslim publics and, 142; permissibility of abortion in, 123; plural nature of, 184n69; sacralized nature of, 114n44; on unnecessary movement in prayer, 73
Islamic literacy, 88
Islamic Medical Association of North America (IMANA), 156, 179n12, 196, 218, 219n17
Islamic medical ethics, 39, 40
Islamic moral theology, 167
Islamic Organization for Medical Sciences (IOMS), 7, 23, 26, 84n15, 213
"Islamic Perspective on the Plight of Americans without Health Care Coverage, An," 159–60, 169–70, 171, 185n77
Islamic Society of North America (ISNA): documents of, 153, 159–60, 164, 169; funding of, 159; healthcare equity messages, 164–65; human rights vocabulary, 174; mission of, 158–59, 179n12; partners of, 159; support of healthcare reform, 156, 160, 173–74
Islamic tribunals, idea of, 142

Jambet, Christian, 102, 103
Jaṣṣāṣ, Abū Bakr al-, 60
judicial processing: clinical terminology in, 135; expert consultations, 134–35, 143; knowledge of clinical psychology/psychiatry and, 145; mental status and, 124, *129*, 129–30; peer consultation, 134; prophetic tradition regarding protocols of, 138; psychological factors in, 135, 138; recommendations for improvement of, 141–42, 143; scope and context of, 130–32, 133
junūn mutbiq (absolute insanity), 137, *139*
juridical thinking, 97
juristic theology, viii, xii
Jurjānī, Sayyid Sharif al-, x
justice, concept of, 170, 171, 184n75

Kahf, Monzer, 153, 162, 163, 172, 181–82n37
Kawthari, Muhammad ibn Adam al-, 54n30, 161
Kenny, Anthony, 90, 94
Keshavarzi, Hooman, 27
Khaleel Babakr, Ahmked, 61
Khalil, Mohammad, 3, 21, 210, 211
Kholwadia, Mohammed Amin, 26, 213, 216
knowledge/knowing: being and, 101, 111; of God, 42–43, 45, 51; modes of, 95–96; of physicians, 42–43, 45, 51; practice and, 92; revealed, 92, 104; sources of, 92; theory of, 26, 95
Kobeisy, Ahmed, 159

legal cause, 73, 75, 83n5
legal insanity, 138
legal interdiction (*ḥajr*), 137
legal liability, 137
legal maxims, 60, 75, 127, 162
life-giving breath (*nasama*), 106–7, 108, 115n76
life threat, concept of, 64, 65–66, 215, 216

Majlis al-ʻUlamā,' 77
Majlis Ulama of South Africa, 24
majnūn (a person who has lost intellect), 137, 138, *139*
majnūn ghayr mutbiq (temporarily insane person), 145–46
Majusi, ʻAli ibn al-' Abbas al-, 6
Malabou, Catherine, 109, 110
Mālik ibn Anas, 73–74
maqāṣid (overarching objectives of Islamic law), 13, 229
maṣlaḥa (benefit), ethico-legal construct of, 46, 47, 231
McMahan, Jeff, 108
medicine: benefits of, 51; ethics of, 39; God's revelation and, 44, 46; in Islamic law, 46; religion and, 48–49, 51–52, 150
Medline database, 21, 210, 211
mental health experts, 135–36, 141, 142, 143
mental status: categories of, 144–45; in Islamic law, 122, 123, 124, 136–40, 145; legal assessment of, *129*, 140–41; religious duties and, 48
mercy, concept of, 170
metaphysics: of death, 103–7; definition of, 88–89, 94; Modern Muslim, 97–100; vs. other branches of philosophy, 95; of positivism, 90; realist and idealist, 99; sources of, 96; spiritual and mental spheres, 99, 100; theology and, 96; world and, 91
Moazam, Farhat, 22
Moosa, Ebrahim, 26, 214
moral theology, 229
mubarsam (person who is not psychologically sound), 137, *139*
muftīs (private jurisconsults): definition of, 41; difference between the *qādī* and, 131–32; on God's intervention in medical treatment, 43–44; importance of, 52; judicial reasoning of, 130; medical treatment proposed by, 41–42; relationships with physicians, 42, 50
murshids (spiritual guides), 130
Mushidd, ʻAbdAllāh al-, 45
Muslim bioethics: impact on clinical practices, 209; vs. Islamic bioethics, 5, 9
Muslim ethical tradition, 101
Muslim health professional organizations: documents of,

153–54; healthcare reform and, 152, 155–60; Islamic bioethics and, 23–24
Muslim hermeneutics, 98
Muslim jurists: on definition of death, 77; as producers of Islamic bioethics, 75–76, 232; rhetoric of, 97
Muslim physicians: abortion services and, 194–95; brain death conceptions and, 81, 198, 206, *206*, 212–15; capability of doing *ijtihād*, 78, 213–14; community involvement of, 194; ethical considerations, 195–96, 211–12; familiarity with Islamic bioethics, 21, 193–94, 195, 196, 197–98, 203, *203–4*, 209, 210, 218, 227–28; Islamic law and, 210–11; knowledge of, 42–43, 45, 51, 194; moral obligations of, 15–16, 214; *muftīs* and, 42, 50; publications of, 21; recommendations of medical procedures, 195; religiously of, 194, 195, 199–200, 202, *203*, 208–9; sociodemographic characteristics of, 200, *201*; trustworthiness of, 48, 49, 194; use of bioethics resources, *204–5*, 205–6, 209–12, 227, 232; view of life threat, 215–16; views of *ḍarūra*, 64–65, 66, 67, 198–99, 206–7, *207*, 215–16
Muslim physicians survey: bias of, 208; data analysis, 200; data collection, 196; discussion of, 207–18; instruments of, 197; key measures, 197–200; methodology of, 196–97; participants of, 196, 200; results of, 200–207
Muslim population: growth of, 121; religiosity of, 208
Muslim studies, 10
Muslim World League (MWL), 7, 24
mutakallims (discursive theologians), 130

Nagarwala, Jumana, trial of, 1
nature, technology and, 93–94
Nawawī, Abū Zakariyyā Yaḥyā ibn Sharaf al-, 79
Neiman, Susan, 88
neuroscience, 94, 109–10
Nietzsche, Friedrich, xi
Nijm, al-Sayyid, 48

"Obamacare." *See* Patient Protection and Affordable Care Act (PPACA)
ontology, 89–90, 94, 103
Organisation of Islamic Cooperation (OIC), 7, 24, 77
Organisation of the Islamic Conferences' Islamic *Fiqh* Academy (OIC-IFA), 26, 213
organ transplantation, 46

Padela, Aasim, 76
Patient Protection and Affordable Care Act (PPACA), 152, 156, 157, 164, 169, 176–77
personhood, Islamic perspective of, 26–27, 107–8, 109
philosophical concepts, 100–101
Plato, 89
Potter, Van Rensselaer: "Bioethics, the Science of Survival," 7
pregnancy: posing a life threat, 216; rubella and, 62. *See also* abortion
Presidential Commission for the Study of Bioethical Issues, 165
prevention, vs. treatment, 48
Prigogine, Ilya, 90
proto-self, 110
public health ethics, 11

qāḍīs (judges): authority of, 131; judicial reasoning of, 130; vs. *muftīs*, 131–32
Qaraḍāwī, Yūsuf al-, 43, 52n7, 63
qarārāt (collective resolutions), 57, 66
Qudah, Main al-, 161, 162, 181n37
Qur'an: sacred texts of, 168–69; as source of revelation, 10, 170–71; verses on dire necessity, 58–59

Ramadan, Tariq, 13
Rāzī, Fakhr al-Din al-, 109, 116n81
reality, 93
reason, 92
religion, medicine and, 48–49, 51–52, 150
revelation, 10, 102–3, 170–71
ribā (usury), 161, 162, 163, 172
Rispler-Chaim, Vardit, 21, 22, 25
Robert Wood Johnson Foundation, 159, 181n32
Robinson, Marilynne, 94
rubella, 62
Ruhawi, Ishaq ibn Ali al-, 6

Sabzawārī, Hādī, 101
Sachedina, Abdulaziz, 22, 214
Ṣadr al-Dīn Shīrāzī, Muḥammad ibn Ibrāhīm (a.k.a. Mulla Ṣadrā), 101–2, 103
Sa'dullah Khan, Imam, 158, 168
safāha (foolishness), 138, *140*
Ṣaqr, 'Aṭīyah, 43, 48
Sawy, Salah al-, 162, 181–82n37
scholastic theology, 229
science, 40–41, 89–90, 94
scientific naturalism, 100
scriptural approach, 97–98, 99
Searle, John R., 99
sex selection, 43, 44
Shabana, Ayman, 179n5
Shāfi'ī, Abū 'Abd Allāh Muḥammad b. Idrīs al-, 73
Shanawani, Hasan, 3, 21, 210, 211
Sha'rāwī, Muhammad Mutawalli al-, 42
Shariah. *See* Islamic law
Shāṭibī, Abū Isḥāq Ibrahīm b. Mūsā al-: on legal cause, 75; model of *ijtihād*, 26, 72–74, 76; on truth and error, 74
Shurunbulālī, Ḥasan ibn 'Ammār al-, 79
significant harm, concept of, 215
Skovgaard-Petersen, Jakob, 166
spirit, 104–5, 106
Stengers, Isabelle, 90
sterilization surgery, 49
Stodolsky, Muhammed Volkan Yildiran, 26, 213, 216
substance (*jawhar*), 90, 91, 94
Sufi practices, 9, 234n3
Suhrawardī, Shihāb al-Dīn al-, 101
Suleman, Mehrunisha, 24
Sunnah, 10, 168–69, 170
Suyūṭī, 60
Syeed, Sayyid, 159

takāful (Islamic health insurance), 163, 177
taklīf (legal responsibility), 136, 137
Ṭanṭāwī, Muḥammad Sayyid, 46, 51
Ṭawīl, Sayyid Rizq al-, 49
therapeutic treatments, vii–viii
Toffler, Alvin, 89
Tyndall, John, vii

'ulamā' (Muslim scholars), 71, 72, 80
ul Haq, Ikram, 161, 162, 163, 181n37
Uniform Determination of Death Act, 198, 212
Universal Declaration on Human Rights (UDHR), 167

uṣūl (sources of Islamic jurisprudence), 60, 229

vaccination: ethics of, 61, 65; Islam and, 61–62; with porcine products, 61, 217
Van den Branden, Stef, 21
vapor in the heart, 104–5
vegetative life, 108

Walīyullāh al-Dihlawī: description of death, 103–4, 106–7; on extraction of the *nasama*, 115n76; on knowledge acquired from revelation, 104; on spirit, 104–6; on vapor in the heart, 104–5
waswasa (obsessive-compulsive disorder), 137, *139*
Wittgenstein, Ludwig, 95
worldview, 10, 96

Zarka, Mustafa al-, 162, 182n45
Zarkashī, Muḥammad ibn Bahādur al-, 60

Aasim I. Padela is professor of emergency medicine, bioethics, and humanities at the Medical College of Wisconsin. He is also director of the Initiative on Islam and Medicine and co-editor of *Islam and Biomedicine*.